Enduring Strength

The Story of the Other Hansbrough Brother

Greg Hansbrough

TIPS Technical Publishing, Inc.
Carrboro, NC

ISBN 978-1-890586-57-7 (print)
ISBN 978-1-890586-58-4 (ePub)
ISBN 978-1-890586-59-1 (mobi)

Cataloging-in-Publication Data on file with the Library of Congress
Names: Hansbrough, Greg.
Title: Enduring strength / Greg Hansbrough.
Description: Carrboro, NC : TIPS Technical Publishing, Inc., 2017.
Identifiers: LCCN 2016050720 (print) | LCCN 2016052275 (ebook) | ISBN
    9781890586577 (print : alk. paper) | ISBN 9781890586584 (ePub) | ISBN
    9781890586905 (mobi) | ISBN 9781890586591 (mobi)
Subjects: LCSH: Hansbrough, Greg. | Runners (Sports)--United
    States--Biography. | Brain--Cancer--Patients--Biography. | Ultra running.
Classification: LCC GV1061.15.H36 A3 2017 (print) | LCC GV1061.15.H36
(ebook)
    | DDC 796.42092--dc23
LC record available at https://lccn.loc.gov/2016050720

TIPS Technical Publishing, Inc.
108 E. Main Street, Suite 4
Carrboro, NC 27510
www.technicalpublishing.com

Copy editing: J. K. Maxwell
Design and composition: Robert "Kerndog" Kern
Cover image: Rachel "Wisp" Kelley
Back cover author photograph: Martha "Sidetrack" Hoelzer

Printed and bound in the United States of America

To my grandfather and all the people I call friends and family

Ron,

Thank you for being such a great person. I am so glad we became friends. I hope you like the way I describe you in here.

your friend,

Contents

Foreword

I was five years old when it happened. I'd been at a friend's house goofing off and having fun, but when I got home that cold fall day, I knew something was off. The house seemed empty. No Greg, no Mom, no Dad, just Pawpaw, Mimi, and Ben (our youngest brother). Pawpaw was never one to hold anything back. He told me Greg wasn't feeling well so our parents had taken him to the hospital in St. Louis. I don't think anyone in our family wanted to acknowledge how sick Greg was and I was too young to realize that driving two and a half hours for a doctor meant something was seriously wrong.

The doctors informed my parents that Greg had a terminal brain tumor. They gave him about six months to live. Our dad must have called every brain surgeon looking for an expert to perform a miracle. He got lucky and found a doctor at the Mayo Clinic in Minnesota who was willing to try to help Greg.

While our parents where in Minnesota with Greg, Ben and I moved in with our grandparents. We had no idea what Greg was going through or that he was about to begin the biggest challenge of his life.

I remember Greg coming home after surgery and rehab in Minnesota. I couldn't have been happier my bro was back—now we could start doing all the things we did before he left… play basketball, throw the football, and have fun like every young kid. But it wasn't long before I realized that Greg wasn't like every young kid. As a result of the surgery, his left side wasn't working the way it should. He was clumsy, tripped over things, and generally did not move well. Presurgery, we had done everything together: played basketball and football, raced, everything you could think of. So it was tough and confusing to watch Greg struggle with even the simplest of tasks. I went from playing all these different sports with my skilled older brother to watching him relearn how to pick up marbles with his left hand and put them in a cup, over and over again. I watched the whole process of him relearning to use his body: how to walk, pick things up, basically everything. He worked hard and gradually improved. He even tried to ride a bike, struggling over and over again until he finally got it (he only used the front brake so you can imagine the damage he took). Through his hard work, his walk turned into a jog, jog into a run, and run into finishing an ultramarathon. While Greg's left side would never return to "normal," he is now doing all the things the experts said he would never do again.

I'm most proud of Greg for never giving up or making excuses for what he was going through. He got bullied and made fun of, but it never held him back or made him quit; it only motivated him. Yes, he could get discouraged and emotional, but never gave in or gave up. Greg is one of the toughest competitors I've been around. The best way to describe Greg's approach to most things is to say that he is an absolute bulldozer. One of my favorite stories about Greg happened during one of his high school basketball games. It was a good ol' ass kicking. Greg's team was down by more than twenty-five points with less than ten seconds to go in the last quarter. (If you don't know basketball, the game was way beyond over). Suddenly, there was a loose ball and Greg comes out of nowhere, takes a long leap and dives right on the ball, and calls timeout. Was it funny? Absolutely! You've got to understand, that's how Greg approaches everything, whether it's running, basketball, ping-pong, you name it. That's just how my big brother rolls.

Enduring Strength is a book that anyone can connect with. It's a great story of someone overcoming obstacles and proving naysayers wrong. Regardless of what your struggle is, this book can show you how to find motivation to persevere. This book shows you the rollercoaster of emotions that is involved with such a recovery as Greg's. It gives you the raw experience, the "no holds barred" stories that most people don't hear about when things are tough. This was a particularly tough read for me, as I'd watched Greg go through all this and yet never heard the in-depth details. Before writing this book, Greg rarely talked about what he went through, and I think a big reason for that is that he never wanted to use his struggle as an excuse (not that he ever needed to; even with a partially impaired left side he was still better than most of the kids at any sport he tried).

—Tyler Hansbrough

Introduction

I first started to write this book when I was in my mid-twenties as a way to gain a true sense of myself through an activity that I enjoyed from struggling to learn to walk again to finishing my second ultramarathon. During the process, I discovered a lot about myself by looking at my life and the random yet strangely connected events that have shaped me into the person I am today.

Growing up in a small town in southeast Missouri, there were lots of the characteristics inherent to small communities everywhere in the country: There was a notion that only small things and accomplishments could come out of this town. Everyone wanted to know everything about everybody else; it seemed that everyone knew everything about your personal life.

In many ways, my family was a stark contrast to the normal mindset of the town. They shaped the man I have become without limiting my aspirations to the hometown mindset. My mom and dad always told me I could be whatever I wanted in life. I feel this is different from the mindset of most people in Poplar Bluff, a town where the standard for excellence was placed incredibly low. But my mom and dad are anything but typical small-town people.

My mother had been Miss Missouri in the Miss America pageant when she was younger, and has a talent for singing—her pageant talent—which most people will never get the opportunity to experience in their lifetime. One of the joys I remember as a child is hearing her sing songs as she walked around the house. I still believe my mom has one of the most beautiful voices in the world. The older I became and the more I heard her voice, the more I realized my mom was a great singer.

My dad, a local surgeon and former collegiate high jump champion, was and still is a passionate athlete. He would wake up early every day of the week to exercise. Three mornings of the week, he would open the junior college gym for a group of guys to play basketball at six in the morning. After basketball, he always lifted weights. He swam laps after work and rode his bicycle as well. He still mountain bikes a lot today. Each of my parents had a rare talent that brought them accolades beyond what most people thought possible in my hometown. Growing up, I noticed my parents living out their passions in their own ways. It is no wonder that they always told me I could be whatever I desired, even if I wanted to do something greater than anyone in Poplar Bluff thought possible.

From a very young age, I always felt a connection with my brothers. Despite this, while we were young boys I did not like them, we fought constantly, competed against each other in everything we did, and were always butting heads over everything under the sun. It was not until we were all past high school that I realized how important my bond with them was. I began to realize that I was closer to them than anyone else. My brothers went from being my rivals to my best friends.

During my journey to where I am now, I have struggled with a few bouts of depression and, as you will read, I have felt as though my life was not worth living and almost took it. But in writing this book, I have gained a sense of perspective about what I have accomplished that has allowed me to be proud of everything I have overcome to get to where I am. I guess the best way to describe where I am now compared to my younger self can be summed up in a trail run I had a couple years ago.

The trails that I have come to know as my "home trails" are located in the towns of Chapel Hill and Carrboro, North Carolina. This particular patch of woods is almost in the middle of Carrboro and has all the familiar scenes of a local forest. There are trails carved through the thick stands of tall deciduous trees, with hills rolling across creeks, meadows, and pine trees. The majority of the people on these trails are locals who have hiked, biked, or run the trails for years. Almost every time I venture onto the trails in these woods, I see someone I know and find myself in a quick conversation before we both disappear down our own paths through the trees.

The trails here have names that are different for different people, but my running group, the Trailheads, has a naming system for the different trails that is understood throughout the group. There is almost always a story behind the name. There is a trail named "Nader Valley" for the abandoned car marking the entrance, which, legend has it, was abandoned by Ralph Nader many years ago. The "Forbidden Trail" is so named because of the signs on either end stating that running is not allowed on this trail. These names are something that I have gained intimate knowledge of through running with the Trailheads.

One day, I was out for a run down the Forbidden Trail on a warm morning, the kind of morning inherent to North Carolina, with sticky humidity and temperatures that start high and rise steadily throughout the day. The route I was running was a six-mile loop from the Wilson Park parking lot and I was looking forward to pushing myself through the challenges of the run.

To pause in the story and provide some history, ever since I first started running in high school, I have enjoyed the aspect of challenging myself through running. I looked at every uphill as a challenge of my strength and told myself that I was tougher than this hill, I'm the fucking alpha male! The hills were nothing compared to me! Keeping in line with this mentality, I told myself that I had no weak points, I was tough enough to do anything. In reality, ever since I was seven years old, I have tried to hide the left side of my body, as it had (and still has) limited functionality due to the effects of a brain surgery. I walked around self-conscious about my left arm and on several occasions got into fights due to my insistence that there was nothing wrong with my left arm.

As I made my way down the wide trail I refer to as the "interstate" toward the Forbidden Trail, I fell into the familiar mindset of pushing myself over hills and feeling as if I were tougher than every hill I ran over. I navigated the creek, hopped across the rocks, and cruised down the interstate toward the Hundred Years' Flood bridge marking the unofficial entrance to the Forbidden Trail. I gazed over the beautiful creek running alongside the trail, then turned up one hill. I found myself on a relatively flat section, and it was then that I felt it—I was incredibly happy. I loved the place I was at in my life. The realization came into my head: "I am this incredibly happy because of the journey my life has been. I would not be this happy if I hadn't had all the experiences that led to this moment." In that simple thought, I came to appreciate myself as a pretty incredible individual. I had come from a boy lying in the hospital unsure whether he would live or die to a trail runner in love with life and full of joy. It was right there on the trail that I stopped feeling insecure about my left arm. As I ran beside the creek bed, it felt like I was giving myself a huge hug as I completely embraced myself for who I was. I decided that I was an extraordinary person who would not be this happy without the life I had lived.

As the trail turned up another hill and I hopped over the fallen tree that had been chewed and forgotten by a beaver years ago, I instinctually reverted back to the mindset of a conqueror, seeing this as another battle between me and the hill. Halfway up the hill, I thought, "This hill doesn't want me to avoid it. This hill was put here for me to run. The hill wants me to run up it!" As I put that mindset into practice, I felt my muscles relax and I seemed to be floating up the hill instead of my normal straining to conquer it. I started bounding up the hills with the sense that the hills were working with me instead of against my strength. I took these two realizations with me the rest of the run. For the rest of the run, I swelled with pride at the life I had built and the accomplishments I had achieved. By the time I arrived in the parking lot, marking the end of the day's run, I was full of pride and walked away from that run with a new mindset and concept of self that I still carry with me today.

In the chapters that follow, you will read about the journey that led to my becoming such a happy individual. It is filled with struggles, strife, and odds against me. You will see how I used to grit my teeth to overcome difficulties by carrying with me the mindset of being tougher than all obstacles. You will see how I came to the point I am at today, where I have gone far beyond what I had previously believed possible. And you will learn that I have gained these accomplishments by learning that the difficult tasks in life were placed there for me to overcome.

Start of Something Special

I am a seven-year-old boy. I slowly open my eyes to see my parents gazing down on me in my hospital bed. My vision is blurry and nothing looks as clear as it had a few hours ago. There is a throbbing feeling in the front of my head; it feels as if someone stabbed a fork inside my scalp. I feel the air conditioner blowing air on it, which is very painful. As I glance around the room, I see doctors and nurses looking down on me with serious faces. The back of my head, right below the midline of my skull, also feels painful and I have an intense headache. Even though the middle section of my brain is pounding with pain, it also feels strangely lighter, as if an invisible weight has been lifted from my head. My gaze travels toward the doctors, away from my parents' concerned faces. Even as a child, I can see that the doctors are considering about what their next move should be. They're watching me like I'm some great accomplishment of theirs. Just then, one of the surgeons tells me that I need to get on my feet.

I think, "This should be easy enough; I can run, jump, and do things all day long." As I start to get to my feet, the pulsing headache gets even worse. Doctors have to support me on both sides to keep me from falling.

In this moment, I make the terrifying discovery: my left leg will not extend. For the first time in my life, my legs have failed me. All I can do is hop slowly and painfully on my right leg a couple times. As I hop, I feel the headache getting worse. I'm also afraid that somebody's going to bump the incredibly tender ridge on the front of my head. After a few hops, I can't hold my head up anymore, so the doctors lay me back down in bed. I lie there in extreme pain, all from the once-simple act of standing. My head feels as if my brain is trying to break through my skull. The empty space that I felt in the middle of my brain is overcome with intense pain and I start to feel light-headed. My vision darkens and I drift off to sleep, with no idea that my life is never going to be the same.

***

My entire life, basketball was the top sport in my house. My dad had a small Nerf basketball goal for me to shoot on in the living room from the time I learned to walk. We talked about the sport all the time. He played in basketball games constantly and would take me to the gym to shoot. He taught me the proper mechanics for a jump shot, how to dribble a ball, and the rules of the game. It was in these early moments that I developed a desire to play this game.

Our basement was the ideal setting for a young athlete. One half of the basement featured a weight room complete with dumbbells, bench press, stationary bikes, and curl bars. The other half had been converted into a miniature basketball court complete with two baskets screwed six feet high into each of the opposing walls. The only glitch in the court was a support beam that stood in the center of the court. After a few weeks of games, my dad put padding on the walls in order to keep us from getting hurt by bashing into the cement walls.

The majority of the day was spent in the basement playing imaginary games. Once we walked down the stairs, we were no longer in our house on Autumn Road; we were in the game's most exciting arena. I would go into the basement and pretend to be playing in a huge game against the greatest players in the world. Soaring through the air and dunking the ball through the hoop on our six-foot goals, it was easy to get caught up in playing an imaginary game against Michael Jordan, Charles Barkley, or Dominique Wilkins. I played these pretend games for hours. Tyler even took it to the extreme by running through the basement screaming "BAM-BAM-BAM!" and telling everyone the band was playing for him as he lost himself in the imaginary games.

But every night after dinner, the music faded and it was time to play some real games. My dad would follow us to the basement to watch while Tyler and I played our daily game of basketball against each other. I was always excited and looked forward to the games because I knew I was going to win, since in the whole time we had been playing, I had never been defeated and won every night.

The backyard of our house also featured two basketball goals: one was a ten-foot goal that was immovable and connected to a concrete wall and the other was a side goal that was called the "dunk goal" because it could be moved up or down with a broomstick. The games that were played out there were against much older kids from the neighborhood. At age six and four respectively, Tyler and I were playing twelve-year-old boys in intense games that would last into the sunset. I can remember playing hard, getting knocked down, having my shot blocked, and not playing very well. After a few days of playing the older kids, I would occasionally score. As I improved, these games became fun because they were challenging and I was taking on the older kids in the game that I loved.

Once I entered kindergarten, I went to the playground and played basketball against kids my own age and was able to score all the time. I would watch the older kids, the same kids who played games in my backyard, walk by on their way to their section of the playground. Occasionally, one of them would stop and say hello. They all knew I could play and I caught them watching me hit left- and right-hand jump shots as I played the kids on my part of the basketball courts. It was not long before I gained some good friends and recess teammates from kids in my class.

Kyle and Josh were two of those friends, and we began playing basketball games together every time the bell rang for recess, completely dominating the kindergarten and first-grade basketball courts. I started scoring whenever I wanted. Kyle was a good player as well. He could pass the ball, score, and play great defense. Josh was a good scorer but was never really one to play defense. When we played together, there was no one our age who could beat us in a game of basketball. Kyle and Josh then came over to the house, I showed them the basement basketball court, and they began to join in on the imaginary games I had been playing against the NBA greats.

Every time we were down there playing, Tyler joined in the games and they became two-on-two games with me and Josh on one team against Tyler and Kyle. These games were intense contests featuring hard dunks, hard falls, and the occasional fight. Although he was two years younger, Tyler was able to hold his own against us in the basement. I was secretly proud that my little brother was able to do so well, but would never tell him so.

It was in one of my basement basketball games against Tyler that my dad made an observation: I had quit dribbling the ball with my left hand because it was difficult to control. The next day, my dad asked me to eat dinner with my left hand. I tried as hard as I could, but was unable to hold the fork well enough to eat my meal. As a precaution, my dad called the local radiologist and asked him to meet at the hospital for a CAT scan on my brain.

Over the past few months, I had been getting headaches, but thought it was nothing to worry about. I was making great grades, was the most athletic kid in my grade, and had never had any illness worse than the flu.

Walking down the hallway to the radiology room was not a new or intrinsically frightening experience; I'd walked there countless times with my dad whenever he was called in for work. My dad was an orthopedic surgeon who led an incredibly active life. Every Sunday at the gym, we would shoot baskets on side goals while my dad played in basketball games. He also played every Tuesday, Thursday, and Friday morning before work. As a doctor, he would be on call for the hospital, so if we were at the gym with him when he was called, we just rode with him to the emergency room where he saw patients.

On this trip, for some reason, they wanted to see an image of my brain. I lay on my back and a machine slid the table I was on into a small tunnel. As I lay there, the machine took images of my brain, which were being shown to my dad and mom and the radiologist on the hospital's imaging system. After a few minutes of lying in the tunnel, I looked up after the table slid out of the tunnel and saw my mom and dad with incredibly somber faces. We drove home. I expected to go to bed like I always did, but my parents packed a bag of clothes for me and we drove straight to St. Louis to check into Barnes Jewish Hospital. I found out later that the location and position of the tumor was incredibly serious, and the radiologist had suggested we leave for St. Louis immediately.

Upon arrival at the hospital, my parents and I were shown to my room. It was a typical hospital room with a little window, a bed with raised arm barriers, and a television. I looked around the room, still stuck on the fact that I didn't have to go to school the next day. In my mind as a seven-year-old, there was no better day than one where I got to miss a full day of school.

The next day, after a few tests, I began to get nervous and restless before my MRI. The doctors wanted to use morphine to calm me down, but this decision was met with a loud objection from my dad and uncle, both of whom are respected medical doctors. The reason they were so loudly against the injection of morphine was because one of the side effects is increased inner cranial pressure. And to a boy with a brain tumor, any increased pressure could have very serious consequences. But, the doctors chose to ignore my familial objections to my receiving morphine

The next day, I noticed an increase in the severity of my headaches. The doctors decided I needed a shunt placed in my head to help relieve the pressure caused by the morphine. A shunt is a device that is placed in a person's brain to help drain fluid from the brain to the stomach where the fluid enters the excretory system. It is essentially a long plastic tube that goes from the brain down the front of the body and ends in the stomach.

The night before surgery, my parents sat up late with me eating junk food. I loved it; I was eating all my favorite candies and we were laughing, playing games, and watching TV.

The next morning, before I was rolled into the operating room, my dad asked me if there was anything I wanted; anything at all I wanted him to get me. I told him I wanted the newest pair of Air Jordan basketball shoes in red and white colors. He told me okay, and as they wheeled me off to surgery, I saw him leave with my uncle. My mom stayed with me until they took me to surgery. She kissed my head, told me she loved me and watched as they wheeled me down the hallway to surgery.

The operating room was a very scary place. I was lying on the cold table when the anesthetist placed a mask over my mouth. I freaked out because I realized I couldn't breathe with this thing covering my mouth. It took every doctor and nurse in the room to hold me to the table. Finally, I drifted off to sleep under anesthesia.

I awoke in a room that was closed off with a curtain on all sides. As I opened my eyes, I became aware of an extreme tenderness on the top of my head. The surgical sutures were pulsing and felt as though someone had inserted an electrical plug into the top of my head. As soon as I awoke, the doctors came into the room and, with no regard to the tenderness of my head, started pushing next to my scar. They were making sure the shunt they had put inside me was working, which they do by pushing down on the bulb on the top of the head. I didn't know that then, and was dazed with the intense pain caused by their pushing right on my new puffy wound. Once they were sure the shunt was working, they wheeled me down to my larger hospital room. Even though my head was sore from the doctors' pushing, I understood they were trying to help me.

On the way to my room, the sutured area on my head was so sensitive that I could feel the air conditioner blowing on my bare head, which caused me to be very cold and made my head even more tender to the touch. Once I had arrived in my room, I was greeted by my parents. My mom just looked at me with fond eyes, but I could tell she was worried about me. My dad looked at me with the same loving glare. He then told me he had a surprise for me. I leaned up carefully to see the surprise, as I was hyperaware of my wounded head. I looked over and saw him holding a box of brand new shoes. He told me the closest size he could find was a size too big, but as he opened the shoebox, my eyes widened with joy at seeing the exact pair of shoes I had asked for before my surgery.

That night, I put my new shoes on and walked with my dad around the hospital. As I walked tall in my new shoes, we entered a walkway that led to another section of the hospital, a section I'd never seen before. We then came to a nearly empty room that had in its center a crazy contraption in a glass case. I watched the large metallic ball roll down a track then move back to the top, incessantly continuing its journey. My dad told me it was a perpetual motion device. As I stood there in my hospital gown and brand-new Air Jordans, I became entranced by this ball and its smooth, continual cycles. It was not until I looked up that I noticed my dad was not looking at the machine. Instead, he was watching me.

The next day, I was lying in my hospital bed watching cartoons with my mom when I had a visitor walk through the door. It was Skip, one of my parents' good friends from Columbia, the town where my dad and mom went to college. I was born there and knew Skip relatively well. Skip's daughter Robyn was an early childhood friend of mine and I had missed her a lot. Skip gave me a gift from Robyn—a message hand stitched on fabric and framed wishing for me to get well. That immediately became my favorite gift. I looked at it and was elated that Robyn had made something for me.

The next day, I got a gift that my seven-year-old mind could hardly fathom. As I looked at the plain brown box, curiosity filled my entire being. I tore through the tape and stared, slack jawed, at a ball that had been signed by Michael Jordan, the legend himself. The greatest basketball player on the planet had actually sent me a gift. There were a lot of other goodies in the box, but a

Gatorade hat and that signed ball had quickly become my two most prized possessions.

While I was in awe of these things from Michael Jordan, I still loved the gift Robyn had given me and glanced toward it occasionally to renew my smile. A gift from Robyn meant the world to me because she was my first true friend and she had made it for me.

A few days later, it was time to leave the hospital and make the trip back to my hometown. So with my head shaved, scarring, and tender, we made the two-and-a-half-hour trip back to my hometown. The whole drive home I was looking forward to playing my brother in basketball downstairs in the basement. As soon as I got home, I headed straight to the basement for a basketball game. Once we were in the basement, we started playing, my head throbbing as I dribbled the ball toward the basket. Every time I bumped into Tyler, my head throbbed. Every time I changed direction, my head throbbed. When he accidentally hit my incision on my way to the basket, I struggled to keep from screaming, but I couldn't let him know how much pain I was experiencing. I had to win this game. When I would jump for a rebound, he would barely graze my head and it would send waves of pain through my entire body, but after a few hits I became used to the awful sensation. I won the game, but realized it was a lot harder to beat my brother now than it had been before I went to the hospital. After that game, my head was an epicenter of pain, but it finally quit pulsing by the time I went to bed.

After being home a few days, my headaches began to get really painful, and every little movement and slight change in my surroundings could trigger one. I tried coping with them by ignoring them as I continued to go through my day. I then became used to the constant pain, in the same way I had in order to win a basketball game. My parents told me I was going to Minnesota in a few days for more surgery. I was still excited to be missing school, but on the drive to St. Louis, I began getting even more intense headaches. This time, there it was very difficult to put the pain on the back burner; it was almost too intense to avoid. As I lay in the back-seat, my head began pounding and I could feel the wheels turning in the van. Every motion of the car caused the pain in my head to worsen, but I eventually became used to the constant pain as we arrived at the airport. We boarded a plane bound for the land of ten thousand lakes. I had no idea that this trip was going to completely change my life.

I later learned that while we were at home, my dad had combed the medical community for surgeons who would attempt to remove my tumor. Because of its location, there was a very low chance that I would survive the surgery, and most surgeons didn't want to take the chance. He finally found a doctor in Minnesota who would attempt to remove the tumor, even with the high probability that I might not survive the surgery. The doctors in St. Louis had not been willing to attempt the surgery because it was too risky. They told my parents to enjoy me while they could, as I probably only had a few months to live.

Once our plane landed, there was still a rental car ride to get to the Mayo Clinic in Rochester, Minnesota. This car ride was a continuation of my rationalization and tolerance of pain, as an intense headache began to develop, creating the sensation that my brain was slamming against my skull with every sway and turn the car made. Every stoplight made my head feel as though there was an anvil crashing into my skull. I told myself that I had endured the trip from my hometown to St. Louis, and this was a shorter trip so of course I could handle it.

On that trip I learned a technique to deal with pain that was going to help me get through many painful episodes in the future: dissociation. As I stared out the window, I began to look at myself from afar, it was an almost out of body experience. My eyes glazed over as I dissociated further and further from my body as my head thundered and ached.

Once we arrived at the hospital, I began a barrage of MRIs, CAT scans, and other tests. This process seemed weirdly normal as I had done it all before with the doctors in St. Louis. I decided to use my new dissociation technique with the injection I received midway through one of my MRIs. As the nurse came in the room, I rolled my arm over, turned my head, and began to dissociate from the pain of being injected. It worked; my pain wasn't as sharp as the last time I had received the same injection. It clicked in my mind: by dissociating I could endure pain and have only a dull perception of the displeasure being caused to my body.

After the tests were completed, I met my new doctor, the surgeon who would remove my tumor. He was a cerebral and serious man with an all-business mentality. He said very few words to me, but the words he did speak were carefully rehearsed and had a clear meaning, they were not just reassuring filler. I decided that I had no opinion of him because he chose to keep himself at a distance from me.

After a few days of tests and visits from various doctors and nurses, it was time to have surgery again. This time, the operation was to remove the tumor and involved a much more difficult procedure.

Before I was wheeled into the operating room for surgery, both my parents were with me in my room, talking and holding my hand. The nurse came in and told my parents she was going to take me in for surgery. Both my mom and dad walked the hallway beside my bed as I was being moved to the operating room. They held the bars of my bed the entire time, and my mom held my hand. Once I arrived at the entrance to the operating room, my parents let go of my hands and I was wheeled toward a set of double doors. I looked up from my bed to get one last look at my parents and saw both of them crumple into each other's arms with sobs and tears. They knew that there was a good possibility that that was the last time they would see me alive because my surgery was still a very new and uncertain procedure.

Once inside the room, the nurses moved me onto the operating table, which was cold and chilled my skin. I looked up and saw a circle of masked doctors and nurses looking down at me. I then saw the lady with the mask moving toward my face. I knew what to expect and tried my new disassociation technique. It didn't work. The sensation of being in oxygen denial sent me into overload. I tried the technique again and was able to begin slipping away from my body in a dissociative lapse. I felt myself drift off to sleep as the nurse told me all the different flavors of anesthesia that were available to patients.

***

As I awoke, I found myself in a new hospital room with curtains for walls and I was alone. Before I had time to notice my surroundings further, I began vomiting violently over the side of my bed. My stomach would rise and fall in involuntary successions ending in my oral excretions. I was scared because I could not get my stomach to stop heaving. My disassociation was useless because I had switched into panic mode trying to stop puking and catching my breath between bouts of vomit. I noticed nobody was coming to help me as I violently vomited in this small room. The floor was covered in puke and I could not get my stomach to stop heaving. After a long time, my stomach finally ceased its spasming and my puking came to a stop. I was exhausted from this episode and closed my eyes for a nap.

When I awoke, I was in a normal hospital room, the kind that looks like every room in every hospital in the country. It had a bed, television, bathroom, and a couple of chairs for people to sit. I looked over and saw my parents sitting in the chairs beside my bed. I also noticed Dr. Kelly standing beside my bed. He immediately wanted me to get out of bed and try to walk. As soon as my head left my pillow, I felt the familiar tenderness of surgical wounds on my head, but my headache was different. Instead of the heavy, pounding headache I had grown used to, my head felt light and I felt a dizzy feeling instead of the familiar pulsing. As I tried to stand, my left leg would not lower and I stood on one foot as Dr. Kelly and my dad held me upright on either side. My vision was blurred and Dr. Kelly asked me to walk. I tried to take a step, but all I was able to do was take a short hop on my right leg. My left leg simply would not move. This simple inaction was enough to send alarms through my head, which began to hurt with a fury. As I lay back down on my hospital bed, I drifted off to sleep as I tried to detach from my headache and surgical tenderness.

The next few days floated by in an endless blur of IV injections, drawn blood, and countless nurse visits. The IV injections were always painful because they had to "clear the vein" before giving any drugs to my system. The process of clearing a vein involves injecting a saline solution that moves blood through the vein in order to allow for immediate transport of drugs into the bloodstream. This process is incredibly painful because it makes your veins feel as though they are on fire. Every time my bag of fluids was getting low, I knew it was almost time for another painful vein clearing. I continued using my strategy of disassociation to dull the pain. When a nurse entered to start a new bag of drugs, I turned my head and stepped away from my body until the pain subsided.

My dad had gone back to Missouri at some point during one of my blurry days. He needed to get back to take care of my brothers and work. This left me with my mom watching over me in the hospital. It was during this time that I discovered what a wonderful mother I had in this world.

Most nights she slept in the recliner by my hospital bed and kept me company through the day as I watched television and got injections. My mom did a great job trying to keep my spirits up while I lay in my bed. I had so many drugs and fluids coursing through my body that I never got dehydrated. Unable to walk, I was forced to urinate into a plastic bottle. To a seven-year-old, this was a difficult task. I had to wiggle my body to keep from missing the bottle. Watching my clear and sometimes grayish urine, my mother and I decided we would call my urination into a bottle the silver wiggle, which brought uproarious laughter to both of us. Every time I needed to pee, I'd say, "It's silver wiggle time." We would both laugh and laugh until I was finished.

After a few weeks of being in my bed, I was informed that I would start therapy. But, before going to therapy, I told the nurse that I was feeling some discomfort because of the location of my IV. My IV began to cause me discomfort because it was always getting snagged on my gown, which compromised my arm movements because of my fear of it snagging. I told my pediatric neurologist, Dr. Groover, of my discomfort and he told me they would put a PICC line in to help me be more comfortable.

A PICC line is a device that is more comfortable than an IV because it is a tube placed in a vein that is more central to the body, which allows for the extremities to move more freely without worry of ripping an IV out of the arm. It allows fluids and drugs to be more easily injected into the body because it uses a larger vein. Little did I know the implantation of this device was going to teach me a major lesson in my ability to dissociate from pain.

As I was wheeled into a room, I saw a group of medical students standing around me with clean, white aprons over their stomachs. As they started to rub skin cleaner on my shoulder, I knew they were about to stick me with a needle. I turned my head and began to disassociate from the pain immediately. But I still noticed the sharp pain associated with a large needle punching through my skin. I then heard one of the students curse, which even I knew to be a bad sign. They tried to place the PICC line into my shoulder again. Once again, they failed to implant the device. I continued to disassociate as they stuck me again and again. After some time passed, I decided to look toward the students. As I turned my head, I noticed that the aprons of everyone in the room were smeared with blood. It took me a few seconds to realize that it was my blood! In an effort to escape my mounting fear of what I had just seen, I turned my head and disassociated further into a dream-like trance. Just as I began to dream, I heard the door to the room burst open violently and saw Dr. Groover explode into the room like an atom bomb. He yelled at the students, "What the hell are you doing!? Get out of here!" The room cleared until it was only me and Dr. Groover. He installed the PICC line inside five minutes. He then cleaned up the blood from my sheets and sent me back to my room. I could see that there was a sorrowful look in his eyes as he watched me lying in my bed having blood cleaned from my sheets.

***

A couple days later, I was met the two ladies who would be instrumental in helping me to get back on my feet. My first therapist was an occupational therapist named Angie Austin. I thought she was the coolest person on the planet, probably because she made an effort to be cool. She was an attractive woman with short blond hair, a well-built figure, and a smile that seemed to expose the playful mentality of a child. Her job was to help me learn how to take care of myself with the limited abilities I had from my surgery. The thing that struck me most about her was her attitude; she was incredibly positive and seemed to believe that I could do anything. I decided that I was going to do anything she wanted me to accomplish because she was such a cool person.

My physical therapist was a lady who seemed very boring to me. Tonya was an Asian woman with an average attitude and she behaved like a normal adult. Her job was to help me to regain some of the abilities I had lost from my surgery. I did not look forward to meeting with Tonya because not only was she a boring adult, but the things she wanted me to do were very difficult and caused me a lot of frustration.

Each day I went to a therapy session with Angie and another session with Tonya. In my sessions with Angie, I tried to accomplish all the tasks she asked me to achieve because it all involved activities I was confident I could tackle, such as tying my shoes with one hand. Tonya asked me to do things that made me very frustrated because I tried as hard as I could but could only accomplish a few of the tasks she asked me to achieve.

I came to detest the exercises Tonya performed with me and did them with the mentality of just trying to get through it until one day Tonya came up with a deal for me. She looked me in the eyes and said, "Greg, let's learn to walk." I asked her if this meant I wouldn't have to do all the little exercises in the main therapy room. She agreed and told me that all we would be working from here forward was going to be walking again.

This deal almost made my heart do back flips because it meant I would no longer be in the dusty therapy room doing little frustrating exercises. The next day, we agreed to try for one lap a day around the physical therapy section of the hospital.

At first, things were challenging. She simply raised my foot rests on my wheelchair and told me to take small steps while still seated in my chair. She followed behind me as I slowly started wheeling myself around the therapy section. We continued this day after day and after a couple weeks, this had become easy and I was able to do two laps around the hallway per session.

As I arrived at my physical therapy session on day, the nurse wheeled me down the hall as usual to meet Tonya. She then asked me to do something I hadn't done since the day following my surgery. Once I arrived in the physical therapy hall, Tonya told me I was going to stand. I must admit, I was a bit skeptical because I hadn't tried to do that since my dad and Dr. Kelly got me up from my postoperation bed. All I had been doing was "seat walking" for the past couple weeks. She placed both her arms on either side of me to catch me if I fell. As soon as I got my feet solidly on the ground and pushed myself off my chair, I was able to stand without much trouble. Tonya then asked me to walk, which proved to be a bit more difficult than standing. As I tried to take a step forward, my right leg went normally, but my left leg dragged across the ground. I was happy to be able to stand, but I really wanted to walk again.

The next day, Tonya asked me to focus on moving my left foot forward. With all my concentration, strength, and everything inside my being, I focused on moving my left foot forward. And it did. It went through the correct stepping motion and swung forward to meet my right foot in the first step I had taken since my surgery.

My foot thudded to the ground awkwardly, but it was a huge accomplishment and I immediately followed up with the next step while Tonya followed closely behind me as I made my lap around the therapy area. This was the first time I had walked since my surgery and I could not have been a more happy kid.

Each day, I struggled to complete the lap around the room. It was incredibly difficult at first, but it became easier each day. Tonya then told me she wanted me to walk around the hallways of the hospital. My fear of falling in the hallway caused me to have some apprehension about doing a lap outside the room. I was also afraid of getting tired and the lap around the therapy room was enough to cause me to be exhausted the rest of the day. We started around the hallways of the hospital walking tentatively. I felt that since I had left the therapy room, the pressure was on for me to be able to walk normally in front of the rest of the people in the hospital.

While I was learning to walk with Tonya, my therapy sessions with Angie were becoming progressively more successful in establishing my independence with my own dressing. I had progressed to tying my shoes one-handed.

Tonya and I continued walking the hallways of the hospital, going progressively farther each session. We were now able to talk as we walked the halls, but she continued constantly monitoring my steps. She then told me I needed to swing my arms as I walked in order to promote a more natural motion. She mocked me by telling me I was walking like a mummy, so I started throwing my arms awkwardly in rapid succession as I walked. Tonya applauded me and told me to keep swinging my arms. The more I swung, the more natural it felt for me to move my arms as I walked. I had gone from the wheelchair steps to awkwardly swinging my left foot forward, to walking normally in a matter of a few weeks thanks to Tonya.

The whole time I had been in the hospital, my life consisted of nothing but television, therapy, disassociation, and hospital food. My mom brought a picture from home with my dad, Tyler, and Ben (my youngest brother) and I put that picture on the arm guard to my bed and looked at the faces of my family. I was happy to have my mom with me, but seeing that picture jarred something loose within me. I started crying through the pain of missing my dad and brothers. They were the people who meant the world to me and I hadn't seen them in over a month. With one look at their faces, I missed fishing with my dad, playing basketball with Tyler, and picking on Ben. I think that picture made me realize how much my family meant to me.

The next day, Angie came into my room with a huge smile on her face; she looked so excited she might burst. She looked down at me and told me that she saw an eighty-year-old woman get dressed by herself that morning and she wanted me to do the same. It was a challenge; I fumbled with my fingers, dropped my clothes a few times, but eventually I had completely dressed myself without any help from anyone. Afterward, Angie told me she was proud of me and that me she had a surprise for me the next day.

As soon as I walked into Angie's office, she threw a Nerf basketball at me and told me to shoot some baskets. I turned to find a small Nerf basket on the back of her office door. I was ecstatic to say the least. This was the first time I had shot a basketball since having surgery. I shot baskets, one after another until our session was over and my heart was doing flips in my chest as I returned to my hospital room.

A few days later, I had another surprise waiting for me. My mom had found some friends from the community who wanted to take me to the mall. This was finally my time to show people how well I could walk. In my hometown, there are no malls, so in my mind, a real mall was a place of unimaginable coolness. All the kids in the popular television shows I watched hung out at the mall. And I was going to be at one of the coolness epicenters in a couple hours.

Once we arrived at the mall, I was amazed at the number of people and the trendy stores. Then, I saw the one place in the mall a guy like me needed to spend his time: At the top of the stairs was an arcade, which had been depicted in countless shows as the coolest spot in the mall.

Once inside the arcade, I found a game that involved getting into a simulated helicopter and shooting objects from the chopper. This game quickly became my obsession. I pumped quarter after quarter into this game until my mom told me she was out of money. I left the mall with my spirits higher than they had been since arriving in Minnesota.

Back at the hospital, my routine continued as usual, but I noticed that I was receiving fewer drugs and that they had stopped drawing my blood for testing. The length of my therapy sessions began to increase, with longer walks with Tonya. During these walks, I started talking and soon noticed I could walk comfortably for longer and longer distances until I started actually walking to my therapy sessions. My sessions with Angie became more focused on practical functioning activities such as getting dishes off shelves and using my hand to negotiate my way through everyday activities like washing my hands and taking a shower. All these things continued to get better until I eventually had no drugs and was comfortable dressing myself and accomplishing the demands of daily living by myself.

Then, my mom gave me great news. She told me that in a couple days we were going home. Inside, I was screaming for joy and excited to finally get to see the rest of my family. My thoughts became focused on what I was going to do once I was back in Poplar Bluff. Thoughts of basketball in the basement with Tyler and wrestling with Ben were all my mind was capable of entertaining. Images of playing games with my best friends Kyle and Josh were constantly whirling inside my head.

When we left the hospital, there was no tearful good-bye, just a road trip to catch the flight to St. Louis. I left my hospital room in an excited walk. The road trip to the airport was not the least bit painful. As I boarded my flight with my mom, I was so happy to get back to the rest of my family.

***

Once our flight landed, my mom and I were greeted by my dad and brothers in the airport. I joyously walked to my dad and brothers, immediately embracing them in a big, family hug. My dad seemed extremely happy to be holding me there in the airport. Instantly, time started again for me. For some reason, everything I had been through in the past few months was not real and it seemed as though, unbeknownst to me, time had stopped until I was back in the company of my family. The world began to spin again with that hug. I had finally arrived back to reality.

Once I arrived in my hometown, I expected things to be the same as when I left town. When I walked back in my room, it was decorated differently, with smiling flowers and bright colors. I thought to myself that it was nice that my parents had tried to make my room more lively, but I was pretty happy with it before they spruced it up with colorful plastic flowers and happy colors.

I began to let my mind wander toward returning to school to visit with my classmates and school friends. I could not wait to return to the playground basketball court and dominate the place just as I had always done. I also missed my teacher, Mrs. Norman, who had also been my kindergarten teacher a couple years earlier. I missed being in the classroom making great grades and waiting with anticipation for the next recess on the playground.

I did eventually return to school and found it to be a much different experience than I remembered. After arriving to school late, I walked the empty hallway to my classroom, a path I had traveled many times during my hospital daydreams. I opened the door to the class and saw everyone in the room look toward me as I entered the room. As I looked at my classmates I saw that each one of them had a gaping stare in my direction as I walked to my seat. After sitting at my desk, class began as usual and I paid attention in the same manner I always had. Then the bell rang for recess. I was finally back on the playground, a place I had longed for while lying in my hospital room. Once outside, I heard the voice of my best friend Kyle yelling for me to meet him on the basketball court for a game as we had always done. But once I caught the ball, I struggled to dribble and shoot. It felt very awkward trying to move on the basketball court. I ended up walking off the court after being unable to catch a pass. I wandered the playground in an awkward manner, settling in a spot under the balcony in the shade. As I sat there, I began to feel the chill of the ground moving through my body. After a few minutes, the bell rang to go back to class. After returning to the classroom, I noticed that the pace at which the teacher was teaching us seemed very fast. The rest of the day went by in a blur.

The next day, I awoke ready to head back to school, but instead was told that I was going to the Harper's house to learn. Mrs. Harper was a very nice lady and reminded me of Mary Tyler Moore, the main character of a show I had watched on Nick at Night. She had wavy brown hair, sharp cheek bones, and soft eyes that made me feel completely at ease sitting in her kitchen. She presented the lessons in an understanding and gentle manner that made me feel calm and relaxed as she went through the material she wanted me to learn. The room I studied inside was a neat and plain room with a small table and a chair, decorated in a soft, relaxation-promoting manner. We met every day for a few hours and I began to notice things were incredibly easy in her house. Everything I was learning was easy to understand and I quickly realized that my lessons were not very challenging. It was because of this that I began to daydream as soon as she left me to finish my lessons. After a few months of lessons with Mrs. Harper, I realized that it was getting close to summer. I had longed for the summer days of riding my bike to the pool, eating ice cream, drinking Kool-Aid, and playing outside.

My dad learned I wanted to ride a bike again so he went to the local bicycle shop and bought a bike called the "banana bike," which looked a bit ridiculous and appeared to be nothing at all like a bicycle. It was a recumbent bike with a seat close to the ground, two wheels on either side of the seat, a wheel below the seat, and a wheel in front of the bicycle seat. He took me to an empty parking lot then had me sit on this contraption and try to pedal. As I pedaled, I realized the bike was hard for me to maneuver. My dad took me and my brothers to the parking lot a few times per week to let me practice riding the banana bike around the open asphalt. Tyler and Ben would fly around the open parking spaces, whizzing by me on their bikes. I tried to keep pace with them, but my banana bike was hard to move and even harder to turn. I then told my dad that I wanted to try riding a real bike. He gave me a puzzled look and told me he would let me try riding on the football field in a few days. I later found out that the doctors in Minnesota had told my parents I would never be able to ride a bicycle.

A few days later, my dad took me onto the football field. He put a helmet on my head, wrist guards, and shin guards for protection. I climbed on my bicycle and tried to pedal, but fell to the ground. After getting to my feet, I mounted the bicycle again and started pedaling. I got a few yards, then toppled over after trying to make a simple turn on one end of the field. I then remounted the bike and began pedaling again. This time, when I came to a turn, my wheel wobbled and I fell again, landing in the grass.

On that fall, I noticed something: I had almost completed the turn and if I turned the wheel at an angle that was less sharp, it would probably allow me to make the turn effectively. I was right. As soon as I got up and started pedaling, I made the turn at the other end of the field. My front wheel wobbled, but I stayed on my bike. I then rode to the other side and made a turn again, this time with less wobble in my wheel. I continued riding around the field with less and less wobble until I was able to make the turns around the field with confidence. I was ecstatic. I was able to ride my bike with confidence as I had always done. I would be able to ride my bike around the neighborhood with my friends and brothers again.

My lessons with Mrs. Harper were also rapidly improving. I learned that I was going to return to the classroom. I went to Ms. Norman's second grade classroom. The first assignment she gave us was to read a book, then do a book report on it. As I began reading, it was evident that I could not finish the book in the allotted time for class. Ms. Norman told us that we could finish the book at home and turn in our report the next day. I had only finished a couple pages and felt incompetent because most of my friends had already finished the book and had written their report.

That night, I read the assigned book and it took a long time. I then completed my report and turned it in, expecting to receive an A on the assignment and regain my academic confidence. I got the paper back and saw that she had given me a C. I then thought, "Oh well, I'm still passing." It was then that I began to think I was unable to make good grades in school. The rest of the day went well until she handed out the times table assignment. We had one minute to do thirty quick problems. I hurried as quickly as I could, but when the time was up, I was not even close to having completed my assignment. I turned it in anyway, and received another C. We had physical education class that day and I flashbacked to memories of fun and exciting activities that allowed me to exhibit my athleticism. But, once again, I struggled to keep up with the other kids in my class. Instead of crab-walking effectively, I wound up awkwardly flopping on the floor trying to do the crab walk without the use of my left arm. It was no use, so instead of playing crab soccer, I sat and flailed my legs at the ball anytime it came close. It began to become clear to me that everything I had been able to do before leaving for Minnesota was going to be much more difficult now that I had returned. I felt as though I had been left out of the fun. I wanted desperately to get back to being the best at everything I did, but was unable to even keep up with the rest of the class.

Before heading to Minnesota, playing with the neighborhood kids was easy and fun. I was able to outrun anyone and jump off walls on the sides of my neighbors' driveways with ease and never get tired. Upon returning from Minnesota, I had to learn to run again. My dad would take me to a field and attempt running races. One day, my brothers and I lined up on one side of the field and were going to race to the other side. My dad yelled go, and we took off. I ran as hard as I could. Then my left leg took an awkward stumble midway through the field and I fell to the ground and broke my wrist.

Once my wrist healed, I began learning to play basketball with limited use of my left hand. After lots of practice, I felt confident in my ability to run and jump, but what I really wanted was to play basketball. Because I had religiously practiced using the correct shooting form since I was four, I knew that my left hand was only needed to support the ball. My right hand and my legs were the important part of a fundamentally sound jump shot. I began practicing shooting in the backyard. I learned to catch the ball and dribble. I slowly became a basketball player again. My dad then decided to remove me from physical therapy sessions.

His decision to quit taking me to the therapy sessions was because I viewed it as exercise for weak people. I always considered myself to be well above the curve in my ability to perform athletic tasks, with a desire to be one of the best and toughest dogs in the pound. I'm going to call this the alpha-male mentality. Looking around the physical therapy area made me feel like a wolf that had been wrongly placed in a pen full of poodles. After a few days removed from therapy, my dad told me he wanted me to lift weights with him on Monday, Wednesday, and Friday. Of course I agreed; lifting weights was a thing that badass wolves did to get bigger and stronger.

The following Monday, my dad and I went into our basement weight room to begin a workout routine. We first did bench presses with only the bar. He then showed me a series of lifts that we were going to do three days a week. At the end of the weight workout, we had a series of fine motor things I had to do with my left hand. I had to use tweezers to pick up pieces of paper and move a ball along a track with my left hand. While the majority of the workout was directed toward a strength training program, the tweezers and ball exercises gave me the most difficulty. My favorite exercise we did in the basement was "machine gun passing." This involved my dad passing a basketball to me in a chest pass while I passed a ball to him at the same time in a bounce pass, we continued in this manner of rapid fire successions until our allotted time for this drill was over.

Every few weeks, we added a little more difficulty to the workout. My dad had found two heavy balls that bounced like a basketball to use for machine gun passing. While I loved lifting weights at first, it became tedious and there were many times I did not want to do it. My dad made me go down there and complete the routine anyway. It didn't matter what the day brought us, we ended the day with this weightlifting routine. After school, we lifted weights. After a long day at the pool, we lifted weights. We would even lift weights before playing night basketball games in the backyard with the neighbors. I began to notice that I was becoming a good athlete again. While I wasn't the fastest kid in school, I could handle the athletic skills needed for basketball. I once again had become one of the better basketball players in my grade school.

When I was growing up, there were seven grade schools that taught kindergarten through sixth grade.

Each school had a basketball team made of the best fifth- and sixth-grade basketball players in each school. I was excited to get to try out and play basketball for my grade school because it meant that I, along with my friends, would be viewed as the best players in the school. It also meant that we would carry on the tradition of basketball dominance that came with being an O'Neal Elementary Blue Jay.

After the first week of tryouts, I was notified that I had made the team and was excited to be able to play. Even with basketball practice, my weight routine continued at the house and I did not look forward to it. But we continued with our routine. The grade school basketball league included the local Catholic grade school, Sacred Heart, which was where my brothers went to school. My dad coached that team and Tyler and Ben were on the team. The games between O'Neal and Sacred Heart became a household rivalry and I was confident we were the better team.

We faced my dad and brothers' team in the championship game of the grade school tournament. The game was broadcast on the local radio station and I was sure my team was going to win. As a fifth grader, I saw very little playing time because the sixth graders got to play the majority of the minutes. At the end of the first quarter, O'Neal was down to Sacred Heart and my brother Tyler and Travis Tinsley were the leading scorers in the game. I went in the game at the start of the second half, blocked Travis Tinsley's shot, and scored a layup with him guarding me. I then returned to the bench and watched as my family's team beat my team for the championship. I was determined to not let that happen the following season.

Playing for O'Neal came with an air of arrogance, as we thought of ourselves as the best basketball players in the grade school league. Even with our loss, I believed we would return O'Neal to the basketball powerhouse it had been before losing that championship.

Around the dinner table at my house, my dad talked about the mighty powerhouse falling to the little Sacred Heart Hawks and his team being led by a second grader who outplayed the dominant O'Neal sixth graders. I told him that the next season was going to be different and we would crush the Hawks.

That summer, I began to practice in my backyard every day. My imaginary basketball games began to take place on the ten-foot goal as well as the side dunk goal. I developed a shooting routine involving drills I had learned at basketball camp. I shot this routine every day that summer and played against my brothers and the neighbors. My dad installed lights on the roof so that we could play basketball at night.

These lights meant that we could play as late as we wanted into the night. That summer we would play games sometimes until ten o'clock at night. It was a lot of fun, as those lights gave me a feeling of playing in a major outdoor basketball venue. My neighbors were always stopping by to play and without fail, we would almost always beat them in whatever games we were playing.

The next year, my friends and I were in the sixth grade and we prided ourselves on being the best and toughest players in school. We found a group of kids on the playground that played physical basketball and had a tendency to foul a lot during recess. One day, I got pushed to the ground shooting a jump shot and skinned my knee. This was not a new thing to me, I was frequently sitting in class after recess with a paper towel trying to get my knee to stop bleeding. So I'm not sure why my best friend, Kit, told me to not take that from Paul, the kid who pushed me. I punched Paul in the face, which started a fight on the basketball court between us and the group we were playing against. Because Kit fought to keep Paul's friends from hitting me, we both went to the principal's office and were paddled for our actions. While the paddling hurt, I felt a little bit of pride in knowing that my best friend and I had been in a fight and won.

Then, the basketball season began and we were playing really well, beating most teams by over ten points. I was finally getting to play a lot and we cruised through the tournament until the championship game. Our grade school league had rivalries and our rival was the Oak Grove Panthers. We met the Panthers in the championship game. During the season, we had beaten them by five points and I was confident we would win by more this time. But the game was close; I was not playing my best and neither was the rest of the team. The final buzzer went off and we were up by one point. I began running around the gym in celebration. I had not noticed that there had been a foul called and they got to shoot two free throws. The wind immediately left my sails and I watched as they made two free throws to win the championship. I was very disappointed in this loss, but at least I hadn't lost to my dad and brothers.

The rest of my sixth grade year went well, except for a scuffle I got in with my best friend over a poker game during indoor recess. I thought Kyle had cheated me out of a glue bottle so I jumped on him, and the teacher came into the room and found us fighting. I was paddled in the hallway for this scuffle. Luckily, this scuffle did not affect our friendship and we graduated from O'Neal Elementary as best friends.

Going to junior high was a big deal because all the kids from all the grade schools went to the same junior high once they reached the seventh grade. It was also the first time we would get lockers and get to switch classrooms with each class. I had no idea that I was entering a time of tremendous struggle in my life that would make me a much stronger person.

Junior High

As I went to my first day of junior high school, I was excited to meet the other kids from the other grade schools and wanted to make sure I established myself as a cool and popular kid. In my mind, a cool kid was the kind of person that was incredibly tough, disliked by the good kids and respected by gangsters. Basically, I felt a cool kid was the type of person portrayed in rap music. However, as I walked to class, I was shoved into a closed locker by a tall kid who appeared to be much more physically mature than me. At thirteen, I was a little over six feet tall and slightly heavyset. I looked up at him, surprised, and he told me, "Get out of my way!"

I went from class to class enjoying the fact that I was changing classrooms and teachers with each hour. I enjoyed having a locker and felt cool opening a locker the same way kids on popular television shows did. I was also excited to see that I had been placed in athletic PE because it meant that I had been recognized as one of the athletes in the school. It also fed into my belief and understanding that I was the alpha male and could accomplish feats that most people in the world would not be able to accomplish.

I feel the reason I considered myself an alpha male comes from my father and early successes in life, before my brain surgeries. My dad always strove to be the best at everything he did, especially when it came to sports. He was always pushing himself to work out harder than other people. And before my surgery, I was able to win at everything I did with minimal effort. Every time I gave maximal effort, I succeeded by a large margin. Just like any leader of the pack, I needed a great nickname.

In switching classes, two of the teachers asked what I wanted to be called in their class. I told one teacher to call me Snake and another to call me Diesel. Both times it brought uproarious laughter from the rest of the class. Some of my classmates started calling me "Snake Diesel" and I then had a great nickname worthy of an alpha male.

As I walked into the PE locker room, I was given a basket and locker to put my clothes in while I was in class. We were told to keep our PE clothes in the basket and change into them every day for PE. It was in this class that I began to feel self-conscious about my left arm and my inability to use it very efficiently.

In that first week of school, I heard another kid in my PE class picking on me about my limited ability. I stood up for myself and told him to leave me alone. He immediately grabbed me by my neck and twisted it to a point where it felt as though it would snap. He said in my ear, "Say you're sorry or I'll snap your neck." I was terrified of having my neck broken because I knew that would mean I would not be able to walk anymore. I apologized and felt my neck go back to its original position. As I rubbed my neck, I looked up to see my PE coach, Strum Bufford, staring down on me with a look that said the interaction was my fault. I immediately contemplated fighting back, but thought that could cause me to be dismissed from athletic PE class.

After a few weeks, I was hanging around kids in the hallways that I thought were tough and cool. I began to think it was cool to wear my shorts low and recite rap music as I walked the halls. I also loved talking to people so it was difficult for me to be in class before the bell rang. I loved the social aspect of school. In continued efforts to gain recognition as a popular and cool kid, I singled out kids in class that I thought were tough and cool to talk with in an effort to boost my own popularity. In my home economics class, I tried to align myself with a boy named Rine. He was incredibly rude and mean to me in the school. I continued to endure the ridicule at the expense of my self-confidence. I placed a fake smile on my face and continued trying to align him as a friend because I wanted to be seen as a cool and tough kid in the school.

Before my surgery, I never thought about being the tough guy, I just always knew I was the best at anything I tried. After returning from Minnesota, I was struggling to keep up with the other kids in class. As a result, I tried to hide my shortcomings under the veil of toughness. Portraying myself as a hard or cool kid was a way to hide that I was having more trouble succeeding in life than I had before surgery.

After a few weeks, my PE class went up a flight of stairs to a locked door. The only people who could go up the staircase were coaches and students in athletic PE. The stairs led to the school weight room which featured four platforms holding four Olympic bars, squat racks, and bench press benches. We were going to learn proper weight room techniques for the different lifts in class.

On the second day, I was spotting a student doing the power clean lift. As a spotter, I was supposed to stand behind him with my arms extended to catch him if he fell backward. While I was focusing on the person I was spotting, I felt an Olympic bar hit me in the back with a force that knocked me down. I then felt a lot of pain in my back from the impact and began crying. As I began to cry, the football player who had thrown the bar began laughing at my tears. His laugh became uproarious laughter from the entire class. I walked away and saw Strum, the PE coach, laughing at me as I walked to the wall in pain. I thought the boys who had thrown the bar would be punished for their actions, but instead the class went to the locker room still laughing at my pain. By the time I had reached the locker room, the pain from the bar was gone, but there was a sharper pain from the ridicule I was receiving for crying in the weight room. It seemed as though every couple minutes someone would make a comment that caused hilarity from the rest of the locker room. It made me feel as if I were the butt of a hilarious joke. I did not feel like the alpha male at that moment; instead I felt embarrassed about not being as tough as I pretended.

The next day, Strum had me switched to regular PE because he claimed I was a liability in the weight room because of my left arm.

In my hometown, it was understood that the athletes in school would be in athletic PE, which meant they would lift weights three days a week during class. It was understood that the kids in this class would be representing the school on a sports team. A student not in athletic PE would have a more difficult time making one of the sports teams because they were not immediately recognized as an athlete by the school.

Since the start of school not a day went by that I didn't get picked on about my left arm. Each time it happened, I thought about fighting back, but then decided against it because I didn't want to lose a spot on the basketball team the next year. I had this belief that getting suspended would keep me from playing basketball. I thought this because none of the basketball players on the team were getting suspended from school. Plus, my grades were not the best, and I thought I could be held back a grade if I were suspended, meaning I would be ineligible for sports. It was for these reasons I continued getting picked on and refused to stand up for myself.

In my new PE class, there were three boys who were sixteen years old. They gained a lot of respect from the classmates because they were in multiple fights throughout the school year. It seemed at least once a week, one of my PE classmates would be involved in a school fight.

While I may not have been in athletic PE, I was still playing in the seventh grade intramural basketball program. Since seventh graders were not allowed to play for the junior high school team, we would play in an intramural program. Every seventh grader that signed up was assigned to a team and the teams would play each other during the basketball season.

I knew I was one of the best players in school, and I was going to show that every day on the basketball court. That season I was confident I had established myself as one of the best basketball players in the seventh grade. I honestly thought I was the best, but I knew there were other players in my grade who were good also. The season ended and I was sure that I was going to make the basketball team the following season. I decided that over the summer, I was going to lift weights at the high school and become better at basketball so that I would easily make the basketball team next year as a member of the eighth grade Poplar Bluff Mules basketball team.

***

The summer before the eighth grade, I went to a Fellowship of Christian Athletes (FCA) basketball camp in Indiana with my neighbor. This camp was a blast. I was able to play a lot of basketball games, but I also gained a sense of Christianity while at camp. I am still proud to say that I started a camp-wide pillow fight that spilled into the field beside our cabin. I also felt I was one of the best players in the camp. I was excited to return to school and show off not only my basketball skills, but also my Christian faith.

In the days before I entered the eighth grade, my dad advocated for me to be in the athletic PE class. Strum told the administration that I was a liability in the weight room. My dad argued that I was not a liability and deserved to be in that class. After a few heated arguments, the principal agreed to put me in athletic PE against the wishes of Strum.

As I entered the eighth grade, I was filled with the desire to behave in a positive, Christian manner. I sat quietly in class the whole first week and paid attention. In my athletic PE class, the first week we learned the drills before every class. One of the football players instructed the class to do a push-up before Strum gave the direction. The whole class performed a push-up and Strum thought it was hilarious. I thought it would make for a funny trick a few days later during class.

The following week, the good Christian boy syndrome had worn off. I was still a Christian, but my desire to behave as an angel was gone. It was replaced with my desire to become a comedian. I tried to get laughter from everyone in class and also try to be the coolest and toughest kid in school. In PE, I performed the same joke as the kid had a week earlier by instructing the class to perform a push-up before Strum. Strum told me to move to the side of the class and do one hundred sit-ups as punishment. As I moved to the side of the class, I didn't understand why I was punished for an action that another boy did without any consequences.

In the locker room, the other kids ridiculed me for everything they could think of, from my arm, to my clothes, and even my weight. I began to become incredibly insecure about my coolness and felt as though I was not a very cool or valuable person. Every time I was called something derogatory, if I retaliated in any way, even by simply telling them to stop, Strum would tell me to do one hundred sit-ups.

After our second week of lifting weights, we were walking back to the locker room and a boy started pushing me. I turned and he yelled, "You're just a big pussy" then punched me in the head. This pissed me off and I turned around to retaliate, but before I was able to turn around, he grabbed me by my right arm, pinned my arm to my body, then threw me headfirst down the flight of stairs leading to the locker room. Once I had finished bouncing off the stairs and landed at the bottom, I looked up to see Strum staring down at me, once again with a look that said it was my fault for plummeting down the stairs. I turned to the boy who had thrown me down the stairs and he was standing there wanting to fight. He slapped me in the face, and said, "C'mon bitch." I considered defending myself, but changed my mind because I believed if I got into a fight, I would be suspended and not allowed to play on the basketball team. Strum watched as I was punched again by the boy, this time in my gut, causing me to bend over. As I stood upright again, the boy finally left me alone and began to change clothes for regular classes.

In the wake of this attack, I felt humiliated and helpless to defend myself. In a way, I was restrained by my desire to achieve athletic success. And to add insult to injury, the boy called me a "one-armed pussy" as he dressed. As I dressed, I could feel tears welling into my throat and knew I wanted to cry. I didn't want to get caught crying at school, so I swallowed hard and buried the pain from this attack deep in the pit of my stomach. The other boys in my PE class also called me names, usually in reference to my left arm, on a daily basis.

I began to try to make fun of the other kids in my class as a means of retaliation, but always failed to ridicule them as harshly as they had ridiculed me. I then resorted to threatening to beat them up in a show of bravado. After a couple months of this, it was time for basketball tryouts.

I was confident that I was going to make the team because I was in athletic PE, knew how to play, and considered myself to be one of the best players in the school. Tryouts were every day before and after school. In the morning, practice would start at 6:30 and go until ten minutes before school started. After school, practice would last until 5:30. These practices were difficult. We ran a lot of line drills and I was paired with a boy named Ed for a lot of the drills. I hated going against him because he was always the most difficult player to guard. In the morning, we did a lot of individual drills, then in the afternoon, we ran a lot and did more team-oriented things. Coach Vagrun was the eighth grade coach and he was an angry, short man who seemed to always be yelling profanities toward us as we played. He told us to pick our asses up, stomped his foot if somebody did some-thing wrong, and screamed if we did not perform a drill to his liking.

After that first week, tryouts were over and I had made the team, as I expected. We received our team practice jerseys that consisted of a maroon and white reversible tank top. We also placed orders for the team basketball shoes, for which each player had to pay sep-arately. Another huge perk for making the basketball team was getting assigned a larger locker in the locker room. I was excited because my athletic locker was large enough to hold my clothes and shoes easily while the regular lockers would not hold my shoes. For the next two weeks, we continued to have practice before and after school.

Coach Vagrun began to make us run more during practice and continued yelling at us in a hostile manner, stomping his foot and telling us how poorly we were playing. He reminded me of an angry, stereotypically hot-headed coach, as it seemed that the only way he knew to get the best from his players was to scream profanity at them.

During school, I was still called names and picked on about my arm and how uncool I was, but I was too tired to care. I continued telling them stories trying to make myself sound like a hard-ass, a person capable of winning any fight. I once told somebody that I was in a gang and if I turned my hat backward, it meant I was going to fight. Truth was I just wanted to fit in with the tough kids in school to hide the fact that I was struggling to be successful. The difference between me and the tough kids in school was that I did not want to lose my spot on the basketball team. In the classroom, I wanted to make grades that kept me eligible to play.

Our first game was quickly approaching. We opened the season in an away game and I was excited to get to play against another school as a Poplar Bluff Mule. The first game, I discovered I was not going to start and sat the bench the majority of the game. After that first game, we only had practice after school, eliminating the morning practice. The weeks began to fly with basketball practice, games, and school. Coach Vagrun continued to yell and scream at us, I continued to keep my grades at a level that allowed me to play. I was still getting beaten up in PE, even thrown down the stairs once more. I was still trying to falsely present myself as a streetwise, mean kid. And my self value continued to plummet. However, even with all these negative messages being sent to me by other kids, I still considered myself an alpha male because I was on the basketball team and in athletic PE. Strum still allowed me to be picked on by his football players and he still gave me harsh punishments anytime he could—I once did four hundred sit-ups during a PE class for talking during warm-ups.

At home, I was fighting more and more with my brothers. I was taking out my frustrations in school on them. I drew away from my family in order hide from them the hardships I was enduring at school. Part of me was afraid that if I voiced my struggles at school, my mom would try to talk to the coaches, which would only add to the ridicule I was already receiving from my teammates.

One day in practice, one of the other players on the team, Nick, complained about a hard foul during a drill. Coach Vagrun turned bright red and began violently striding toward Nick. As he strode across the court, he ripped his whistle from around his neck and threw it across the floor, then got in Nick's face. His body was so strained with anger that I could see his carotid artery throbbing with hostility. He then screamed, "Nick! You big fucking pussy! If somebody fouls you, you take their ass through the fucking hoop with you!" After practice, the entire team laughed at Nick about receiving Coach Vagrun's outburst, but I stopped laughing after a few minutes because I could tell Nick felt humiliated. In a way, it was nice not to be the one getting laughed at, but once I saw how hurt he was, I remembered how much it hurt me every time I was picked on and I immediately stopped picking on him about the coach's violent outburst. Nick transferred schools shortly after this incident.

The basketball season came to an end and I was exhausted from the season, looking forward to being able to relax after school instead of going to practice. Meanwhile, in school, I continued with my bravado of being a great fighter, until one day it was tested.

One of the boys I considered popular, Ryan, was offended at something I had said about his mother. We met in the bathroom to fight. I stood there and got punched in the face repeatedly as I waited to throw a punch. After a couple minutes, the fight was over and I was standing there with a bloody lip having never thrown a punch. In Poplar Bluff, there was a culture of violence everywhere. It seemed as though everyone wanted to be the tough guy. Which meant that winning fights established a boy as being a tough guy. Fights at school were a big deal, there was at least one fight a week in the junior high. After any fight, both kids were immediately suspended for a week. Luckily, my fight had not been discovered by the teachers. Unluckily, I had undoubtedly lost the fight. When I told my dad what had happened, he seemed a bit disappointed with my performance, telling me to defend myself next time. He told me that next time I got in a fight, I should do anything I could to win. Bite, kick, punch, anything I could to hurt the other person.

Later that year, our PE class went roller skating during class at the local roller rink. One of the boys in my class, Danny, had been one of the main culprits in calling me names and degrading me during school. At the roller rink, Danny began popping me with a rubber band as I skated. I told him to stop multiple times, and he then popped me in the back of my neck. The hair stood up on my neck, and I felt a year's worth of being called names and degraded bubbling up in my gut. I turned around and saw him laughing. I snapped. I punched him in the throat as hard as I could, causing him to land on his stomach in the middle of the rink. I then skated off. Danny quit picking on me.

A few weeks after the roller skating incident, I was sitting in class, and once the teacher left the room, Danny told me to turn around. He then pulled a large bullet out of his backpack telling me that it could kill a person, all he had to do was hit the tip of the bullet hard enough and pieces of lead would explode through the person's body. This terrified me. I was in fear for my life. The rest of the year, I avoided Danny at all costs, and he also avoided me. As I watched Danny interact with other kids in the school, I noticed he was not being rude to them. It seemed as though I was the only one he picked on.

As eighth grade came to an end, I was told that there would be a basketball PE class over the summer and they wanted the players expecting to play basketball as ninth graders to take the summer class. I immediately signed up for the summer class and decided that I would do anything necessary to make and stay on the basketball team in high school. The little playing time I had received on the team in eighth grade made me believe that I had to do everything in order to stay on the team. This meant that every time there was an event involving Poplar Bluff Mules basketball, I was there ready to play.

This summer PE class met every day from eight until noon. In this class, we lifted weights, played games, and did jumping and agility drills, all inside a gym without air conditioning. In the weight room, I considered myself capable of lifting as much weight as anybody my age. I quickly learned that I was not as strong as many of the other kids my age in this class. I watched as my classmates were able to lift more weight in the different lifts during our class. I was also having trouble getting my left wrist to lock into place for some of the lifts. For bench press, I would grasp the bar with my left hand, then hit my left wrist until it locked in a position that would allow me to perform the lift with both arms. While I had learned to do this efficiently in the basement of my house with my dad, I struggled to keep my left wrist locked in position for lifts such as incline bench press and I was unable to perform power clean lifts. It was always embarrassing and scary when my left wrist would slip out of position during a lift because it made the bar come crashing down on me. One of my teammates was usually spotting me and would grab the bar after it hit me. At this point, I had become such an athlete that everyone on the team knew about my left arm, but they still expected me to be able to perform on the same level as the rest of the team. So, when I would drop the bar, they would yell at me for not helping them lift the bar back into the correct spot on the incline bench press rack.

Since the third grade, I had been figuring out ways to assimilate my left side in order to keep up with everybody else on the basketball team. I was now confident in my ability to play sports as an equal. The high school weight room was a new assimilation challenge and I was determined to become one of the better athletes in the class. By the end of the summer, I had learned that if I felt my left wrist slipping on the incline bench press, I just had to force my arm to position itself underneath the bar while concentrating on forcing my wrist back in the correct position. This would help me to keep my wrist from slipping about half the time, but the culture in the locker room was one that continued to create insecurity.

High School

As an incoming freshman, I expected to get picked on a little bit by the players on the team, but for some reason it was not as painful as the hazing I had received from my eighth grade PE class. I was still picked on and called names—one of the seniors called me "one-armed wonder"—but I was not maliciously picked on, as I had experienced in the junior high locker room. By the end of the summer, all the players on the high school varsity and junior varsity teams knew me by name and understood that I was a physical and tough basketball player.

As I started the ninth grade, I once again attempted to align myself with the kids I thought were the popular kids. I sat with the seniors and tried to joke with them in the halls. The only time I really spent with the other ninth graders was in classes and basketball.

I was placed in basketball PE, which meant that I was expected to make the basketball team and got to lift weights and work out with the other players on the team. The first week of PE included an exhausting schedule consisting of hill running, wind sprints, weightlifting, and more sprints. After the first week, I noticed that a lot of kids had switched from basketball PE to regular PE. But I loved basketball PE for some strange reason, I enjoyed pushing myself through the sprints and drills. I think part of my enjoyment of this intense class was knowing that it was tough and that I was able to handle myself in the toughest class in school. By the time basketball tryouts began, our PE class had dwindled to about twenty students.

The freshman coach was Tuck, a tall, thin, bald, middle-aged man who seemed to enjoy coaching. I could tell right away that he wanted to see who was going to be tough enough to stay on the team despite the excessive amount of running we endured during practice. After the first week, half the players who had tried out stopped coming to practice. After the second week, we received our practice uniforms, which were again maroon and white reversible shirts.

I had done it, I was a member of the freshman basketball team. While I was still picked on in the locker room for being uncool and my left arm not working as well, the head basketball coach allowed me to defend myself and treated me as an equal member of the class instead of trying to make things harder on me than the other students. If one of the older players intentionally pushed me or jabbed me in the chest, I would jump on them and defend myself in wrestling matches. I usually lost these matches, but it was nice to be able to attempt to defend myself.

I was still not a starter on the team, but I was getting in the games a little bit more than the previous year. Practices were very difficult, requiring a lot of running mixed in with the drills. By the time Christmas break had arrived, I was completely used to running sprints during practice.

While I was trying to make my way as a high school athlete, my parents were going through a break up. My parents' divorce was a difficult time for me and I avoided the situation by hanging out with my friends away from home as much as possible. While at home, I saw my parents arguing constantly and watched their marriage end in a nasty divorce. In the aftermath of their split, I dove deeper into spending time with my friends and poured my emotions into athletic training. I learned that I could channel my emotions into a positive action such as lifting weights, running, or playing basketball.

The first week of the two-week Christmas break we did not have practice, but Coach Tuck told us it was important for us to stay in shape. During that week off from practice, I went to the gym, shot baskets, and lifted weights in my basement. I was lifting weights in the basement barefoot the Saturday before practice began again. I was moving a forty-five-pound weight from the squat bar back to the weight rack when my grip slipped and the weight came crashing down on my bare toe nail. I jumped up and down in pain and noticed a lot of blood pooling underneath my nail. I hobbled upstairs and showed my dad what had happened, and he immediately drove to the hospital and returned with an instrument that was designed to burn a hole through the nail in order to relieve pressure. One perk of having a doctor as a dad. Upon drilling the hole in my toenail, blood immediately spilled onto the towel below my foot. While the pressure was lessened from the hole in my nail, my toe continued to bleed and it was extremely painful to walk.

When basketball practice began the following Monday, I told Coach Tuck what had happened and that I wanted to sit out of practice until it felt better. That whole practice, I sat and watched my teammates run drills. Every few minutes, I would see Coach Tuck looking down on me, not believing that I was hurt. The next day, I made the decision to practice. My foot still hurt a lot, but I did not want to lose my spot on the team. And I really didn't want Coach Tuck to look at me the same way he did the players who feigned injuries to miss practice. During drills, Coach would mockingly ask how my terrible toe was feeling. I winced each step I ran during practice. Every step I took running on the court, I could feel blood pulsing under my toenail. I could only continue to practice by using the dissociation techniques

I had learned from my time in the hospital. I concentrated on playing so hard that I put the pain to the back of my head. Every few minutes, I was reminded that my toe was still injured by the screaming pain. If I had to quickly change directions during practice, it would cause intense pain and I could feel blood leaking out of the hole in my toe nail. At the end of practice, coach told me I had to run three extra sprints for missing practice the day before. After running the makeup sprints, I sat in a chair on one end of the gym, slowly loosening up my shoe in preparation to slide it off my foot with a minimal amount of pain. As I began sliding my shoe off, Coach Tuck asked in a mocking tone, "Let me see that toenail you hurt so badly." I slowly and painfully slid my shoe off, revealing a sock that was soaked from toe to heel with my blood. I looked up at Coach Tuck and saw his face lose all expression. He had expected to see my white sock and confirm that I was faking an injury to miss practice. When he saw my bloody sock, I could tell that he felt badly about not believing I had been injured. I didn't miss a single practice or game the rest of the season. The rest of the season, Coach Tuck smiled down on me because he understood I had endured excruciating pain to practice and stay with the team.

***

During the second half of the season, I noticed that I was receiving a lot of criticism and ridicule from some of the juniors on the team. They began to call me anything they could think of to lower my self-esteem. One senior believed he was giving me a positive nickname by calling me the "one-armed bandit." I took the senior's nickname as another derogatory method of poking fun at my left arm, so I told him to shut up. He told me I should be proud of that name. The entire basketball season I endured jokes at my expense, once again causing me to become extremely self-conscious about my left arm.

As my freshman year came to an end, I became extremely self-conscious about everything I did. In many ways, I felt like an outsider being tolerated by the older, cooler social groups I was attempting to join. I started playing basketball every time the gym was open.

While I was trying to be the best basketball player I could, other areas of my life were in the periphery of my focus. I still picked on my brothers at home in an effort to relieve some of the pain I was feeling from being picked on by my teammates. I was incredibly interested in girls, but could never get a date. It seemed I was a little bit too interested in them to win their attention. Most nights, I sat at home with my brothers watching TV and wishing for a social life like the cool kids on the varsity basketball team.

By the time summer arrived, I was known by name by every coach in the school. I began to plan for team basketball camps at the University of Mississippi State and University of Missouri. These were the two camps Coach Pat decided we would attend in order to improve as a team over the summer.

Coach Pat was the head basketball coach for the varsity basketball team, which also meant he was the basketball PE coach and decision maker on what our summer schedule would look like as a basketball program. He was a very friendly and fun-loving man. He frequently wrestled with his players and joked with them constantly. Although his demeanor was playful off the court, I could tell that he was a tough coach on the court and that he wanted us to be the best teams possible. Since he was a young coach, he would occasionally jump in and play in games with us during open gym.

While Coach Pat was the head varsity coach, the assistant and junior varsity coach was Coach Maroon. Coach Maroon learned to coach under former University of Missouri men's basketball coach Norm Stewart. He was a short heavyset man with glasses. He had earned the reputation as a tough coach on the court and was famous for pushing his players to work as hard as they could on the court. He was also famous for his outbursts when one of his players did something wrong. In a way, he kind of reminded me of a fatter Bobby Knight, with loud outbursts of correctional criticism and a reputation for screaming at his players.

That summer, both coaches were at summer basketball, which meant we were going to have tough practices before going to Mississippi State for our first team camp. The hot gym seemed to have a way of making me sweat instantly. I had long grown accustomed to having a coating of sweat on my body every day from playing basketball in the gym.

The weight room at the high school was the place to be for a high school athlete in my hometown over the summer. We would lift weights three days a week in the weight room, then return to the gym for basketball games and drills. The other two days of the week, we went to the building that held the weight room for drills designed to improve our quickness and vertical jump.

These drills involved lining up with the other members of the basketball team behind a line of boxes with about two feet separating each box. One by one, we would jump from the ground to the top of the box, then jump off and bound onto the next box in the line. It was inevitable that every time we did these box jumping drills, I would trip and land chest first on the ground. When I hit the ground, I would hear laughter from my teammates. I felt frustrated that I fell so often on these drills, I wanted to believe that I was one of the most athletic kids on the team, but falling so much on box jumps made me feel like I was not as good as the other players on the team. I would hear them laugh as I returned to my feet. Each fall over the box slowly chipped away at the inner confidence I held about being an extremely talented athlete who stood above everyone in my athletic ability. But I would rise from the ground every time to get back in line with the rest of the basketball players.

While box jumps were difficult to me, Coach Pat would occasionally take us to a large dirt hill on the side of the school to run hill sprints. And I was great at sprinting hills. When we were told to jog to the hill, everyone on the team would grumble and groan on our way to the hill. I enjoyed these hill sprints because for some strange reason, I was one of the fastest guys running these hills. I loved lining up on the bottom of this hill, because while I struggled to keep up with the group in all of our other drills, I could keep up with the team on the hill sprints.

After a few weeks of summer basketball, it was time to load into the buses and head to Mississippi State to play against the best teams in Mississippi.

I thought we would be riding to Starkville, Mississippi, in school buses, but instead we loaded into three large vans and settled in for the five-hour trip. On the trip down, we would tell crazy stories, listen to music, and laugh about inside basketball jokes. I was in a van with Coach Pat and he was telling stories along with the rest of us. We went from stories about high school parties, to crazy times, and then to camp.

I enjoyed these trips because I felt as though I was a part of the team. One of my biggest fears was that I would not be on the basketball team. This fear was the reason I was in the gym every time it was open. As a bench warmer, I believed that the only way I would stay on the team was to always be playing and doing all these little things to ensure a position on the team. In doing all these things to stay on the team, I developed a love for being a part of the team, not only because it set me apart from the rest of the school as an athlete, but also because I loved working out and playing basketball. It had become my passion. It was out of this hard work and the enjoyment of hard work that I had created such a passion for the game.

The Mississippi State team camp was a blast. After checking into camp, we went to our dorm; each team had rooms in the same section of a dorm. The dorms were not air conditioned and each room consisted of two small twin-size beds and a small sink. There was a community shower where everybody took showers at one end of the hallway. After putting our stuff in our dorm rooms, we had a couple hours before dinner and games. During this down time, we would jokingly pick on each other in the dorms. This quickly became wrestling matches and playful scuffles with my teammates. I received a lot of jokes about my left arm and would immediately jump on one of my teammates in a playful manner. While I smiled and playfully jabbed the person who had called me a one-armed bandit or called my left arm the snake, I pretended that it didn't bother me and allowed it to happen. I would repeatedly get beaten in wrestling matches with my teammates and received punches in my chest from jumping into a wrestling match with someone who had insulted me. To say the least, I lost a lot of these scuffles. I was scared to complain about receiving jokes about my left arm because I thought it would give them a reason to remove me from the team. Again, I desperately wanted to stay a member of the basketball team. After dinner, we split into two teams, the junior varsity (JV) and the varsity, to play games in different gyms. I was on the junior varsity team and Coach Maroon was going with us to our game. The teams we played that first night caused me a lot of frustration. I was working as hard as I could, but I still had a lot of problems guarding the quicker and smaller guards. I began to think I may not be good enough to play with the JV team.

The next day was a lot better. We played teams from all over Mississippi. I was guarding players who were bigger than me and I was able to keep them from scoring while making lots of shots as a post player. I felt as though I was a good player again, and was able to be a valuable member of the team. The camp went by in a blur of games, wrestling matches, and jokes. The coaches were getting into the wrestling matches as well. I would see Coach Pat and Coach Maroon jump on players who would pick on them and wrestle them to the ground and hit them playfully in the chest, arm, or even the face.

During the day, I would sleep between games on the hard floor in the gym. Near the end of the day, I would often trip and fall hard on the floor. Whenever I became tired, my left foot would not land correctly and my toe would catch the ground causing me to fall hard on my face. I would simply get up and keep walking as my teammates erupted in uproarious laughter. It was here that I realized they did not see me as a disabled person, but laughed because they considered me as an equal person on the team; if they had seen me as disabled or not accepted me as an equal, they would have immediately helped me to my feet with the utmost care. I started to love the tough joking of my teammates even though a lot of it was at my expense and at the expense of my self-esteem. While this seems like a lot to lose, I was a part of the basketball team and this meant I was one of the best athletes in school. I wanted to have that distinction because I still had the belief that I was an "alpha male."

I did not want to miss a thing that was going on and forgot to shower for the first three days. I was laying on my bed Wednesday night after camp. We had been playing five to six games a day in the Mississippi summer and I am a heavy sweater. One of the older players, Grant, stormed into my dorm room, told me he could smell me on the other end of the hallway—he carried me by the arm to the shower and told me to take a shower. As I was rinsing my body, he threw a bottle of soap over the curtain and told me to use it. I took that as a sign to shower the last two days of camp.

After playing so many games at camp, I was exhausted and slept most of the car trip home. As a younger member of the team, I had one of the least comfortable seats in the van. I had bags of basketballs on both sides of me and gym bags crowding in on me from every angle. I even felt the sharp point of one bag poking me in the rib. I was able to easily disassociate myself from the uncomfortable seat and went to sleep. I awoke just a few miles from home. As my dad picked me up from the high school parking lot, I felt I had further established myself as a member of the team, yet I still felt as though I had to do everything right to stay a member of the team.

The rest of the summer went by in a haze of swimming at the pool, backyard basketball games, lifting weights in my basement, and shooting baskets in the backyard. My dad had also added a great new feature to the basement weight room: there was now a hanging punching bag along with a speed bag against the wall. I began hitting the bag on a regular basis to try to become a tougher guy. Although my dad had bought boxing gloves to use when we hit the bag, I chose not to use them because I wanted my knuckles to be tougher and believed that not using the gloves would make me a tougher person. After a few weeks of regularly hitting the punching bag, I began to consider myself tough and was not afraid of any of the guys on the basketball team who had previously intimidated me as a freshman. I was excited to start back to school.

***

As I entered my sophomore year of high school, I was ready for basketball PE, which I knew was an incredibly tough class. This year, the class was smaller than the year before and it seemed to have been handpicked, with only the basketball team. I knew what to expect and was ready to run the sprints and struggle through PE. As the first few weeks in this class came to a close, I noticed that we were not running as much as the previous year, we were instead doing a lot more plyometric drills designed to improve athleticism.

I also noticed that for some reason the other sophomores on the team started making fun of me relentlessly, and I was becoming more self-conscious about my appearance and athletic abilities in addition to my insecurities about the left side of my body. I received torrents of joking criticisms about the way I dressed, my struggles with picking up girls, and, as always, my left arm. I had changed the way I dressed to try to attract girls, but it seemed the harder I tried, the less interested in me they were. I had a bunch of phone numbers, but never got any dates. These girls became my friends and I was unable to move to anything beyond a friendship with them. Girls I did not know, I approached, but found out they were in no way interested in me. I became increasingly insecure each time I was turned down by a girl I thought to be attractive.

Every time I was made fun of for my left arm, I was secretly very hurt and it created a feeling of incredible self-consciousness. I developed a coping mechanism in regard to my left arm: I laughed away the tears that I felt at the countless remarks I received about it.

My nickname, Snake Diesel, had become another way for my teammates to joke about my arm. Since I was a very physical basketball player and would sometimes cut people during games on my way to get rebounds and loose balls, my teammates called my left arm the snake and every time they got cut, they claimed they had been snake bit. Each time one of my teammates made a remark, I choked back tears and grew increasingly uncomfortable with myself.

My teammates took the snake joke further than I could have imagined. One would hold my left arm up and claim that it was a mythical creature that bit and scarred people of its own free will, as I had no power over it. I laugh along with the jokes and even added my own jokes about the "snake," causing further jokes and remarks about my left arm. I felt as though I was the butt of the entire team's jokes. While the pain from those jokes began to lose its sting, the damage it had done to my self-esteem was still prevalent. I began to think of myself as a person that did not deserve the best things in the world. I thought that no matter what I wore, girls would never find me attractive and that I could never be one of the cool kids in school. While all these things were happening, I began to think that I was not one of the best basketball players in school and believed I was only on the team because I was always around and involved with every event from summer basketball to camps. All the confidence I had gained from basketball camp seemed to fade away in the first couple weeks of school. I was even having trouble running fast enough to finish the basketball sprints in the time acceptable to Coach Pat.

Then, one day, Coach Chrone came into the basketball PE class and asked if anyone wanted to join the cross-country team as a way to get in shape for basketball. Coach Pat added that anyone on the cross-country team was exempt from running preseason sprints. I knew I was a little bit out of shape and the thought of not running preseason sprints appealed to me. I told Coach Chrone that I would be at practice. TJ and Ronnie were members of both the basketball and the cross-country teams. They never had trouble finishing basketball sprints and TJ told me you needed "big balls" to run cross-country, which made me feel as though running cross-country would help me gain respect from TJ and Ronnie. As Ronnie was one of the main people making fun of my left arm, I thought the respect from running cross-country might cause him to make fun of me less than usual.

I put on my PE clothes after school and met the cross-country team in front of the gym for practice. We were going to run half a mile to the track, run two miles on the track, and run back to the high school. I was eager to try distance running.

As we ran out of the school parking lot, I ran to the front of the team and was in the lead down the first hill. I started thinking this might actually be my sport, I could be built for distance running. As I arrived at the bottom of the first hill, I was running slowly and doggedly behind the team. By the time I reached the track, the guys on the team were already running laps trying to finish their two miles. I slowly began running laps, my body feeling tired and miserable. I hated this practice more than I had hated any sport I had ever tried. Coach Chrone told me that I could walk a few laps if I needed to, and I think I probably walked one of the two miles on the track. I then slowly trudged back to the high school from the track with the most miserable feeling I had ever experienced in a sport. While walking away from the track, I thought I would quit the cross-country team. It was then that I remembered my dad giving me one of my earliest pieces of fatherly advice; I don't remember why he told me this piece of wisdom, but I remember him saying, "Greg, never quit." I remembered him telling me this and I decided that I could quit the team after this first year of the cross-country team. That way I would not be a quitter, the season would be complete, and I would never have to run long distance again.

As I reached the high school, I expected the cross-country team to react in a way that would make me feel terrible about being such a slow runner. Instead, the guys on the team gave me high fives and told me good job on the run. I told them thank you and went home in complete exhaustion, thankful that it was Friday and we did not have practice again until Monday.

As I woke on Saturday, my entire body was incredibly sore. It was a struggle to walk to the bathroom. It seemed as though every muscle in my body was screaming in pain and all I wanted to do was lie on the couch. Sunday, my muscles were even more sore than the day before and I had no idea how I would manage practice on Monday.

Monday morning, my body was a little less sore and I struggled to complete the weight workout in basketball PE. As I stiffly made my way through the day at school, I had no idea how I was going to run that afternoon in cross-country practice.

I met the team in front of the gym for practice. We were going to run two miles from the high school to

O'Neal Elementary and back to the high school. My muscles screamed in pain as I began trying to run on the road. I had decided that I would not walk this run, but this goal quickly faded as I reached the first hill. I walked up both hills on my way to O'Neal. The way back, I ran the last downhill into the school so that I looked as though I was a real runner finishing in front of the high school gym. Those two miles were exhaustive and I absolutely hated it.

The next day, the team ran a four-mile route around town, but I was told that I could take a shorter version. I ran the three-mile route and saw the team waiting for me in front of the gym. Again, they told me good job. I was also told that our first cross-country meet was that Saturday and it would be a three-mile course. I thought to myself, "Oh shit! I have to run again on the weekend." The weekend was my time to relax and now this stupid sport was making me run on Saturday as well! This means I would only have one day of the week to not run. There were a few members of the cross-country team who only ran during practice because they were using cross-country as a way to train for their main sport. I had thought I could run only in practice too, but now I thought this would be a cop-out and the only way I could truly quit this team with no regrets after this season was to do all the meets and practices. So Coach Chrone gave me a pair of running shorts and a jersey to wear in the meet.

As I tried the uniform on Saturday morning before the meet, I found the shorts to be very small. Coach

Chrone, with his relaxed country humor, told me that my shorts looked like two bobcats fighting in a toe sack. While my shorts were too short, my uniform shirt was too big and had to be taped in the back to keep it from falling over my shoulders. After we had our uniforms on, we loaded the bus and left for Jackson for the meet.

On the bus ride, I tried to hang out with the two guys from the basketball team, but Ronnie and TJ treated me the same way they did in the basketball locker room. As I looked around the bus, I noticed wide-eyed, thin people with smiles on their faces and a laugh that always seemed to be on the edge of belting out of their faces. One team member I noticed in particular was Tony, an olive-skinned boy who had an inner flame that burned brightly from his eyes. I started talking to the other guys on the team. I couldn't help but notice that the girls on the team were beautiful and were talking to Tony during the trip. I began talking to him too because I thought that maybe some of his charisma would attract the attention of the girls on the team. As we talked on our way to the meet, I felt as though I had made a friend.

Once at the meet, we all put our gym bags in a shaded area close to the other teams. The teams from other schools all had team tents where they placed their things and wind suits. Once our bags were placed together in one spot, Coach Chrone told us we were going to walk the course before the races were to start.

I couldn't help but think, "Holy shit! We have to walk before running! The race is three fucking miles! Isn't that far enough?" But I sucked it up and went to walk with the team. As we walked the course, I saw other teams jogging the course in their warm-up suits. I thought those teams were crazy and we were crazy for walking before the race. As we walked, Coach Chrone showed us the flags and which directions we would need to run to successfully complete the race. As a member of the junior varsity, my race was going to be the second race of the day. As we finished walking the course, Tony pulled me aside and told me that there was one thing about the meets he needed to tell me, then explained in no uncertain terms that I could not walk during the race. It did not matter how slow I was running, but I could not walk. He explained that walking during a race was embarrassing for a team and I represented the Mules. I told him I would not walk, but thought I was going to be incredibly slow.

The girls' junior varsity race started and the boys' JV race was ten minutes after the girls. I nervously walked to the starting line, unsure of how well I could run three long miles. When the starting gun fired, I shot to the front of the race pulsing with adrenaline and as I crested the first hill, quickly began to slow with heavy breath and legs. I did not walk though. As I ran with my pack of runners through the park, I noticed we were catching a few of the girls from the girls' JV race. I saw a few of the girls on my team walking and I ran past them with Tony's words beaming through my head: DO NOT WALK. I wanted to walk but one of my core values is integrity and I knew that I could not walk because I gave Tony my word. Through the three miles of this race, I fell increasingly farther behind the large pack of runners that had engulfed me during the first half of the race. By the time I finished the race, I was in front of only a few runners in my race. I crossed the finish line and handed the stick with my place to Coach Chrone. I had finished close to last place. I then walked to the team area, lay on the ground by the bags, and drank a cup of water. I was spent. I thought about how it was going to be incredibly satisfying to see the end of the season and my running days.

On the bus ride back home, I began talking with Tony and Matt. We were all three absorbed in conversation, mostly about the toughness of running but the conversation ebbed and flowed to a lot of different areas. By the time we reached the school, I felt as though I had made another friend.

As the weeks of cross-country continued, I ran longer runs and even finished one four-mile run. Each week I continued hating the sport. One night I hated it so much I began crying because I knew I had to run in a meet the next day.

Yet after that meet, for some strange reason, my mind began to change. I began to take pride in knowing that my runs were hard and not everyone could run a cross-country race. I began to feel as though my toughness made me different from other people. I also started stretching and doing sit-ups after practice to increase my strength.

Each practice, I became closer to Tony and Matt. While they were faster than me and I never saw them during practice, we began hanging out after practice. Their personalities were incredibly charismatic to me and I started incorporating a few of their traits into my own personality.

Tony was a dark-skinned Italian boy who prided himself on being the toughest. He was always choosing to do things at practice that were tougher than anybody else's feats. Instead of finishing a race at a nice pace and cruising into the finish, he ran with a grimace and pushed himself as hard as he possibly could. I remember seeing him puke after a few meets. I think the transition in my mind toward priding myself in doing something that is tough came from Tony. It also fit in well with my belief that I was an alpha male capable of doing things most people could not.

Matt was a thin boy who was rebellious and enjoyed playing the role of the guy who did things at social extremes. He wanted to gain recognition as a bad boy. I enjoyed that he pretended to be a badass while I knew full well that he was a good person with a good heart and all his rebellion was a textbook façade to attempt to gain recognition. This area of his personality fit with my image of myself because I saw through his façade as a rebel to see the insecure person beneath. I was incredibly insecure myself and it was comforting to have found a friend that seemed to have as many hidden insecurities as myself.

As the season progressed, I began to take more and more pride in my ability to run and felt as though I had become an incredibly tough person because of my ability to finish cross-country practice. By the end of the season, I had developed a love for running and had found a new group of friends. I had already made the decision to run track after basketball season. And basketball season was quickly approaching.

***

Once the cross-country season had ended, I was looking forward to getting my driver's license. In Missouri, once you are fifteen years old, you are already eligible to drive with an adult using a driver's permit. Once I was sixteen, I could take the test to drive by myself with a valid license. During my time driving with a permit, I had to figure out ways to use my turn signal without being a hazard on the road. By this point, I had become an expert at adapting to situations so that my left arm would not be a hindrance to my activities. After a few clumsy attempts, I was able to put my turn signal on with my left arm. It was a struggle and I was afraid of having an accident, but before long, I was able to signal without a problem and felt confident about my abilities as a driver.

A few weeks before my sixteenth birthday, my dad took me to look at a number of trucks for me to drive. One of my favorite test drives was from a small used lot in town. After a ten minute drive, the truck ran out of gas.

We had to coast into a gas station and put a little gas in the tank. We finally settled on a red Dodge Ram truck with forty thousand miles on it. I guess after sitting in a car with me as I drove using my permit, my dad felt as though my truck needed more protection than a standard vehicle, so he had a cattle guard placed on the front of the truck to protect me and the truck from accidents. While I understood his logic with the cattle guard, I was excited because I thought it looked badass. All I had left to do was pass my driving test.

My mom picked me up from school a couple days after my birthday so I could take the driving portion of getting my license. I was confident about my abilities as a driver in every aspect except parallel parking. I began the test calmly, then failed miserably on the parallel parking portion of the test. I didn't pass the test. I was upset, but my mom was prepared. She drove me to another town where we saw a person taking the driving test. My mom and I followed the car the entire route. Once he had finished, we practiced the course a number of times before I took the test again. During this test, the test administrator told me to turn right at the stop sign. I was eager and had the turn signal on before he instructed me to make the turn. This time, I had passed the test and became a fully licensed driver.

I was excited about driving because now I could drive to my friend Tony's house and hang out a lot with him. While I still had my basketball friends that I hung out with around school and practice, I began to develop a strong friendship with Tony and his friend Rustin.

After school, we would run together, then hang out at his house. Tony's mother was a hardworking lady who ran the maid service at a local motel and that left Tony, Rustin, and I in the house by ourselves. We all three began to rub off on each other; I began styling my hair the same way they did, using lots of hair spray and making triangles out of my bangs. We began to think alike—while Tony and I were obsessed with being great runners, Rustin thought of himself as a great basketball player and believed he deserved to be on the basketball team. As a member of the basketball team, I knew he did not have a good chance to make the team because he was not a presence during any of the open gyms, camps, or PE classes. Even with these realities, he still believed he was a better player than most of the guys on the junior varsity team.

One thing that Tony and Rustin held within themselves was the belief that they were great; they had even louder alpha male complexes than I did. Tony was a cook at a fast food restaurant and prided himself on being the very best cook in the place. He was proud of everything he did and believed he could do things better than any- one else. One day, he even worked a twenty-four-hour shift as a cook. Tony was convinced that all the wait- resses at the restaurant wanted him, and from the flirt- ing I had seen from girls on the cross-country team, he was probably right. Rustin believed himself to be a musical talent destined to make millions as an R&B star, along with his belief in his basketball abilities. As for me, I began to pride myself on being one of the toughest runners in school. Every day, we hung out together and we believed ourselves to be the toughest and most talented people in school.

Another thing I liked about us was that we took up for each other if we ever heard anyone talking trash about someone in our trio of friends. It was well known in school that I was a slow runner and near the back of the pack when it came to the cross-country team. One of the baseball players in school made a remark about how if he ran cross-country, he would be running back there with Greg, using a tone that indicated he thought very little of my ability as a runner. Tony was immediately right in his face and told him that I was his friend and that I had a lot more heart than him. When Tony told me about the remark and his reaction, I thanked him and then moved on. While I had developed coping mechanisms to deal with the relentless ridicule I received from my basketball teammates, it was nice to have a friend who stood up for me.

I had developed an emotional callus in dealing with my basketball teammates, but one guy kept getting under the callus and striking deep, painful blows. Since the eighth grade, Brum had a knack for finding the most cruel ways to hurt my feelings. One day after an open gym, he made a few too many remarks and I wanted to beat the living daylights out of him. Walking over to pummel his skinny frame into a bloody pulp, I thought about losing my spot on the basketball team. After all, Brum had a lot more playing time than I did last year and at the summer camp games. I changed my mind and went home furious. This was the kind of rage that got people into trouble. As soon as I walked into the house, I went straight to the basement and saw my dad lifting weights. He said hello and I did not answer, I looked at the punching bag and imagined it to be Brum, I started punching and cursing with all my might, even using his name. Every hit, I would say "Fuck you Brum! Take that!" and so on for about ten minutes. As the heavy bag swung wildly, I felt my knuckles bleeding as I continued to hit the bag in a steady stream of ferocious blows. As I finished and stood there bleeding from my knuckles, I no longer felt the furious rage that had consumed me when I left the gym. I looked to my dad, who was staring at me in bewilderment. He had watched me during my rage-driven attack on the punching bag. He asked if I was okay and I told him I felt better. As he looked at me, I could tell that he was proud I had released my anger in a manner that kept me out of trouble. It seemed as though I had released years of anger I held against Brum in one furious flurry in my basement. And basketball tryouts were only a week away.

After putting in the work over the summer and being in basketball PE, I was still nervous about not making the basketball team. As a sophomore, I was looking forward to playing under Coach Maroon. I had learned over the summer that he was a demanding coach; I had heard him countless times yelling for some of the team to play harder and run the plays and drills correctly. This year, there were a few new kids trying out for the team, but the number of guys trying out was less than my freshman year.

The new guys on the team included Brent and Maurice. Gone were the troublemakers. This meant that the senseless teasing I had received since eighth grade was gone. The locker room began to take on a different feel, a more positive atmosphere. I was proud to be a part of the team, but in many respects, I still felt insignificant compared to the other players.

Maurice and Brent were both stars on the football team. Maurice cherished a belief that he was God's gift to football and was destined to go on to major collegiate fame. Brent thought he was pretty great too, but he was a nice and polite person who stood behind his moral convictions. It was rare for him to step in and make fun of my left arm with the rest of the team. As I received a lot of jokes about my arm and was being made to feel as though I were insignificant, Brent would not partake in the team ritual of making fun of me, he stuck to jokes about normal things without taking shots at things resulting from medical hardships . I was glad he wouldn't, and drove him home after a lot of practices.

As I drove him to his uncle's house, we talked and made jokes about funny happenings in practice. I began to see him as a friend and respected him because he was intelligent, articulate, and proud of himself, while I was still battling the inner frustrations of a continually lessened sense of self-worth.

As we moved closer to our first game, I could tell we were going to be a good team. During practice, we played against the varsity team so they could work on their plays. I began to realize that Coach Pat was upset because our junior varsity team was almost evenly matched with his varsity team. During practices, I remember being able to stop the post player for the varsity team and having confidence in my ability to score on the other end of the floor. Our first few games were easy victories and we beat almost every junior varsity team we played. We were playing well and I was also gaining a few friends from my teammates.

Even so, I continued to be picked on in the locker room. My coping mechanisms were beginning to wear thin, and I felt vulnerable and unhappy that I was still receiving such demeaning remarks. One of my teammates, Ed, sensed I was getting upset. He told me something that made me feel a little better. He told me that no matter how mean they were, anyone outside the team would have hell to pay if they made fun of me. This made me feel as though the ridicule was okay and made me a part of the team.

After practices, I would give a number of guys rides home. This allowed me to create friendships with Ed and BJ. On the days we had home games, BJ, Ed, and I would hang out before going to the gym for games. I enjoyed this because it made me feel as though I were a part of a close-knit team, regardless of the abuse I had to endure to be a part of it.

While I enjoyed playing and hanging out with my basketball teammates, Rustin and Tony were becoming my best friends. After I had driven my teammates home,

I would go to Tony's house and we would hang out, watching TV and playing video games as well as getting into wrestling matches that resulted in a number of household furniture items being broken. One match, Tony dove into me in a tackle and I hit the couch, breaking one of the support boards. In retaliation, I threw Tony on the coffee table, causing one of its legs to break.

All the messages I received from Tony and Rustin were completely contrary to the messages I received from my basketball teammates. Instead of implying that I was an uncool and crippled person lucky to be a part of the team, Tony and Rustin considered me as a part of our trio of the coolest and toughest kids in school. Whenever they made comments about potential future adventures, or jokes about hypothetical situations, they always included me as a positive part of the group, rather than making me the butt of the joke. I began to see myself as a part of this group of three friends who were always there for each other and knew we were great. We would walk around town with our heads held high and our inflated egos puffed out. Near the end of the basketball season, I had quit hanging out with my basketball teammates outside of practice and games and hung out with Tony and Rustin almost on a daily basis.

Although the basketball season ended with a record of 20–4, I was ready for track season. I could not wait to lace up my new track spikes and join my old cross-country teammates for track practice.

As I shifted my focus from basketball to running, I remembered a few things from the previous cross-country season. I remembered Tony clapping for me after I finished my first road run, Matt telling me good job during hill intervals, and the team cheering me on as I ran toward the finish line. As I recalled these things, I also thought about the sport and remembered that the runs made me a tough person and set me apart from other people in school.

The cross-country bus rides were a lot more fun than those on the basketball bus. On the basketball bus, everyone was somber and preparing for the games in their own way. There was not a lot of talking. The cross-country bus was anything but somber, from peeing into Gatorade bottles and throwing them out the window, to getting one of the girls to flash a truck driver. Trips were anything but tame. I could not wait to see what kind of stories I would get from the track team.

The first day of track practice was amazing; not only were most of my cross-country teammates there, but there were also a number of soccer players who decided to run with the distance team. The distance team coach was Coach Coly, a laid-back person who always seemed to have a gleam of fun in his eyes. He made jokes during stretches, but instead of poking fun at someone on the team, he made jokes about theoretical circumstances that made everyone laugh. After stretches, he would send us out for a road run. Instead of following us through the route, he simply told the older members to guide us.

That first run, I tried to stay with one of the senior girls, but she was too fast. I slipped to the back of the pack and finished the run there. The next day, we stayed at the track and ran quarter mile intervals. This meant we would sprint a lap around the track, then relax and walk a little while before sprinting another lap. In these intervals, I discovered that at first, I could keep up with the faster guys in the distance group. But after the third interval I was back of the pack again. Every other day we would do a road run and the rest of the week we would run intervals of differing distances. After a few weeks of this routine, we had our first meet. Coach Coly asked us what events we wanted to run, and he chose the relay teams. As one of the slower runners, I was not asked to be on a relay team, but I could sign up for three distance events. I chose the 3,200-, 1,600-, and the 800-meter races.

That first meet was extremely humbling. I was last in every event but the 800. Even with my slow performance, my teammates still congratulated me and kept my spirits up with crazy stories and jokes. After crossing the finish line, they patted me on the back and we would walk off the track reveling in the accomplishment of finishing the races that were harder than any other track event. It was this camaraderie of toughness that became intoxicating to me. As the season went on, I became a lot faster in the intervals during practice.

One practice, Coach Coly told us to go for a two-mile run. I thought it must be an easy day so I ran hard trying to hang on to the main pack of runners. Halfway into the run, one of my teammates told me we were going to run intervals after the run. I thought there was no way, two miles is too taxing to run intervals after. I was wrong! Once we completed the run, we lined up to run four sets of two-hundred-meter intervals. These were all-out sprints for half a lap of the track. Throughout the season, I had been getting faster on the practice intervals. This was the day that I ended near the front of the fast runners on every interval. I was finally one of the fast guys on the team. After practice, the distance team was told to jog a half-mile to Sonic, order a slush, and drink it while walking back to the track. Normally, this would be amazing; I love slushes, especially free ones. But I was exhausted from the intervals. The jog to the fast food drive-in was difficult. I could feel the heat from the sun radiating into my body and my legs felt like lead. But I continued my miserable jog to Sonic. After ordering my slush, I took a sip and immediately felt better. After my third sip, my mood had completely changed and I walked back to the track with the rest of my distance teammates telling jokes and laughing, in great spirits. Upon arriving at the track, the rest of the track team looked at us with envy. The high jumpers were jealous and the shot-putters almost salivated at the sight of our drinks. We walked with our heads held high and our spirits higher. We all felt as though we deserved the drinks more than the rest of the team because our events and practices were harder than the rest of the track team's events and practices.

Once we saw Coach Coly, he called the junior varsity runners over and told us that we only had to pick two events for the next day because it was an invitational and so we were only allowed two events. I chose the 1600 and 800 meter races because I had confidence in my ability to run fast from my intervals.

The Farmington Invitational was held on a black track and it featured teams from St. Louis as well as southeast Missouri. My first race was near dusk and I stepped to the line feeling as though I had a secret. No one in this 800-meter race had any idea that I could fly around the track because none of them had been at the practice where I kept up with the fast guys on our team. As the starting gun went off, I exploded out from the starting line, quickly moving to the front of the race. After almost a full lap of the two-lap race, I was in the middle of the pack. I was completely exhausted from running the first lap so hard, so the second lap I struggled to finish without walking and crossed the finish line in last place. I felt exhausted but proud that I had finished my race and was on my way to finishing the toughest races at the meet.

The mile or 1,600-meter race was the last event and they had to turn the lights on around the track. I stepped to the line after a few hours of recuperation ready to run the best race I could and decided to run easier on the first few laps. As soon as the gun exploded, I took off from the line at a fast pace, but not a sprint. For the first time I felt as though my legs were moving at a pace that was neither a sprint nor an exhausted trudge. Instead, my stride felt smooth and I ran all four laps in this rhythm. I loved the feeling in my legs—they were in absolute cruise control and I moved at a fast pace that seemed easy and hard at the same time. I did not care that I was in dead last place, my legs were in cruise control and I felt smooth and comfortable. After two sports seasons as a distance runner, I had finally found something that felt amazing. Gone was the feeling of hacking and plodding. I had found my stride and it felt great. With two hundred meters left in the race, I heard the fans at the race clapping for me as I made my way around the last turn. I resented the applause because I was incredibly self-conscious about my left arm and believed they were cheering because they saw me as a disabled athlete. And the only thing I hated more than being ridiculed about my disability was special treatment.

Even though I resented the applause, I could not help but grin about finding my stride for the first time. It was as though I was moving in fast-forward, my feet hitting the ground in a beautiful rhythm. I crossed the finish line and realized that I wanted to feel that stride again.

The rest of the season, I felt that stride every time we ran on the track and loved it. I even began feeling my stride during road runs. I took pride in doing tough road runs, but also in knowing that I had a beautiful, rhythmic stride regardless of how slow it was compared to the other runners on the team.

***

After track season, I still spent more time with my track and cross-country teammates than my basketball teammates. Rustin and Tony had become my best friends and we went everywhere together. Matt and his brothers were also good friends. I loved hanging out with them because they did not pick on me and instead were encouraging and helped improve my self-confidence.

Tony and Rustin were always up to crazy antics and we all three believed ourselves to be uncommonly tough. One day, there was a wasp that had flown into Tony's house, so I grabbed a huge knife off the counter and told them I would take care of the wasp. As I jumped through the house slashing at the wasp with the knife, I noticed Tony and Rustin had left the house. I got lucky and sliced the insect in two. I called Tony and Rustin into the house and they both called me crazy and we laughed all afternoon about my knifing the wasp.

By the end of my sophomore year, things were starting to look up. I began my summer in basketball PE in the un-air-conditioned gym. I felt as though I were in a routine and began to go through the class feeling confident that I could handle the drills. I also noticed that I was quite a bit stronger than most of the other players on the basketball team. I began piling more weight on lifts and was lifting more weight on all the lifts with my legs. I was able to squat three hundred and fifteen pounds and muscled up more and more weight on hamstring curls and leg extensions. My upper body strength was somewhat limited because my left arm was weaker than my right side. Every time I performed the bench press, a lift requiring me to lay on a bench and lower then push a weighted bar up, I had to force my left wrist into a position so that I could support the weight with my left arm. Luckily, I was already used to putting my wrist in this position from the times that my dad and I lifted weights in the basement. While in the previous years I had to position my wrist in the same way, I was now trying to lift more weight. Occasionally, my left wrist would pop out of position and I would drop the bar on my chest which caused me to always have a bruise across my sternum.

On the basketball court, I was able to score more effectively. I was getting better as a basketball player, and I began to enjoy working out and the feeling of sweat pouring down my face. During these hot June days, I relished the feeling of being saturated in sweat, with sweat pouring down my whole body. It was common to see me pushing myself by lifting weights, performing agility drills, and playing basketball games with my clothes soaked with sweat.

Within a couple weeks, it was time to go to Mississippi State team camp with the team. This year, I was looking forward to it.

***

After the first camp dinner, we split into varsity and junior varsity to head to our first games of the camp. I was excited because I would finally be able to show my skills as a varsity athlete. As we went to play these games, I was pleased that I was finally being seen for the wonderful athlete I knew I was.

That year, the camp was buzzing around a player that was the best high school player in Mississippi and expected to go to the NBA after his upcoming senior year. Between our games, I watched Travis Outlaw play and couldn't believe the things he did on the court. As I watched, I thought about ways that I could stop him if I had to guard him in a game. During one of our afternoon games, I saw him watching us play the same way we had watched his team.

The next day, we played his team and though I was not a starter, I checked in to the game and was guarding Travis. Sean immediately told me to switch and guard their post player. I felt relieved because the post player for this team was bigger than Travis and did not move very well, which meant he was a physical player. In a physical basketball game, I always knew that I could hold my own. I bumped and banged their post player and kept him from scoring as best as I could. I even got a few jump hook shots to go in the basket. Every time Travis would drive to the lane, I made sure to meet him with a physical bump to keep him from dunking. I knew if I bumped him before he jumped, he would not be able to dunk and I would not injure him. I noticed that he started shooting jump shots and scored a massive amount of points without going into the lane. After the game, we went to dinner and then collapsed on our dorm beds after playing eight games that day. The next couple days flew by in a blur of basketball, heat, and sweat.

On the next to last day, we played a team called Moss Point. They had the biggest guy in camp, standing tall at six feet, eight inches and weighing well over three hundred pounds. I loved it because his weight kept him from being mobile and I thought I could unleash my physical style of basketball on him. But this guy was bigger than me by a lot. I tried to bump him out of the lane and he did not move! I thought, "Wow! First time that has ever happened." I then tried to move him out of my way using my body, which did not work at all. I was forced out of the lane! Me! I luckily had a good jump shot and was able to score a few points. Then, in the middle of the game, my teammate Grant dove for a loose ball and the big man for Moss Point dove too and landed on top of him. Grant was a six foot one guy who notoriously played physically. As soon as he got up from being crushed, he punched the giant in the jaw. I am not usually one to shy away from a fight, but this brawl was going to be painful. Luckily, the giant just looked at Grant and ran down court as if nothing had happened. I was incredibly relieved that I did not have to jump into a brawl with him and his team. At dinner that night, everyone exclaimed about Grant's unthinkable punch of the giant.

The next day, we finished our games and loaded back in the van for our trip home. On the car ride back, I was so tired, I slept most of the way, only catching a few of the stories gained from camp. Once back in town, we returned to basketball PE for a week before heading to the University of Missouri for another team camp. That week included a lot of agility drills and weightlifting. I was enjoying the fact that we were getting to play so much basketball and could not wait to go to the next camp.

While I was not getting picked on as much as my previous years, I was still receiving a lot of jokes in the locker room. But one day in practice, I discovered that one of the seniors was a true friend of mine.

While outside of the gym I usually hung out with Tony and Rustin, Ed was also someone I considered a friend. Ed was one of the guys who continually made fun of my left arm by calling it "the snake" and was one of the lead writers of its fictional life. While he repeatedly picked on me, I considered him my friend because he was the one who had told me that if anyone outside the team made fun of me that person would have hell to pay. I also gave Ed rides to early morning practices or practice on days that school was not in.

One day in practice, Ed pushed me after a play and said, "Get the fuck off me." I did not think anything of it because I had gotten the rebound, and I had grown callous to Ed's trash talking long ago. William, one of the seniors, told Ed not to pick on me. Ed told William to shut up and William punched Ed in the face. After a few punches were thrown, we broke up the fight. After seeing William stand up for me, I began to realize that I needed to stand up for myself more because I was getting picked on too much by the rest of the team.

The next day in the locker room, I was getting picked on by Ronnie, one of the senior players on the team. I told him to stop picking on me or else. He immediately started hitting me in my chest with a rapid volley of blows. The punches did not hurt very much because I was used to being hit in the locker room from the guys on the team. Usually it was in a joking manner, but it seemed as though Ronnie was trying to teach me a lesson about talking back to a senior. I remembered William standing up for me the day before, and as soon as Ronnie paused for a split second in his punches, I punched him in the chest as hard as I could throw my fist. He flew backward into the wall and looked stunned at my punch. Once he had gathered himself he started hitting me again, but every time he paused, I hit him again in the chest. After a few minutes of this, he quit throwing punches and went to his locker to change. I walked back to my locker and changed into my clothes as well. I was not angry with Ronnie and he was not mad at me anymore. I think after that exchange of punches, he left with a new (and painfully learned) understanding of me.

A couple days later, we left for our second team camp and I was excited to play against the teams from around the state and see how well we matched up to them. During the trip to camp, I could not help but notice that the guys coming to this camp were different from the guys who went to Mississippi State a couple weeks earlier. As I looked around the vans we were climbing in for the trip, I saw that the guys on this trip were mostly the same guys who picked on me in the locker rooms. This did not bode well, and as you might expect, the trip to camp was just a rehash of one embarrassing story after another, many of them involving me. With every joke and mean comment they made about my arm I became more insecure and the strength of my suspicion that I was not a good-looking or cool person grew. Even though I was poking fun at myself and laughing along (my go-to coping mechanism in these situations), inside I was losing self-esteem and self-value by the minute. A couple of guys on the team held my left arm up, pretending to have charmed "the snake." I laughed to keep from crying every time. It was on this trip that all the self-esteem I had gained from hanging out with Tony and Rustin and being part of the cross-country team came crashing down.

Once camp started, I felt I was ready to play and could hold my own with anybody on the court. The second day, as I walked toward the court to play, one of the players on the other team asked if I needed any help catching a pass after motioning to my arm. After the past couple days of experiencing blows to my self-esteem from my own teammates, this comment from an outsider dropped my self-value to rock bottom. I muttered no and went to warm up. Once I got in the game, I hit two jump shots over the kid who had made the comment, and I saw it click in his head that I was a good player and had proved myself on the court. Although his comment had hurt me, the knowledge that I had owned him on the court almost made up for it. After the game, when we shook hands, he looked at me with awe in his eyes and I felt I had proved something to him.

During meals at camp, most of my teammates would not talk to me unless they were mentioning me in an embarrassing story. I noticed my left arm a lot more than normal as I ran down the court. It was as if my teammates' ridicule had made me more aware of my left arm's actions. Every time I took a jump shot, I felt it dangling below my waist. Despite this, on the court, I still believed I was capable of greatness. Off the court, however, the sickening feeling I had that I was one of the least cool people at the camp was constantly reaffirmed. I looked around at the rest of the campers and it seemed as though my insecurities were right: Everyone but me was attractive, strong, and cool. I, on the other hand, was over-eager, too outgoing, and unattractive. I felt alone within my team and as though my comments were not as suave as those of my teammates. I began to speak out less because I felt as though my voice was unimportant and worried that speaking up would cause me to endure more ridicule compared to the rest of my teammates. As I sat there quietly listening to stories and occasionally getting picked on, I missed my cross-country teammates and friends Tony and Rustin.

On the next–to-last day of camp, I received a lot of jokes at my expense during breakfast and went to find an empty bathroom in the gym. I broke down, crying my eyes out from all the verbal abuse I had received throughout the week. I bawled and did not stop for almost half an hour. Once I left the bathroom, I felt better from unburdening myself of the emotional load I had received from my teammates. I was looking forward to camp coming to an end and spending a lot of time with Tony and Rustin.

***

With basketball PE over for the summer, I was determined to become a better runner and looked forward to running with Tony. I began running a few routes from my house around town and got exhausted by the heat. One afternoon at Tony's house, we were talking about the brutality of the heat when we looked at each other as if lightbulbs had turned on simultaneously in both of our brains.

Since we both considered ourselves to be two of the toughest people in the world, we agreed to start running in the hottest part of the day to showcase our toughness. That afternoon, we went to my house and ran a two-mile route to the local gas station and back. While I considered myself to be pretty resilient, I was absolutely dying during this run. Once we finished, we both collapsed on the couch in utter exhaustion. But the next day we did it again and doggedly lifted weights in my basement afterward. We continued running in the heat of the day the rest of the summer, even adding a few longer routes into our training. I was getting in shape; every step I took made me feel like a stronger person. I gained pride in being able to finish these runs and felt my ego of being a badass grow as a result of these hot runs. I believed that since no one else was out running, that meant we were harder than everyone not running, making us the most tenacious people in town.

Tony was a much faster runner than me and I knew he had to slow down to run with me, but every time we ran together that summer, he encouraged me, giving me praise for running, and it made me feel good about myself.

When we were not running or lifting weights, we were talking about how good-looking we were and how any girl would be lucky to have one of us. Although we usually sat around Tony's house watching TV, Tony, Rustin, and I occasionally ventured into town to try to pick up girls.

One night, we discovered that there was a keg party in a field close to Tony's house and all the hot girls from our school were going to be there. We all dressed in our most stylish outfits then headed to the party. One of Rustin's friends came with us as a designated driver so nobody would drive drunk. While we had been pumping ourselves up about how great-looking and desirable we were to girls, on my part, it was false bravado, as I still did not believe myself attractive in any way to the girls in my school. Tony and Rustin, on the other hand, truly believed they were the most desirable guys in school. And they believed I was in that boat with them.

Once we arrived at this field, I couldn't believe it. All the members of the hip crowd from school were there drinking beer and talking. After parking, I let the tailgate down on my truck and we started drinking beer from the keg. This was the first time I had ever tasted beer and it tasted gross to me. But I thought I should keep drinking to see what it felt like to be drunk. After my third beer, I saw the girl that I had a huge crush on standing about twenty yards from my truck. She looked beautiful in her jeans and shirt. As I talked with Tony and Rustin, I could not help but keep an eye on her gorgeous figure. I stood in awe of her beautifully sculpted skin with a slight tan, big brown eyes, and smile that seemed to melt me to a puddle. After my fifth beer, I decided to talk to her and I had the best thing to say to her to woo her. As I started walking toward her, I drank half of another beer to try to gain confidence. I then told her that the reason I had gotten drunk was because I thought she was beautiful and needed to be drunk to tell her how I felt. She politely smiled and said thank you. I began to feel insecure about being drunk and felt as though I was not worthy to talk with her. I felt as though she was just politely tolerating my presence. I turned around and staggered back to the tailgate of my truck. Jason, our designated driver, then drove the three of us home for the night.

A few days after the party, I saw the girl at the store and hid in embarrassment because I was sure she had no interest in talking to the guy who had made a drunken idiot of himself a few days earlier. But, as I walked by I caught her gaze and she waved. I waved back with a grin and felt my heart doing back flips in my chest. I could not believe that a girl as beautiful as her would even waste a wave on the laughing stock of the basketball team. The first thing I did after leaving the store was drive to Tony's house to tell Rustin and Tony about waving to her.

Tony and Rustin both told me I should ask her out, but every time I prepared to ask her out, I never had the courage to do it in real life, regardless of how many times I asked her out in my imagination. They reemphasized to me that we were the three most eligible bachelors in town and any girl would be lucky to have us on a date.

Tony and I ran that day from his house and we were both scorched by the heat. We collapsed on the floor of his house and relished in the cool air. We lay there exhausted with satisfied grins on our faces. While drinking water, Tony explained that no other people in our class were as fit or good-looking as we were and that we were the true badasses of our school and town. This was the same thing I had heard from Tony and Rustin since we started being friends. It was slowly beginning to take hold. Once we had recovered from that run, Tony told me there was going to be a cross-country camp starting on Monday. I was excited and Tony and I agreed that as upperclassmen, we needed to be good leaders for the other guys at camp. Coach Chrone told us that camp would start from the new fifth and sixth grade school, which was still under construction, at noon.

The temperature that Monday was over ninety degrees and you could see the haze of humidity rising off the horizon. Coach Chrone told us that we were going to run the three-mile out-and-back route on a highway that was being built. The road was going to be the bypass around Poplar Bluff and it had not been paved yet. I wanted to run the route and show off the training

Tony and I had done earlier that summer, but Coach Chrone asked if I would lead the small group of new runners on a shorter route. At first, I was upset that I wouldn't get to run the full route, but as soon as I started running, I realized that the full loop would be incredibly difficult. I took the less experienced runners on a short two-mile loop down the hot path, and we finished before the group that took the long route. I stood there clapping for everyone as they finished their run. The rest of the guys in my group also cheered the other runners into the finish of their loop. After the run, we all huddled in the shade guzzling water as Coach Chrone told us to come back the next three days for camp.

Every day was the same loop and I eventually convinced my group to run the long route by the last day. It was on the long route that I realized it was incredibly difficult to run in the heat, despite my training with Tony. By the time I turned around to run back, I was in last place and was not close to any of the other runners. I continued running and as I got close to the finish of the run, there were the rest of the runners, most my cross-country teammates, all clapping and yelling encouragements as I finished the run. I could not help but let a grin grow across my face. Then, I became suddenly self-conscious. I remembered all the ridicule I had received from my basketball teammates and thought that they were clapping because I was disabled. In my mind, I had just received sympathy claps from the guys on my team. I hung my head and all my self-doubt started to creep back. But I then looked up and saw Tony walking toward me with a huge grin on his face. He said great job and then told me how hard it was running on that unpaved highway. His praise immediately cheered me up because I knew he was my true friend and did not look at me with sympathetic eyes. We both piled into my truck and went to his house to hang out with Rustin and enjoy the air conditioning.

The rest of the summer went by quickly and involved a lot of weightlifting, running, and shooting baskets in my backyard. By the time school was supposed to start, I felt prepared for cross-country season.

As I started my junior year of high school, I had developed a bit of an ego. Tony, Rustin, and I had become quite an entourage. The constant proclamations by Tony and Rustin about how great we were had sunk in and made me believe that we were the three coolest and most talented people in school. Any time I told Rustin about something one of my basketball teammates had said, he was quick to discredit the comment and add reasons why we were cooler and better than the person who had made the comment. Tony was also quick to reply to negativity with comments about how we were hardier than anyone else in the school, especially the guys that made fun of me. I recall hearing Rustin say, "He's making fun of you because he's not shit," more times than I can count. It was due to this positive reinforcement that I had developed an ego and felt so close to my best friends.

As I looked at my classes, I noticed that I had chemistry and Mr. Hosmer was my teacher. I had never heard a good word about Mr. Hos, only stories from students about his harshness. From the first day of class, I knew chemistry was going to be extremely hard and that I was going to have to study to do well in the class. Mr. Hosmer was a very serious man who told us his class served as a preparation for collegiate chemistry. I was immediately intimidated by all the stories I had heard from his former students. I heard that he was unreasonably hard in the way he graded and that he made grades unfair. I was worried that I was going to receive grades so low that I would not be able to play on the cross-country or basketball teams. It was in that first week I decided I was going to work hard and do well in this class.

After the first week of school, cross-country began and I was eager to show off the training I had done over the summer. I had made a quiet promise to myself that I would do the long versions of all of our runs and was excited to be an upper classman and leader of the team. The first practice was the same as the year before: we ran to the track, did two miles on the track, then ran back to the school. I was ready for this run and this year I did not have to walk any of the route. I still finished last, but I was not as tired as the miserable drudge I had been a year earlier.

As I finished, I noticed there were some new people on the team. One of the guys I considered popular despite his not being an athlete had come out for the team. Chad was going to try his first year in cross-country. I encouraged him during practice but thought to myself that he wouldn't be tough enough to complete all the practices and meets. But after the first week of practice, I noticed he was doing well and hanging in there with the team, he was finishing the runs and fitting in well. He cheered for me as I finished my runs, gave me words of encouragement, and made jokes with everyone. I started to think he might be a good addition to the team.

There were also a lot of girls who had joined the squad. At first, I was trying to get a few dates from a few of the girls, but the more I ran with them and realized my encouragement helped them, the more I developed friendships with most of them. I no longer looked at them as potential girlfriends, but as my teammates.

I was eager to show off to the rest of the team the hard work I had done over the summer; however, I was still at the back of the pack and finished most runs as the last guy on the team. At least this year I was no longer struggling to finish the routes. I started enjoying the fact that I was running on the road.

Rustin, the other member of our three-person entourage, also decided to run cross-country. This meant that we could hang out on the team trips and practices, and be there for each other during meets. It also meant that we could show off all the inside jokes and familiarity we had accumulated while we had been hanging out over the past year. While Rustin always talked about being a good basketball player, we rarely played basketball together. But he was not a bad runner and I thought it was awesome that we were all on the team together.

As the season continued, I was able to run with the fastest guys on the team during hill sprints and at the back of the team in every other run. But the team still encouraged me and never made fun of me for being slow. I had mimicked the team's satisfying ritual after completing practice runs: I would encourage everyone on the team and help create a fun team atmosphere. Near the middle of the season, I noticed that many of my teammates were looking up to me because I made it through the practices and ran my best during all the meets. There were many practices and meets where I finished so exhausted that I would lay on the ground for a few minutes to recover. Many times, Tony would do the same thing. We fed off each other's hard work. I began to see that I could still be a valuable teammate from working hard even though I was one of the slowest runners on the team. I realized that I was a leader simply because I chose to work hard and maintain a positive attitude.

While my place on the cross-country team was starting to take the shape I wanted it to, I was working hard to make it in my chemistry class. Mr. Hos was the toughest teacher I had had but I realized that he was not an unfair teacher like the stories I had heard from his previous students. He just wanted all his students to be successful beyond his class, so he pushed us. I was studying for his class on bus trips to cross-country meets and at home every night. I grew extremely interested in class and wanted to understand it as well as I could. While my interest in chemistry was increasing, I was still only receiving mediocre grades. But, for the first time in my life, I was interested in class. I think a big part of my interest in this class was because it had a reputation as a hard class. And I love doing things that have a reputation of being hard.

As cross-country began to draw to an end and my work in chemistry class continued, I was excited for the upcoming basketball season because I was now going to be a member of the varsity basketball team.

The first week of practice was considered tryouts and the guys that were left at the end of the week were on the varsity and junior varsity teams. During that first week, there was a coaching change and my former eighth grade coach was now going to coach the junior varsity team, leaving Coach Maroon to be the assistant coach. Once I saw this change, I was glad that I was not going to be on the junior varsity team.

During practice, I felt pretty sure that I was going to be on the team since I had gone to summer PE, both camps, was in basketball PE, and believed I was one of the best players in school. I went through the first week confident in my abilities as an experienced player on the team. I helped guide a few of the younger players through a few drills. I saw the coaches watching me. I was still picked on and yelled at by a lot of the seniors on the team, but I tried not to let it affect my playing.

After the first week, I was told that I would be on the junior varsity team. This caused my world to collapse. It would not have been a big deal except that I did not like the coaching change. Coach Vagrun was not a quality coach in my mind. I remembered incidents from my eighth grade team, including many verbal outbursts and of course the incident where he humiliated a player so greatly that he switched schools.

As the season began, I played a lot more than the previous year. While I did not like being on the junior varsity under Coach Vagrun, I loved getting to play in more games. I may not have been on the varsity team yet, but I was enjoying the chance to play a lot of basketball.

My struggles with Coach Vagrun continued; he was the same hot-headed coach I had in the eighth grade. Every practice was filled with profanity and anger. I never felt as though he wanted me to stay on the team. In a way, it was as though I was dealing with Strum all over again by sticking with the team when the coach was trying to make me quit. During one game, we were in the locker room getting yelled at for not playing hard enough. He looked straight at me and said that nobody was setting hard screens. He said that next screen, he wanted it to be a hard screen. During the first play of the second half, I set a hard screen and knocked the defender into the front row of bleachers. He pulled me out of the game and told me to never do that again. I could not believe this guy—I did exactly what he told me to and I still got in trouble for it.

Near the end of the season, we had one game left and the practice beforehand was incredibly tough, filled with lots of running and scrimmages. As the tallest and strongest player on the junior varsity, the only way the other post player could compete with me was to grab my right arm on rebounds. Since I do most things in life with one arm, this put me at a real disadvantage. I could not get free for a rebound. So I put my strength into action to send him a message to stop intentionally holding my arm. I leaned into him with one shoulder and knocked him on the floor before going to get the rebound. Coach Vagrun stopped practice and screamed at me cussing at me as he told me, "Greg! Quit being a dirty fucking player, you piece of shit!" I told him that I could not get my arm free. Coach Vagrun then told me that if he played against me he would hold my right arm every play. When he told me this, I immediately saw red and wanted to slug him in the face because I interpreted that as him trying to show me that I was incapable of holding my own on the basketball court, making fun of me in his incessant attempts to get me to quit the team. It took every ounce of strength I had in my sixteen-year-old body not to punch his lights out. But I decided violence would be a poor choice because it would mean my immediate dismissal from the team and I had worked too hard for that. After making this deci- sion, my anger turned into a heavy lump in my throat. Since crying in practice would mean absolute ridicule the rest of high school by my teammates, I choked back my tears and swallowed the lump in my throat. After practice I realized that Coach Vagrun's comment was more a reflection of the poor character he embodied than a reflection of my athletic capabilities.

As that season ended, I felt relieved that I would never again have Coach Vagrun. And I was looking forward to the track season. I was going to get to be back with my cross-country teammates for another season of running with my friends.

It was a well-ignored fact that while Tony, Rustin, and I considered ourselves to be great catches when it came to the opposite sex, we very rarely picked up girls. But there was this one night during the weeks before track practice started that Tony found some girls interested in hanging out with all three of us. Luckily, my dad was not home that night, so Tony, Rustin, and I brought these two girls to my house.

We naturally ended up playing truth or dare while sitting in a circle. Everyone had chosen truth instead of dare, but I did not want this game to finish with everyone telling questionably truthful confessions and no one having to complete a dare. My next turn, I chose dare. One of the girls told me to take my clothes off and run around the house naked. As she told me my dare, she looked at her friend with a look that said, "Here's another guy that doesn't have the balls to complete this dare." It was clear that she thought I would not strip down and run around the house. Tony and Rustin looked at each other and shook their heads because they knew exactly what was about to happen. I jumped up, took off every article of clothing on my body, tossing each article at the girl who gave me the dare. I made sure to put my underwear on her head before running a nude lap around the house. I then returned to my seat in the circle with nothing on but a grin. As I sat down, the girls were in complete shock while Rustin and Tony were laughing hysterically. The game ended shortly after my dare. On the drive to take the girls back to their car, they all just stared at me in disbelief that I had completed their dare. Tony, Rustin, and I laughed the rest of the night about that game.

The next day, Tony and I began talking about track season and how we were going to show off our speed to the rest of the state. We talked about seeing teammates, running challenging workouts, and how much faster we were going to be than the previous year. Deep down, I knew I was not going to be one of the fastest guys on the team, but I was looking forward to running faster races than the previous year and I was excited to see what memories I would get from this season.

The first few days of track practice, I started getting headaches and thought it was due to the heat and an electrolyte imbalance. I started eating a lot of salt at home and drinking lots of water throughout the day. The headaches stayed all day everyday. I would especially feel my headache during track practice, which only strengthened my belief I was dehydrated. I began guzzling water everywhere in school. I never walked past a water fountain without drinking from it. Then one night I, along with my family, discovered why I had been getting headaches.

The shunt I had implanted in my brain from my first surgery was designed for someone who was six foot three. I had grown to be six foot five and that caused my shunt to not work. The tube had gotten disconnected from my brain due to my height, causing water pressure to build in my brain. The increased pressure caused the intense headaches I had been experiencing during the past few weeks. One night, the pressure became too much for my body to handle and I had a seizure in the middle of the night. My brother Tyler found me having a seizure and woke my dad and Ben. Tyler, Ben, and my dad then carried me to the car and rushed me to the emergency room where I was loaded into an ambulance and driven to Memphis for emergency shunt repair surgery.

As I woke from surgery, I felt the familiar tenderness of surgical sutures on my head and noticed the doctors had shaved half my head in order to complete the procedure. I turned my head to see my mother sitting beside my hospital bed smiling down on me. The doctors immediately walked into the room and began testing my shunt to make sure it worked. Once again, I felt them pressing down on my tender and new wound. I winced the first time they pressed down and then became used to the pain. I had been through this before, I knew it would hurt and took a deep breath as I forced myself to become used to the pain inflicted by the doctors. After a thorough evaluation, they decided the surgery was a success and they all left the room. I then turned my head back to my mom, who had arrived in my room before I awoke from the surgery. We were the only ones left in the room. After putting me in an ambulance, my dad had stayed home to work and take care of my brothers. As I looked into my mom's eyes, she sighed and started laughing, saying, "Welp, Greg, here we are again." I cracked up and laughed right through the pain my laughter caused to my head. I told her that this time there would be no silver wiggle. I then noticed that other than my surgical site, I had no headache. This made me feel better and assured me that I was okay. This time I was able to walk and did not need help going to the bathroom. As my mom and I talked, I was incredibly thankful she was there and felt as though I had the most amazing mother in the world. She was sitting there holding my hand as I went through another scary moment just like she had when I was in Minnesota. This time, the only side effect from the surgery was a bad haircut and a new scar.

After staying in the hospital a day for observation, it was clear that I was ready to go home. My dad drove down to take me home with him. While I loved having my mom there with me, spending time with my dad was one of my favorite things to do. I looked forward to seeing him and riding home with him in his truck.

He walked into my hospital room and gave me a huge smile and asked if I was ready to go home. I sure was. I quickly changed back into my clothes and we left the hospital. On the drive home, we saw an exit for a greyhound dog track. We both looked at each other with the same idea lighting up our eyes. He asked if I wanted to go to the race track and I said yes. Once inside the track, we saw the dogs racing around the track as fast as their long legs could go. Since I was too young to place a bet, we decided on which dogs we should bet on and my dad placed a modest bet on the next race. We watched and yelled for our dog as loudly as we could, hoping that we could win some money and satisfaction from our bet. We had placed a whopping $2 bet and watched our dog finish near the back of the pack.

While we had lost our bet, I was glad that I got to experience a dog race with my dad. The rest of the trip home was okay, I slept most of the way and woke as we reached the city limit sign for Poplar Bluff.

Now that I was back in my hometown, I began to feel awkward about my haircut. I had school the next day and my dad told me that I could wear a hat to school and to tell the teachers why I was wearing a hat inside the school. School rules prohibited hats inside the buildings, but this was a special circumstance, he told me. This helped me to lose some of my insecurity about my recent surgery.

During school, I kept that hat on for dear life. I did not want to see the looks I would get when my classmates saw my haircut and my embarrassing scars. One teacher yelled at me about wearing a hat and I told her that I was allowed to wear a hat in school. She yelled at me, ordering me to take my hat off. Since this would be the first time I had exposed my scars and haircut at school, I felt my eyes beginning to swell with tears as all my insecurities about my scars, haircut, and the reaction of other students came to rest in a lump in my throat. I obeyed her and then saw her face distort with horror as she saw my suture and haircut. I felt a few tears trickle down my face as I heard the gasps from people in the hallway. She quickly told me she had had no idea and that I could continue wearing my hat. I saw how terrible the teacher felt for telling me to take off my hat, and I understood it was a mistake. Only a few of my classmates had seen my scars.

That night, my truck was getting fixed but I wanted to go hang out with Tony and Rustin. I looked in the yard and saw my mom's riding lawn mower. I decided that I could take the lawn mower to Tony's house so I started it then began the seven-mile trip to Tony's house.

The trip to Tony's was along a busy two-lane road and I had cars whizzing past me the entire trip. I was afraid that I would be hit, but I also knew that driving this mower would make for a hilarious story and decided that a funny story was more important than safety. As I pulled into Tony's house, I saw Rustin and Tony laughing uncontrollably as I drove it into the yard.

Once inside Tony's house, I told them about my surgery and they both wanted to see my scars. I took my hat off and Tony told me that he could give me a haircut to even up the rest of my hair. As was Tony's personality, he believed he was a great barber without ever giving anybody a haircut. I sat on an abandoned car in his front yard and saw him come into the yard with a pair of scissors. Luckily, my wounds were no longer tender and Tony cut my hair for three hours until he had successfully given me a buzz cut with his scissors. I walked into the house and looked in the mirror. I immediately thought I looked like a badass with this new haircut. I then realized because of my height, most people would not be able to see my scars. I thanked Tony and told him he did a good job.

Then I saw a truck pull up to Tony's house with a trailer. My mom's husband had driven to pick me up and bring the mower back with him. My mother's husband was a tough man who had a very masculine approach to life. He told me that I was lucky not to have been hit by a car on my lawn mower ride. I nodded and verbally agreed, but internally I knew that I had a great story I could tell people for the rest of my life. I then realized my mom was going to be furious for my driving the lawn mower down a busy street.

As soon as I walked into her house, she started telling me of the immense danger I had put myself in driving that mower. I nodded and agreed as I heard my brothers laughing in the background. Then my mom turned around from fixing cookies and saw my haircut. She immediately started crying, asking why I had let Tony give me a haircut. I told her that I liked it. She told me that seeing my head like that made her cry. I then realized my surgery and battles had affected her deeply and, in many ways, I think it caused her more pain than me.

The next day at school, I decided to show off my new haircut because my best friend had given it to me. I was so proud, every time I looked in the mirror, I thought I looked like a badass with a buzz cut. As soon as I got to track practice, everyone on the distance team asked if I was okay. Then we went right back to talking about training and getting ready for the season. As always, Tony and I prided ourselves on working harder than anyone, but this year, it seemed as though Tony was taking it to another level. I noticed that near the end of every practice Tony would throw up. I admired that he was pushing himself so hard and decided to run hard enough to puke like Tony. No matter how hard I tried, I never ran hard enough to vomit, but Tony was doing it on a regular basis. This inspired me to work harder and not allow myself to get left behind by the team in practices. I was running faster and faster, and by the end of my junior season I had run a faster time in every event than the previous year. I loved track and pushing myself during practice was something that filled me with pride, just as pushing myself in the hot gym during the summer did. I may have been near the back of the pack on most of the runs, but I was satisfied knowing that I was seasoned enough to finish the practices.

That season went great. I was becoming closer and closer to my track teammates and hanging out with my basketball teammates less and less off the court. The only other basketball player on the track team was TJ and he usually did not pick on me as much as the other basketball players. TJ and I had been friends for years and we played basketball together in church on Saturday nights during the summer. We would occasionally play football in a local park and go to the pool. His comment about needing big balls to run cross-country was one of the reasons I started running. While he never picked on me during cross-country and track, the few times he picked on me in the basketball locker room hurt me more than when other guys on the team called me names because I thought we were good friends and I valued his opinion more than other members of the team.

After a track meet, I was sitting in the middle of the bus with a few of my distance friends and heard a few of the throwers making fun of my left arm and the scars on my head. I ignored them and continued trying to rest. After a while, I had my fill with them making fun of me. I called them fat. Then I heard TJ say something about my left arm. I was already pissed off from being prodded by the throwers and made an unpleasant remark about one of TJ's family members in retaliation. He got out of his seat and punched me in the face. I had taken harder hits in my life, but being punched by someone I considered my friend hurt more than the physical pain. I was also hurting from being picked on by the throwers, and it all boiled over for me. I sat in my seat with my head down on the verge of crying my eyes out. I could not stop the first few tears from falling, but I swallowed as hard as I could and choked back the tears that wanted to burst from my eyes. The rest of that bus trip, I sat in silent introspection as I heard a few throwers making fun of me for being punched and for crying. Tony tried to console me as I sat thinking about things I had gone through and how difficult things were for me. As I started thinking about the comment I had made to TJ, I realized he was standing up for his family and regretted my comment. I put myself in his shoes and realized that if somebody said something about my family, I would always defend them. Although I had gotten punched and was not proud of the comment I had made, I was proud that I had stood up for myself.

The rest of the track season went well and Tony and I were running on a level that we both thought was admirable. One day in practice, we ran two-hundred-meter sprints with very little rest and I crossed the line on each interval in almost the same time. It seemed that no matter how tired I was, I could always run the same time in a sprint.

The last meet of the year was an invitational and I was running the three distance races, which I knew would wear me out. After my last race, I was lying in the team tent relaxing when the sprint coach ran up and told me they needed me to run the final leg of the four-by-four-hundred-meter relay. This is a race where four members of a team run four hundred meters each and hand a baton to the next relay member at the end of their turn. Since I was exhausted from running the mile, two-mile, and eight-hundred-meter races, I tried to get out of it by saying I had not practiced handoffs, meaning when the baton is handed to the next relay member. The coach told me I was running last and did not need to hand it off. I was out of excuses. I climbed out of the tent and walked to the starting line. A couple weeks before this relay race, I had run a four hundred in just under one minute. But I was exhausted from running three races earlier that afternoon.

When I got the baton to run my section of the relay, I ran as fast as I could and felt the fatigue screaming at me from my legs. By the time I reached the halfway mark, I was exhausted and tried to put everything I had into finishing this race. I had to at least hold the lead for my teammates. I decided to run the last curve as hard as I could then try to maintain that speed all the way to the finish. As I pushed, my legs churned below my body and I was able to fly all the way to the finish line. I crossed the tape. As I caught my breath, I heard my time: under a minute. I smiled exhaustedly, proud of myself. I had run four hundred meters faster than some of the sprinters who had made fun of me and further confirmed I could run consistent times on my sprints.

By the time track season ended, I was motivated to run faster and train harder for the next cross-country season. I was also excited because it was almost summer. I was about to be a senior at the high school. As a senior, I knew I was going to finally be a member of the varsity basketball team. But I knew that if I wanted to stay on the basketball team, I had to be in basketball PE, team camps, and open gyms.

One day after school let out, my dad and I went to Memphis for a follow-up appointment with the neurosurgeon that performed my shunt repair. I always loved road trips with my dad because I admired him a lot for his athletic discipline, but I also enjoyed getting to have some father-son time with him away from my brothers. I sat in the passenger seat talking with him about sports.

My meeting with the doctor went well. He told my dad there was zero chance of my tumor returning and that my shunt was functionally sound. I would not need to return again unless I started to hurt. As I inwardly celebrated the knowledge that my tumor was not going to return, I heard him say that if Tyler had not found me that night, I would have been dead by morning. My jaw dropped to the floor. Tyler had saved my life! If it had not been for him, I would have died that night on my bedroom floor. This confirmed in my mind, not for the first time and not for the last, that God had blessed me with a wonderful family, especially my brothers.

I was ready to start my summer with running and basketball. I decided that I would prepare for the upcoming cross-country season by slowly increasing my long run until I could run eight miles by the end of the summer. In basketball, I decided I was going to play in everything so I was assured to keep my spot on the team. I also wanted to be a great example for the younger players on the team.

When I showed up for basketball PE that summer, I noticed that there were fewer seniors on the team than the previous year: I was one of only five. My brother Tyler was about to enter his freshman year of high school and was going to be in all the summer basketball activities as well. While I was glad to have him on the court with me, I was a little embarrassed because I knew he was going to see how mean other people on the team were and I did not want them to pick on him in the same way that they picked on me.

As PE began, I quickly jumped into the workouts as I always had and saw my brother keeping up with me everywhere but in the weight room. He was able to play with us and in many ways outperformed me in a lot of the drills. I was glad he was playing so well and keeping up with us.

One time, I expected to win the team free throw competition by making eighty out of one hundred shots; shooting free throws had become my thing on the team. I thought I had the competition in the bag, and I was immediately pissed when Tyler beat me. But I thought about it and was glad we had finished first and second. One thing was for sure: the Hansbrough boys could shoot free throws.

In the locker room, I was getting made fun of less and less because most of the main culprits who had made fun of me were no longer a part of the team. Some had been forced to quit due to ineligibility from poor grades, a few of them had gotten in trouble with the law, and a couple had dropped out of school altogether. I still received the majority of the ridicule, but it did not bother me as much because I was going to be on the varsity team. As we loaded onto vans for team camp in Mississippi, I was excited to get to play on the varsity team in every game.

That camp was exceptionally tough this year and I fell asleep several times in the hallways of the gym between games. Tyler and I also hung out between games, walking to the cafeteria, dorm, and gym together. He was already showing that he was ready to play on the varsity team. I was playing pretty well and felt confident that I could stop any post player there. I deserved to play on the varsity team. After that camp, I realized Tyler and I would probably be playing together all summer. I was happy because it meant that I could sit with him and walk places without worrying about being made fun of for my left arm. I loved having him around because he was my family. I felt us growing closer and took my social frustrations out on him less frequently. I think he was now seeing why I had been so mean to him and Ben in the past.

Once we made it back from camp, I started running after PE so that I could keep ready for cross-country. I started running two miles every day and wanted to continue running so that I could run eight miles comfortably before summer was over. But this was going to be hard with another team camp quickly approaching. We loaded up and went to the Mizzou team camp in Columbia.

On the trip to Columbia, I got to sit in the front seat this time and had a lot of leg room. The trip seemed easier than the previous summers and I was not getting made fun of as much as previous years. While I still received a lot of jokes about my poor fashion sense and social awkwardness, I noticed that I was receiving fewer jokes about my left arm. Occasionally somebody would comment about "the snake" and I would immediately fall back on my coping mechanism of laughing it off and making jokes. But I was incredibly happy to see that the people who had led the relentless insults were no longer on the team. I was finally being treated as one of the team and not the continual butt of a joke. I held my head high and carried my stuff to my dorm room, excited to see how well we would play against teams from our own state.

We started off playing well, winning most of our games the first day. I was playing well, I was hitting a lot of my shots. I saw Tyler playing well also and loved it every time I got to go in a game to give him a break or we were on the court together.

The next morning before camp, I got up and ran to campus so that I could continue training for cross-country while at camp. That day, after running, I was not shooting well and my legs were not moving fast. While I played decently, I was not the beast I had been the previous day. The next day, I ran before camp again and experienced the same thing—my shots were not going in and I was unable to play very well. At lunch that day, Tyler told me I might want to stop running before camp so I could play better in the games. The next day, I did not run and was able to play well, hitting most of my shots and reverting to the beast I had been on the first day. While I wanted to train for cross-country, I wanted to keep my spot on the team as well. I did not run the rest of camp and played quite well the last couple days.

***

The rest of the summer, I ran with Tony, but there was a new guy who started hanging out with us. Rustin,

Tony, and I had a pretty regular schedule of activities we were going to do throughout the week. I knew Tony and I would run and lift weights then hang out with Rustin playing video games and watching TV. It threw me off that this other person was trying to become part of that schedule the three of us had fallen into. I had always seen us as three extraordinary people alike in our toughness, great personalities, and intrinsic badass factor. So when this new guy tried to become a part of us, I didn't like it because I thought he was a person who lacked the internal alpha male characteristic that was prevalent in Tony, Rustin, and I.

Nate was a short, nonathletic guy who never worked out or played sports. I had never seen him sweat or do anything worthy of admiration. But one day, Tony and Rustin told me they were going to hang out at his house. They told me I should go with them. I decided to go home because I was not interested in hanging out with a person like Nate.

The next day, Rustin and Tony told me they had smoked weed with Nate and that it was amazing. They asked if I wanted to go to his house with them the next day. I told them I did not want to go over there or smoke weed. And I also had no interest in spending time with a guy who just lay around smoking weed all day. I had nothing morally against smoking pot, but I thought it would hurt my ability to do the activities I loved, like playing basketball and running. I noticed that Tony and Rustin were spending more and more time smoking with Nate and less and less time hanging out with me. Although we were still best friends, they tried to get me to smoke with them more often and I kept telling them I did not want to smoke weed.

One night, late in the summer, Tony and Rustin asked me to go to Rustin's house and hang out. Once I got in the living room, I was expecting to watch TV and hang out as usual, but then I saw my two best friends leave the room for a minute. I got comfortable on the couch and turned the TV on. I looked up to see them walking out of the kitchen holding a large joint. They had rolled the marijuana into a cigarette that was filled to capacity.

After weeks of me adamantly stating that I did not want to smoke weed, they had decided to corner me and get me to smoke with them and show me what a great feeling it was to get high. They knew I did not want to smoke and to have them corner me like this caused a fire to rage from the pit of my stomach and emerge as anger when I realized what had happened. I stood up and walked out of the house. On the drive home, I was enraged that they would disrespect my desire to keep the progress I had made as an athlete.

Over the next few weeks, I started seeing my two best friends less and less until we were not hanging out on a daily basis. I felt as though this nonathletic stoner Nate was stealing my best friends. I was not interested in hanging out with potheads. I was an alpha male and wanted to stay an alpha male. I had not worked as hard as I could for years to lose it to smoking weed.

That year during cross-country, I started hanging out with the Lewis boys more instead of Tony and Rustin. While I still considered Tony and Rustin to be my best friends, the Lewis boys were a lot of fun and did not smoke weed.

The Lewis boys were three brothers, Matt, Jeremy, and John-Mark. They lived in a house a couple miles from the school and were badass like me. They all prided themselves on being able to complete difficult and long runs, which I loved because I was proud of my ability to endure tough runs as well. They also prided themselves on being hilarious. We conjured up new running routes around town and talked about hot girls at school and the hot girls on the cross-country team while lying around the house.

By the end of that cross-country season, I had gained all three of the Lewis boys as great friends. We had run a lot of miles together and gained countless stories about our hardiness. There was the time Jeremy talked trash to a group of guys heckling us for running on the road. The time Matt and I decided to put on our coolest clothes and drive around town in my truck picking up girls and I left him in a parking lot for hours as I attempted to charm my way into a girl's heart. The times that John-Mark ran naked around town wearing only his running shoes. I was incredibly grateful that I had found such a great new group of friends.

The mood in the basketball locker room was also different. I was now considered one of the leaders of the team. On the first day before tryouts, Coach Pat told the seniors that each one of us could have one request and asked what we wanted. As I sat there contemplating what I wanted to ask from the team, I thought about the jokes I had endured the past four years, the tears I had choked back, laughing to keep from crying, and my low self-esteem. When the coach asked what I wanted, I told them I did not want to receive any jokes about my left arm. The whole team nodded their heads in agreement that they would no longer make fun of my left arm. I felt a huge relief in knowing I no longer had to endure that ridicule. It was as if a weight had been lifted off my shoulders.

At first, I felt awkward not hearing jokes at my expense. I walked into the locker room the next day expecting to hear jokes about me even though I had made my request. Nobody made a derogatory remark about me and I could finally relax in the locker room. I began to honestly joke around with everyone without feeling self-conscious about my left arm. I finally felt like one of the guys and a real part of the team.

Another big change with the team was that my brother Tyler was going to be on the varsity team with me. I was happy we were going to get to play together that year. Having him on the team meant that we would get to take the backyard games from our house onto the high school courts.

As the season went on, I noticed that the people who had made fun of me for years were no longer picking on me in the hallway. The guys who had made fun of my left arm since the eighth grade were suddenly inspired by my continued efforts and presence on the basketball team. It was as if a switch went off in their minds and they realized that they had mistreated me for years. And this realization caused them to admire me for enduring their cruelties and jokes as I continued with the basketball team. I would look in the stands and see these people clapping and cheering for me.

Coach Vagrun was still the junior varsity coach, but he had little interaction with the varsity team. I was glad to be past him because I never felt that he cared about his players. When he was my coach, I was always scared that he would curse me out or tell me something negative about my left arm.

By the end of the season, I had become a crowd favorite with the school because I had endured so much throughout my basketball career and kept a smile on my face. I could not help but shake my head at some of the people who told me how much I inspired them. Every time I checked into a game, there was a huge uproar from the crowd and I could not hold back a huge smile. On senior night, the crowd chanted for me to be in the game. I can still hear the chant, "WE WANT SNAKE!" (in reference to my nickname Snake Diesel, not in reference to my left arm). While over the years I had become known by my nickname, most of the people had no idea the word "snake" was used in a negative manner. I liked my nickname Snake Diesel but hated it when someone would call my left arm a snake.

However, I knew that most of the people who had laughed hysterically at my left arm having a mind of its own were not in the crowd. Checking into the game to that chant sent the crowd into a cheering frenzy. Every shot I made sent the crowd into a riot as well. Then, when I checked out of the game on senior night, all the coaches gave me a hug and told me they loved having me on the team. Coach Vagrun even hugged me. I did not want to hug him, but thought I should since his wife and kids were seated behind the bench and I did not want his kids to see their father in a poor light. As I walked down the bench giving my teammates high fives, I saw my brother Tyler standing there with a face full of pride, waiting to slap my hand. Seeing his face, I could feel his pride for me as a brother. That made me swell with pride and proved all the persecution and obstacles I had overcome to make this team worthwhile.

We made it out of our district for the state tournament. We played a team from St. Louis in our sectional game. By this time, Tyler was starting and I knew we were going to beat these private school weaklings and move on to the next round. Halfway into the game, Tyler got on a fast break and I could see he was going to dunk the ball. As he lowered his body to jump, I saw him try to jump but land on the ground clutching his leg. I sprinted from the bench to see what had happened. He was loaded on the stretcher to head to the hospital because he had broken his leg. I was pissed. I wanted to go in the game and beat these guys in revenge for my brother's injury. But I was not put in the game. I sat the bench the rest of the game and watched us lose. I hated watching us lose, but I wanted to check on my brother in the hospital more than waiting around for the team. I went with my dad after the game and saw my brother in the emergency room, his broken leg bandaged. I told him we had lost and he sat back in slight disappointment.

On the ride home, I was upset that basketball was over, but was already starting to focus on track. I had decided to try to compete in shot put this year since I already knew how to throw it and was stronger than the last time I competed in the event eight years ago.

The first week of track was going well and I noticed that Tony was not running as well as he had the previous year. He was still one of the fastest runners on the team, but he no longer had the steely glint in his eye I had seen the year before. After a lot of the practices, we would be at his house and he and Rustin would go smoke weed with Nate. I would then go to the Lewis house and hang out with them. I missed my two best friends, but the Lewis brothers were quickly becoming my second family.

During the track meets, I was able to place higher in the shot put than in the distance races, and I exulted in the knowledge that I was the only one throwing the shot put and running distance events. I felt that this must make me one of the most resilient guys in school. I would place in the top five of the shot put before running the mile at most of the meets.

By the end of the track season, I still considered Rustin and Tony to be my best friends, but they were still hanging out with Nate and I wanted nothing to do with him or smoking weed, no matter how much fun they made it sound. One night, however, I could not resist their pressure. I went down to the basement and smoked a joint with them in a circle. Although I did not feel any different, I pretended to be high and laughed at everything that was said in the room.

The next day, I went for a run and felt my lungs working incredibly hard to breathe. As I reached the top of the last hill, I was gasping for breath and vowed to never smoke again because I wanted to continue being a badass alpha male and would need my lungs to do so.

After track season, I started to think on where I wanted to go to college. I was never a great student in high school and did not have a lot of confidence in my abilities as a student. I saw many of my classmates receiving great grades on tests that I had studied and prepared to take while they seemed to rarely study. After taking the ACT, my score was well below the requirements for admittance to a major university. I then realized that going to community college in my hometown would be a great way to see if I were academically competent.

The Decision

Istarted taking classes at the local junior college in Poplar Bluff in the fall. As a college freshman, I decided that I would live in the student housing at the junior college. My dad and I agreed that even though I was still in my hometown, it would be good for me to learn to live on my own as a college student. I would have a certain budget to live on each month and would be working hard in my classes.

As I moved into my dorm room, I met my roommates for the year and was excited to be living with people from other places. The apartments were set up in a suite that included four rooms, two bathrooms, and a small living room. Each student would have their own room and two people would share a bathroom, while all four suitemates would share the kitchen and living room. The first two roommates I met seemed like normal guys, both from a nearby town and they were both ready to start their first year of college. Then my third roommate, the one I would share a bathroom with, showed up, and I was immediately pleased to see that he was a tall guy, like myself. He claimed to be there to play on the basketball team. I felt immediately at ease because I had lived with athletes my whole life. Dexter was from the Bahamas and claimed to be the upcoming star of the junior college basketball team. Immediately after moving in, he loftily announced that he had to leave us for practice. The way he left for practice showed that he felt playing basketball made him a better person than me and the other roommates. This dug into my athletic pride because I had considered myself a great basketball player since I was a small boy. I was one of the alpha males of the world.

Once classes started, it was incredibly apparent that my other two roommates were there to have fun and that was about it. They seemed to never go to class and I barely ever saw them awake during the day, so it was as if Dexter and I were the only ones going to all of our classes.

I noticed that I had a lot of free time after my classes because I didn't have a sports practice to go to or a workout to do for a team. I would leave my classes and go to the gym and shoot baskets for a little while. I knew I should study, but I did not know how to prepare for lectures and assumed that I could be successful by approaching the classes the same way I had in high school.

I was friends with the basketball coach at the college; he had taught me and my brothers the fundamentals of the game since we were small children. After the first week, I told him that Dexter was my roommate. He told me Dexter was not on the team. He told me that he was not good enough to make the team. I thought it was funny that he claimed to be this great basketball player who was here just for basketball when in reality he wasn't even good enough to play on the junior college team in my hometown.

After a couple weeks, I approached Dexter and asked him about his basketball skills. He claimed to have scored twenty points a game in the Bahamas and told me that I would not stand a chance against him in a game of one-on-one. I immediately challenged him. He had no idea that I was a great basketball player.

I knew that he was looking at me as a disabled person and not an athlete. On our way to the gym, he asked me why I walked funny and told me he would spot me some points. I told him that I would not need him to spot me any points and that I was confident I could win without any help.

After shooting a few baskets to warm up, we started the game. It was a game to ten with each basket counting one point. He had the ball first and scored two points so I was a little nervous about being able to win the game. Then I got the rebound from one of his missed shots and scored five straight points. He never got the ball again. I won the game by eight points. On the walk back to the dorm, he was talking about how pathetic it was that he had been beaten by me. He told me that his high school coach would laugh if he knew that I had beaten him. I quietly smiled and thought to myself, "Your bitch ass just encountered the alpha male."

Since I had a lot of free time, I began wondering what I should do with all of it. I then remembered a goal I had set for myself when I first started cross-country. I told myself that before I died, I would run a marathon. It was as if a light came on in my head: I have enough free time now, I should train for a marathon.

Since three miles was the furthest distance I had ever run for a race, I decided to use the knowledge I had gained from building my long run for training to run a marathon. I decided to start with three miles as a long run and build on the distance from that run each week. I made the decision I was going to start training the following week to run my marathon and cross off one of the events on my bucket list.

The Road to St. Louis

As I set out for a plan to train for the marathon, all my friends were still running cross-country in high school. I was going to be the first one from my group of runners to attempt anything longer than a three-mile race. I decided to ask my dad what a good method for preparing for the race. My dad had run a marathon while he was in college and I always thought of him as a great athlete, so it seemed natural to ask him for training advice. He told me to increase my long run by ten percent a week.

I thought this recommendation might work for most people, but I am an alpha male and these rules do not apply to me. I would increase my mileage by one mile a week. Starting with two miles as my long run on Monday, I would increase that run by one mile each week. My runs on the other days of the week would be half the distance of that long run.

The first few weeks went by normally. I was increasing my mileage by a mile with no problem. I began to think my dad's ten percent rule was for weak people, and that I could handle things way better than most people. After thinking this for a week, I started noticing my shins were getting a little sore after each run. I immediately thought I might be getting shin splints.

A girl on my high school team once developed a terrible case of shin splints. Her shins were so pained that I had to carry her off the track after her last track race. While I had never experienced shin splints, I believed that if I ever got them, I would be tough enough to run through the pain because I was way more resilient than she was. Again, I considered myself to be an alpha male who could handle things way better than the general population.

I continued to run with my shins feeling sore every day between runs. The pain continued to get progressively worse and I decided to ask my dad what I could do to get my shins better. He told me that shin splints were caused by the muscle on the front of the shin tearing away from the bone. He then showed me an exercise that involves hanging the majority of the foot off a step and raising your toes toward the sky, forcing the muscle beside the shin bone to flex. He told me that this exercise was a great way to rehab my shins. He also told me to stop running until it was better.

I told myself that I would use this exercise to heal my shins, but I was not going to stop running. I could handle this, I was on a mission to run a marathon and as a badass, I was not going to let shin splints get in my way, I was way harder than that.

After another week of running with shin splints, I could barely walk from the pain. I felt my shins screaming in pain every time I went for a run. I finally realized I had to quit running until my shins healed.

While I was not running, I became obsessed with the rehab exercise drill my dad had shown me; every time I walked up a step, I had to do a set of ten reverse toe raises before continuing on my way. I received a lot of funny looks from people at school as I obsessively did this exercise between classes. After a few days, I asked my dad for advice on how to stay in shape while I was injured and he told me swimming and biking were great ways to stay in shape while healing from my shin splints.

My dad had bought a bike for me while I was in high school that was equipped with all the controls on the right hand side of the bike so I could shift gears like a normal rider. I had only ridden the bike a few times in high school, but decided that I needed to ride it if I wanted to run a marathon. As an avid cyclist, my dad would always tell me about this incredibly hard road he and his friends would ride called O Highway. He talked about the incredibly tough hills found on this highway and how it would wear him and his riding buddies out every time they went to ride there. I decided I was going to start riding there to stay in shape for my training while my shins healed.

I knew my dad was an incredible athlete from being the conference high jump champion while he was at Mizzou, playing basketball all the time, and riding his bike regularly. I admired his toughness and dedication to working out, but I was the badass alpha male and would skip the wimpy rides that most people did before trying to ride on the infamous O Highway. I loaded my bike into my truck and drove to the start of the infamous route.

As I started riding, I came to the first hill and began pedaling up, thinking I could conquer this hill. After a few feet of climbing, I was breathing heavily and my legs began to scream in pain, I then looked up and realized I had only started up this hill. As I neared the top of the hill, my legs were blown, I was completely out of breath and anxiously looking forward to relaxing on the downhill after this climb. I then heard a dog barking violently, I looked over and saw a giant dog flying down a gravel driveway straight for me. As if climbing this hill was not hard enough, now I had to outrun this dog. I started pedaling with everything I had left in my body. The dog snapped and bit my pedal, narrowly missing my shoe. I felt adrenaline shoot through my veins and used it to increase my speed to get away from the dog. Once out of view of the dog, I began to relax and coast down the other side of this hill. I then realized I would have to ride past this dog again on my way back. After this hill,

I noticed the rest of the ride was not very hard and I cruised through it until I reached my turnaround point. On the ride back, I was incredibly tired and struggled to get to the top of the hill again on my way back to my truck. I was now expecting to be chased by the dog and prepared to sprint for my life at the top of the hill, but this time, I was exhausted from riding eight miles on my bike. The dog came tearing after me and I tried to sprint, but instead kept going at the same pace, I was too tired to outrun the dog. As he approached my bike, I saw him try to bite my rear tire and narrowly miss. This miss allowed me to reach the top of the hill and begin on the downhill. I was able to go fast enough down the hill to outrun the dog. As I reached my truck after the downhill, I was exhausted and glad I had outrun the dog. I then thought I would be better prepared to outrun the dog next time I went out there to ride. After loading my bike in my truck, I began to swell in pride knowing that I had conquered the infamous O Highway and drove home with a huge feeling of accomplishment.

Each day after class I went to ride this route and every day it became easier and easier. I realized after a week of riding there that dog had moved closer to the road and I was having to sprint harder and faster each time to escape without being bitten. At one point I was talking with my friend Matt, who lived in one of the houses on O Highway. He told me that dog had attacked his mom and he then went to the house and shot the dog. I felt a wave of relief course through my body. I would no longer have to ride my ass off to outrun this dog at the top of the hill.

The next day, I reached the top of the hill and relaxed from not hearing the dog running for my bike. I returned to the ride, relaxing each time I came over the hill. I told my dad that I had been riding O Highway since getting shin splints. He then challenged me to a race. I jumped at the challenge and was excited to test my cycling skills against my dad. I thought I was going to win because I had been riding this route a lot.

As we started up the first hill, he jumped in the lead and I struggled to stay with him. Near the top of the hill, he told me to be careful because there was a huge dog that sometimes chased cyclists. I was breathing too hard to answer but saw him pick up the pace in anticipation of being chased. I continued at my steady and slow pace a few feet behind him. The rest of the race, my dad stayed right on the back of my wheel. I thought I would win the race by sprinting through the flat section. As I pushed the pace as fast as my legs could pedal, my dad stayed right on my wheel. Then, on the last flat section, I was finally exhausted and he went around me and then increased his lead all the way to the finish. I arrived at the finish completely out of energy and saw him grinning ear to ear. On the ride home, he explained that riding behind someone was a great way to conserve energy and was called drafting because it decreased wind resistance on the trailing rider. He then explained that while I was spending huge amounts of energy to outrun him, he was able to conserve his energy until the last part where he flew by me to win the race.

After three weeks of riding my bike, my shins no longer hurt and I was ready to return to running and continue on my quest to run a marathon. I decided that I would start running at the same place I had left with my shin injury.

On my way home Sunday, I heard a song on the radio from AC/DC called "Back in Black." I loved that song and decided the next day I would wear all black on my first run back since my injury. I pulled on my black running tights, black shirt, and black shorts and started out on an eight mile run. During this run, I noticed it was a lot harder to finish the route than it had been before I had hurt my shins. Luckily my shins were not hurting, but I was really tired and the hills were much more difficult to run. The next day, my run was four miles and I felt back to normal. I thought to myself that the run on Monday had cleared the cobwebs from my legs, as if they were old, unused buildings.

As my miles got longer, I noticed that I was spending over an hour each day running and multiple hours every Monday, which was my long run day. As I had become bored with my old cross-country routes, my mom told me of a ten-mile loop around town she once ran when she was in really good shape. She told me it started and ended at Pizza Inn parking lot. I was incredibly nervous about this run because it would be the furthest I had ever run and the loop went around the entire town. The night before this run, I had trouble sleeping due to worrying about being able to finish this route. As I drove to Pizza Inn, I could feel my stomach churning in nervous knots. I then started running and thought to myself, "You can't stop something you started." I continued running and moved through the town with an intentional effort to finish my long run. I realized I was extremely thirsty. I ran into a gas station and saw the Lewis brothers' sister working behind the counter. I told her I was extremely thirsty and asked for some water. She told me to take a bottled water from the fridge. I asked for two, she said no problem. I guzzled the water and she told me not to worry about paying, she was happy to help. After finishing the second bottle and leaving the store, I realized I felt way better and was extremely thankful she had helped me. I finished the run and was exhausted. But I felt incredibly accomplished to have finished a run that was longer than any run I had done in high school.

As the weeks rolled by, I was nervous each Monday for my long run, each run one mile further than I had ever run in my life. That ten-mile loop began to look easier and easier with each run adding a mile onto the previous week, the town loop working as my base loop.

After finishing my first run of fifteen miles, I decided to find a marathon to run and discovered St. Louis had a marathon in early April. I signed up for the race and then continued to build my mileage.

On my first-ever twenty-mile run, I did not sleep easily for three days before it. I tossed and turned in nervous fits about that run, which would be two loops around town. I drove to Pizza Inn and began my run that afternoon. By this time, I had placed Gatorade bottles at certain points throughout the town loop as well as picked out spots to grab more water so I could drink during my run. I had a bottle on a pillar beside the Lawson's house, carried a dime so I could buy water at a gas station that charged ten cents for a water cup, and could run into a Sonic Drive-in that gave me free water.

I ran through my first loop easily. As I started my second loop, it was getting dark and I began to hear people heckling me from their cars as I ran. I heard honks from people and laughing as I ran. As I ran past the junior high school, I was completely out of energy and was eager to finish this run and take a hot shower. I slowly made my way up the last hill and noticed a car swerving closely toward me on the shoulder of the road. Since it was a busy road, I thought maybe he was just accidentally swerving. It was then that I felt something hit my chest with a thud and heard glass break on the ground. I looked down and saw a broken beer bottle behind me on the ground. This guy had thrown a beer bottle at me while I was trying to finish my first ever twenty-mile route. I felt rage course through my veins and my blood boiled over. I screamed in rage and ran furiously the last half mile to the finish. As I finished the run, I was no longer angry and smiled as I realized I had used my rage to successfully finish my run. I felt proud that I had finished another longest run of my life and understood that if I had not been hit in the chest with the beer bottle, I would not have been pissed off and the last half mile would have probably been more difficult.

While my running was going great, my grades were not. I was failing in almost all of my classes and was scared of flunking out of school. I went to my grandpa, the most academically accomplished person I had ever known, for advice. My grandpa was a general surgeon and prided himself on intellectual accomplishments. He always stressed the importance of education and I knew he could give me advice on ways to make better grades. He told me to read each section multiple times before and after class. I told him that many of my class readings were over thirty pages. He responded unsympathetically, telling me of having to read things when he was in college sometimes eight times.

I took his advice to heart and started reading each reading section in the syllabus twice before the lecture and three times following the class. I was spending four to five hours a day studying for my classes. I heard other students talking about not needing to study for the tests. I took pride in knowing that I was well prepared for every lecture in every class. I was highlighting the readings in different colors, yellow for the first time reading, orange for the second and third time, and blue for the fourth and fifth time of completing a reading. I then noticed that during tests, a lot of the students who claimed to not need to study were cheating off other students when the teacher was not looking. After noticing this, I felt myself swell with pride in knowing I was earning my grades and not cheating to finish the classes. Every grade I received, I had earned. And my grandfather was right; reading the sections multiple times was getting me better grades. I was now dedicating myself to two things: running and studying.

***

I now had one long run left before my marathon, scheduled to happen three weeks before the race. I was going to run twenty-two miles and then run easy the last two weeks before the marathon. A few days before my twenty-two mile run, one of my former high school teammates told me he could still beat me in a sprint even though he had seen me running all over town. I thought to myself, "Prepare to meet the alpha male," which was my mentality at the time. I showed up at track practice that day and challenged him to every interval he was running that day. During the first interval I was twenty yards ahead of him and felt my hamstring tighten with pain. I thought it was nothing serious and continued beating him in every interval during that practice. Once I sat in my truck after running those intervals, I felt my hamstring pulsate with pain. The next day the back of my leg was swollen and purple.

My dad told me I had pulled my hamstring and that I should not run until it was better. This time, the pain was so great I could not even think about running. I hobbled to class and painfully made my way through the halls. My dad told me stretching was the only thing I could do to help my hamstring get better. I started stretching constantly. Every chance I got, I stretched my hamstring. After a week, the swelling had left and the purple coloration had lessened, but I noticed the pain was still there and became nervous about being able to run in the marathon. I decided that regardless of how my hamstring was feeling, I was going to run the marathon. I had not spent months running on the roads to not finish something on my bucket list. Besides, I was never going to run another marathon; I had the rest of my life to let my hamstring heal.

I continued stretching everywhere. My parents were coming to watch me run in the marathon. The day before the race, my hamstring was a little sore, but I was determined to run my marathon. As I packed for the race, I looked outside and noticed that it was a beautiful day, seventy-five degrees and not a cloud in the sky. I put my shorts, shirt, and shoes in my gym bag. I then thought that I might as well grab my tights in case it was a little cool the next morning.

I had bought tickets to the pre-race dinner that night and was excited to be sitting in a room with other marathoners. At the dinner, I found out there was an artistic poster for the marathon on sale. Since this would be my one and only marathon, I wanted to buy the poster, but found out we could not buy them until after the main speaker was finished. Jeff Galloway was the main speaker at the dinner and thought he was incredibly interesting and was immediately drawn in by his speech. He talked about how tough it was to train for a marathon and what an accomplishment it was to train and finish one. By the end of his talk, I was inspired.

On my way to buy the marathon poster, I talked about training with the other runners. They were amazed that I had trained for a marathon at eighteen years old. We swapped stories about crazy runs and strategies for preparing for the race. By the time I had purchased a poster, I had shared and heard almost a dozen stories about running.

When I got back to the hotel with my family, my nerves began to set in. I started worrying about all the things that could go wrong before the race, centered on the thought of losing my race number. A race number is a bib that all the racers pin on their shirts to show they are running in the marathon and can be counted as a racer. That night, I had a nightmare where I could not find my bib number anywhere and was screaming at my brother to move so I could look for it under his seat. When I woke early the next morning, Tyler told me I had screamed at him in my sleep. I apologized to him and he thought it was funny.

I checked the weather and felt my heart sink as I looked outside to confirm what I had read. Overnight, a cold front had come to St. Louis. There were clouds and the temperature was just below thirty degrees with a forecast calling for freezing rain and sleet throughout the day. I pulled out my tights, pissed that I had not packed for colder weather. All I had were my tights and shorts; I had left my gloves and cold weather hats at home. I thought to myself, "Well, this is going to be really cold, but I cannot back out now, I have the rest of my life to recover from this run." I remembered my mom explaining that the doctors had told her that the left side of my body would have more trouble staying warm than the right side of my body. I focused on how hard I had trained for months to do this marathon. If I lost a finger to frostbite, I could brag for the rest of my life about how I had lost it running a marathon, which would make me a badass.

As I made my way to the starting line of the race, I felt the chill of the cold rush right through the thin tights I was wearing. I made my way to the back of the pack because I expected to run close to a six-hour marathon. Luckily there were pace groups for each projected finish time. I ran with the five hour and thirty minute group because it was the slowest pace group. As the race started, I began talking with the other people in my pace group and the conversation was lively; we all shared training thoughts and stories, and then talked about the grittiness of running the marathon. It started to rain as we reached the first couple mile markers. The miles and hours seemed to pass easily as the conversation moved from one subject to another. I was meeting a bunch of new people as we ran through the course.

At about mile twenty, I began to feel incredibly tired and saw the group I had been running with leave me behind as I struggled up the hills. I had packed gum to chew in my pocket so that I would not get thirsty during the race, but my fingers were so cold that they couldn't function well enough to open a piece of gum. As I struggled up a hill near mile twenty-two, I was exhausted and thought, "This is what a flat tire must feel like." I looked over and saw my mom and dad cheering for me as they drove by in the van. I was so tired I could not even mutter a response. I attempted to smile at them, but my face was so numb with cold that I could not give them my usual toothy grin.

I climbed a hill on St. Louis University that had a brick clock tower at the top and felt myself slogging up the hill, complete exhaustion swamping my entire body. On the downhill after the clock tower, I saw that I had passed the twenty-three-mile marker. I coached myself: "You only have three miles left to go, c'mon Greg, you only have a high school cross-country race left to run." I felt my toenails pulsing in pain, but I thought about the months I had trained and everything I had endured to get to this marathon and told myself that I had come too far to quit. I reached the finish line in five hours and forty minutes, shivering from the cold rain. While I was completely exhausted, I felt my soul smile with satisfaction as I crossed the finish line.

Marathoner

After crossing the finish line, I sat in the medical tent sipping water and eating a doughnut with my finisher's medal around my neck. I was completely exhausted and cold, but the weight of that medal was incredible. After a few minutes, I jumped in the van with my family and we headed back to Poplar Bluff. The looks on my brothers' faces told me they were impressed by my accomplishment.

After the high from my run wore off, I noticed how uncomfortable I was in my wet running tights. I had been running for over five hours in freezing rain and was shivering. I told my dad I wanted to change clothes. We pulled into a mall off the interstate and I changed in the bathroom. After putting on warmer clothes, I felt a little better, although my body was still exhausted to its core. I proudly wore the marathon finisher's medal around my neck as I walked back to the van. While I had originally planned to just run one marathon and check it off my bucket list, on the ride home I realized how much I had I loved training for and running that race. I immediately wanted to run another one.

I had planned to wear my medal the whole next day to show off my accomplishment, but as I woke and started to get out of bed, I felt my legs and body gripped with muscle soreness. It was a struggle to walk to the toilet. I had a miserable time taking a shower and getting dressed for classes. I painfully made my way to class. Every step I took felt like someone was hitting my quads with a hammer. I did the best I could to continue my daily routine, but there was no escaping the agonizing muscle soreness. I took the elevator to my study table in the library. As I read my chapters for class, I had trouble concentrating because my legs were in such terrible pain. I hurried through my studying and walked back to my dorm room. I put on my sweats and lay down on the couch trying to stop the unrelenting soreness in my legs.

Each day, my legs felt a little better, but it was clear that I had hurt my hamstring and needed to let it heal before I started to run again. The back of my leg was blue from the injury and it was painful to walk around campus. My dad told me again that stretching was the only thing I could do to get it better and I stretched relentlessly, as I had before the race. After a week, the soreness in my legs was completely gone and I was left with my hamstring injury as my only complaint.

For a while, I enjoyed not running and not feeling as though I had to keep a training schedule, but I slowly began to miss running on a regular basis. I decided to run another marathon the following year around the same time.

Once classes ended, I started reading a book by Jeff Galloway that talked about a training method that included both running and walking. I decided to implement this into my training once my hamstring healed.

A month after the marathon, my hamstring had finished healing and I started training for the Country Music Marathon in Nashville the following year. I started running three days a week and implemented the running and walking into my training. This time I knew what to expect. I understood that training for a marathon meant a lot of long hours running through the town by myself and required the ability to handle injuries and return to training. So it was no surprise to me that a few weeks into training I experienced an injury to my shins just as I had the previous year. Instead of panicking about not being able to work on my training, I started swimming in the pool to stay in shape, substituting for cycling.

Every day I went to the pool and swam laps to stay in shape for my marathon training. One day, I was swimming laps and one of the gym workers suggested I take a course to become a lifeguard. I thought to myself, "Shit, I hate swimming, but she must recognize an alpha male when she sees one." I didn't have the heart to tell her I hated swimming. However, as I finished swimming my laps, I began to think that maybe sitting at a pool would be a great way to make a little money. Once my summer school class ended, I enrolled in the lifeguard training program. During that week, I learned a lot about swimming and passed the course to become a lifeguard. That July, I started working at a local swimming pool as a lifeguard. I thought it was fun because I could run before and after work and get a tan from sitting outside all day.

The pool was located only a couple miles from the Lewis house, which meant I could hang out, run, and relax there before and after work. Jeremy showed me a cool running route from his house that became a staple in my training. The route ran from his house down to the cobblestones on Main Street, and through the city graveyard. One day, I saw a sign for KO Fight Club on the glass window of a large corner building that housed a gym. I filed its location away in my head as we ran. This gym also happened to be on my drive home from the pool.

Soon after, on a drive to work, I stopped at the KO Fight Club gym to see whether or not it would be fun to do a little boxing as cross training. As soon as I walked in, I saw Marquise, one of my basketball friends, who greeted me from a boxing ring. Marquise explained that he was the gym pro and wondered if I would run with him a few days to help him stay in shape for boxing. I was pumped; I had found a new running buddy and couldn't wait to show him the joy I had found in running.

We started running together twice a week. Halfway into the first run, we talked and he explained that his legs were hurting, but he was not breathing hard and since I loved having new company on my runs, I didn't want to worry him with talk about shin splints. After the second week, he complained about his shins hurting too much to run with me so I told him how to rehab them using the exercises my dad had shown me. He stopped running with me but told me to stop by the boxing gym to say hi.

I went by the gym frequently after work because the people there were constantly training to become better boxers; they were training to box with the same focus I had to train for my running. I noticed that many of them were poorly conditioned and wanted to gain better conditioning. Marquise asked me if I would help them increase their running stamina. I could not believe it! I would get to show the boxers how much fun running was! I started them off slowly running two miles as a long run. They all groaned and struggled to complete the run. I then increased their mileage the same way I had for my marathon training until they were all able to run five miles without stopping by the end of the summer. I discovered that I loved showing these boxers the joy of training and they all seemed pleased to have increased their fitness.

In my own training, I noticed that the walk breaks were helping me to not be as tired through my long runs. And this time, I avoided racing my old high school teammates—I had learned my lesson with that one.

However, the Lewis boys were now my best friends and they ran with me a lot. Jeremy and I ran together fairly often. I could sometimes drag Matt out for runs, but he was definitely the social one in the Lewis family so he and I went out together more socially than athletically.

Along with walk breaks, I had also added speed intervals to my weekly training regimen. These intervals were supposed to be fun, so I approached them with a playful attitude. I wore headphones and enjoyed music as I ran.

By the end of the summer, I was deep into my training for the marathon the following April. I thought it would be fun and beneficial to run a half marathon to prepare for the marathon. So I closed out the summer with a new focus: gearing my training toward the Memphis half marathon in December. I loved having a disciplined training program as a major part of my life, and I was pumped to be the first person in my family to run more than one marathon. In completing my second marathon, I was going to further secure my spot in the world as an alpha male.

As school started, I continued using my grandfather's advice in my studies, studying three to four hours a day in order to be ready for my classes. I was able to draw upon my marathon mindset with my studies. Every time I sat down to read a chapter, I understood it would take a few pages before things felt comfortable. In running, the first couple miles are tough because it is difficult to get moving, but during the middle miles, you are in a rhythm and just have to keep cruising through in the same rhythm, then by the end of a run, you see the end getting closer and fix your eyes on the finish. Studying was no different: the hardest part was beginning my reading at the library. I was reading each chapter twice before class and once afterward. After each chapter, I continued moving in my rhythm, then finished the last chapter for my last class with my mind focused on the finish line. I was becoming vocal in the classroom, asking questions and carrying on conversations with the teachers in class. I was still making average grades, but I prided myself on knowing that I had earned my grades with hard work.

While I lived in the dorm, I still went home a lot. I began to notice some positive changes in my brothers. We had always played a lot of basketball, but Tyler had started lifting weights and eating according to a nutrition program designed by an athletic trainer in St. Louis. He and my dad also watched videos and read books on basketball training and were developing a shooting routine based on the shooting drills professional and college players used in their training. I would go with my dad and help rebound in these workouts when I had time. They began shooting every day. My brother Ben had fallen in love with playing basketball and would play any games going on around town. I drove him to many gyms so he could play.

I watched as Tyler became a much leaner and stronger person from keeping a disciplined training and nutrition program. It was clear he was getting stronger, more athletic, and, thanks to the shooting drills, a lot better with his basketball skills. As I watched Ben play against everyone in town, I noticed he could do incredible things with the ball. It seemed that no one in town could keep him from getting to the basket and scoring. And he received a lot of pleasure from the tons of different game situations he found himself in, which taught him new ways to score. Every time I saw him in a strange situation, his facial expressions let me know he was trying to figure out a new way to get to the basket. I saw him go through a lot of defenders to find his way to the basket. I then noticed he was filing these new moves into his memory as moves to be used in the future to get out of similar situations.

I began to use similar methods in my training for the Memphis half marathon, which I decided to run in preparation for the Country Music Marathon. If I came to an icy uphill, I would shamble up the ice by placing my feet in a stable, shuffling step to get up a hill. The first few times I usually fell, but I would find my way up the hill and file the success away in my memory as a way to push through in much the same way that Ben remembered successes to increase his basketball skills. And when I ran with the Lewis boys, I was getting a lot of happy moments from being with my running buddies, much as Ben was with his basketball friends. I thought about Tyler and my dad developing and keeping a shooting routine just like I had developed and stuck to my training program. Tyler and Ben were quickly becoming the two best players in the state of Missouri as far as high school basketball was concerned, and I was becoming a much better and stronger runner. I began to see that Tyler, Ben, and I were all alpha males.

As my race in Memphis drew nearer, I felt even more sure that I was ready to run. I drove there the day before and found my way to the hotel. This would be the first time I had stayed in another town and run a race by myself. After checking into my room, I decided to head to the expo to pick up my race packet. I saw a limo parked beside the hotel. The driver looked bored, so I told him I was in town for the half marathon and unfortunately could not afford a limo ride. He rolled his eyes in frustration and told me for twenty dollars he would drive me to the race expo. I said yes and excitedly jumped into a limo for the first time in my life. On the ride, I thought I must look like somebody special. I thought, "When I get out of this limo, I am going to look like a very important athlete."

Once at the pre-race expo, I realized that this was going to be a larger race than my St. Louis marathon. There were people all over the baseball stadium that would serve as the site for the race. After picking up my race packet, I got stuck in the crowd surrounding the vendors located throughout the stadium. By the time I got back to my hotel room, I was caught up in pre-race anticipation that came from conversations with expo salesmen and other runners, and looking through my race packet.

The next morning, I walked to the starting line in the freezing cold, but this time, I had learned my lesson and was prepared for the weather. I had on tights, wind pants, a long-sleeve jacket, and a pair of gloves. I was not going to be cold in this race.

I looked around at the other runners and felt my nerves begin to creep up on me. But then I thought about my training and felt a wave of confidence as I remembered the miles I had run preparing for this race. I felt confident I could finish this race well.

The gun went off and I started moving, getting into my normal rhythm and feeling the familiar chill of the wind against my face. It was a little different this time, though, since this time I was running with five thousand other people. I looked at the buildings in downtown Memphis and enjoyed talking with the runners around me. By the time I reached my first walk break, I was completely immersed in the character of the race. After my walk break, I went right back to talking with people around me, my joy increasing with each mile. The people in this race had a lot of personality and stories. They seemed happy to have trained hard for the race. As we reached the eleven-mile-marker, I saw the soon-to-be-winner of the marathon running past us on the other side of the road.

As I watched him run past, I saw his pain, his eyes searching for the finish line. The lady beside me said, "Those elite runners are incredible, they all train incredibly hard for this race and run nearly every day." I thought to myself, "I trained hard for this race! We all trained hard to run it, he is simply faster." I reached my last walk break and she moved ahead of me.

As I reached the last mile, I was excited to be finishing my first half marathon. The end of the race was inside a minor league baseball park. Running into that stadium, in my mind, felt just like I was running into an Olympic stadium for the finish. I made it my goal that no one would pass me once I entered the stadium. I put my running into high gear and started chasing down everyone near me all the way to the finish. I crossed the finish line as I passed two women. I was even more excited when I saw that my time was two hours and thirty minutes—about twenty minutes faster than I had expected to finish.

After receiving my finisher's medal, I went back to my hotel to take a nap and then celebrate the race on the town. I put on my Memphis half marathon shirt and went to BB King's Lounge for the post-race party. As I walked into the lounge, I saw that everyone else in the bar was also wearing a race shirt. I drank a soda and watched a blues musician sing, immense pride bubbling up in my chest. I had completed my first half marathon and wanted to stay out all night celebrating my accomplishment, but went back to my hotel room early because I was exhausted from completing the race.

***

On my drive back from Memphis, I began to think about the half marathon and how incredible the winner had looked on his way to the finish. I listened to the Chistmas CD that all the runners had received and decided that I was going to be more ready for the

Country Music Marathon in four months. I knew that the run-walk method was a great way to train and kept to my training schedule week after week.

During these runs in the winter months, I encountered cold conditions and ran through the rain, snow, sleet, and whatever conditions Mother Nature threw at me during runs. I discovered that pain and discomfort were temporary and that if I continued running, I would get used to the pain and discomfort through disassociation. On one of my routes, there was a cobblestone road and I routinely tripped over the bricks and fell. Every time I ran down this road, I usually fell at least once, so I was used to the familiar sting of scrapes from these bricks. On cold days, if I kept running, my body would warm itself to the point where my hands would sweat inside my gloves. I learned to take my gloves off while running and put them back on once they had cooled down. This required a lot of concentration because every time I had to put my left glove on, I had to wiggle each finger into its finger hole using my right hand because I cannot move the fingers on my left hand. The first few times I tried to put my gloves on while running, I dropped my glove and had to stop, wiggle my fingers into place standing on the side of the road, then continue running again once both hands were successfully inside my gloves. After a couple weeks of struggling with my gloves, I was able to remove my gloves, cool my hands off, then put my gloves on again without having to stop.

In experiencing these things, I began to understand that if I did something enough, any action that used to be difficult would become normal. I learned that the wind always hurt more at the top of hills than on the bottom. I knew that my wind-burned face hurt as the wind hit it at these hill tops, but if I kept running, the wind would be less intense as I reached the bottoms of those hills.

Once spring arrived, I had learned to continue running through cold conditions. Now, as the temperatures rose, I used my knowledge of becoming used to discomfort to push through my runs in warmer temperatures. I was able to use my disassociation skills once more.

When I was not running or studying, I was in the boxing gym helping the boxers increase their fitness. The more time I spent in the gym, the more I realized that I liked the boxing culture of toughness. I began joining in on more of the drills and learned a lot about boxing. I would often leave the boxing gym with a smile on my face and the taste of blood in my mouth from a punch I had taken during one of the drills. I continued this routine of running, training the boxers, and studying. It was fun and tiring at the same time. I became close to the boxers and my running buddy Jeremy, who even came to the gym with me a few times to run with the boxers.

While all of this was going on, Tyler was also taking his training to another level. He and my dad had researched and found a trainer who had trained a number of professional football players in St. Louis. The trainer had met with my dad and brother and had given Tyler a strength and nutrition program to help him gain weight and strength and improve his athletic skills. Tyler was becoming a stronger athlete and it showed on the basketball court. He was now the best player in every high school game he played and, along with Ben, had made the high school team the best in the state.

Watching Tyler improve his physical skills and his athleticism through his diet and weightlifting, I wanted to have a program developed for my training as well. After I met with the trainer, he created a nutrition program for my marathon running that required an incredible amount of discipline. My nutrition program required eight meals a day. Each meal was extremely low in simple sugar and was designed to make my body burn fat instead of sugar. This meant that I had to cook eight meals a day on my Foreman Grill, a small indoor grill my mom had given me as a gift. For the last two months of training for the Country Music Marathon, I cooked eight meals a day while running, studying, and working at the boxing gym. There was little time for anything else. But my body felt incredible; I could feel myself becoming stronger and the improvement in my diet had caused me to lose twenty more pounds. By the time I packed my things for my marathon in Nashville, I had no doubt that I was going to be able to finish.

My dad came with me to Nashville and I was incredibly proud that he was coming watch me run. We went out for pasta on the night before the race and I did not know what I should eat. For the past two months, I had eaten a strict and regimented diet. I wanted my last meal to be perfect. I tried to order a steak, but my dad told me pasta might be a better choice. I thought he was probably right so I ordered spaghetti. That night we talked about the upcoming race. He was amazed at how much larger this marathon was than the St. Louis Marathon. I was not nervous at all until I saw the weather forecast for race day. It was supposed to be ninety degrees with high humidity. I thought back to my training and remembered how I had become comfortable with uncomfortable conditions and told myself that the heat was just another condition I needed to make comfortable. I closed my eyes excited to wake the next day and run my second marathon.

My dad walked with me to the starting line and told me he would see me at the finish. As I got closer to the starting line, I saw a huge number of people crowding onto the street. I realized that this marathon was a lot bigger than St. Louis. There were almost three times as many people in this race. I found my place in the crowd with the other runners who were running near my goal time. As I stood there waiting for the start, I felt the heat from the sun soaking into my head. Once the gun went off, it took almost five minutes for my group to cross the line to start the race. Then I was doing it again, sticking to my run-walk method through the race.

One of the cool things about the Country Music Marathon was that there was a band at every mile marker throughout the marathon course. Early in the race, I felt the heat and began trying to get comfortable with the adverse temperature. I talked to a few people on the course and enjoyed the conversations, and tried to listen to each band as we ran past them. Although I was warm, I had confidence that I could complete the race regardless of anything that would happen on my way to the finish line. I noticed that there were fewer and fewer people around me in the race and I stopped talking with other runners in an effort to conserve energy and become comfortable with the heat. I threw cups of water over my head at each aid station in an effort to cool myself. It didn't really work, but I was able to find a small bit of comfort from the heat. I had finally become used to the temperature.

As I continued running and walking, I looked forward to each walk break and smiled each time I heard another band, signaling the end of another mile. I was focused on getting to the finish line and trying to stay comfortable with the heat.

Once I reached the twenty-mile marker, I could see heat rising off the streets in a haze and my vision was blurred by the sweat bucketing from my eyebrows. I tried to stay focused on being comfortable with the heat, and then I felt my right calf muscle start to cramp. I tried to acclimate myself to this new pain and felt the cramp move up my right leg from my calves to my quad and hamstring. I was no longer able to run or walk, but was forced into a hobble as I struggled down the road. By the time I reached mile twenty-four, I was no longer focused on finishing and simply hoped my leg cramp would subside, but each step seemed to make the cramp more intense until I reached the last tenth of a mile. I wanted to finish this marathon at a run, not a hobble. I gritted my teeth and started to run, even with pain shooting through my right leg muscles. My right foot landed in a pothole on my second step of running and miraculously my cramps went away and I ran across the finish line screaming in exhilaration. Not only had I become the only person in my family to run two marathons, I had done so in incredibly adverse conditions.

The next day, I expected to be crippled by soreness as I had the day after the St. Louis marathon, but miraculously, I was not, only exhausted and hot. I felt like a balloon that had been deflated and realized the race had drained all of the glycogen from my muscles. But each day my body felt more and more fueled.

That race taught me that no matter how tough things became, as long as I kept moving, they would get better and I would succeed. By dragging my right leg for almost three miles, I experienced once again what it felt like to triumph over intense pain. And I understood that I could look toward my brothers for motivation.

When I came home from Nashville, I felt like a new man. Not only was I the only person to run two marathons in my family, but I was the first one from my high school cross-country team to run any marathon at all. This was just another thing that made me a badass alpha male.

I continued working at the boxing gym as a conditioning coach and would occasionally run with Jeremy and the Lewis boys. Each day the smell of unwashed boxing gloves became less overpowering to me. I began jumping in and helping some of the boxers do drills. Occasionally I would get a bloody lip and occasionally I would give a bloody lip. I even managed to punch the boxing pro in the stomach for almost a complete minute without getting hit. But the coolest thing was that I had taken people who hated to run and made them into people who were now able to run five miles without stopping. The looks on their faces when they were finished with those runs made me want to become a coach.

I started coaching a local track club for children and found that it was a lot of fun seeing a child smile from doing something better than they would have considered possible before running at track practice. These things sold me on becoming a track coach for a high school. I wanted to become a track coach and improve my athletes so they could smile, emanating satisfaction from achieving their goals.

Once the University of Missouri discovered I wanted to coach track, they put me in contact with the head track coach in an effort to recruit Tyler. I was ecstatic that I had an opportunity to be around Division-I athletes and learn how to coach them to athletic excellence.

After I contacted Coach Mac about becoming a manager for the track team, he replied with an eagerness to have me join the team as the student assistant. I was excited, but before I decided to enroll in the University of Missouri for classes, I thought it would be a smart idea to visit the town, school, and track team to see if they would be a good fit for me as a person. My old friend Kyle was in school there and he told me I could stay with him while I visited one weekend.

On the drive to Columbia, the location of the University of Missouri, my imagination went wild about what the people on the team would be like. I imagined watching these super athletes running incredibly hard and incredibly fast every time they touched the ground. I also thought the world must bend for them because of their prowess. I believed that the athletes on this team would have to be unbelievably disciplined to be able to compete as Division-I athletes.

Coach Mac invited me to come to practice and see whether or not I would enjoy working with the team. Once I walked onto the track at practice, the people on the team were all introducing themselves to me and they seemed to have a warm and pleasant nature to their personalities. I watched them complete running drills and laugh with each other throughout practice. It did not take me long to really want to be a part of this team. Then Coach Mac asked me to help take starting blocks out of a cart for the sprinters. I did it as quickly as possible so I could prove my worth to him as a manager. After loading and unloading the equipment, I was tired and began to think I might not enjoy working with the team because all I would be doing was manual labor.

The next day, Coach Mac invited me to the track meet. This was going to be awesome; I would finally get to see some of the best runners and athletes in the world in action. I knew Coach Mac was a sports psychologist so I expected to see a bunch of strange, new-age psychological techniques being done by the athletes in order to prepare themselves for competition. Instead, I was greeted by the majority of the athletes on the team with a smile. I talked with many of the athletes and with Coach Mac as we watched the meet. After one of the races, Neville, an eight-hundred-meter runner, was going for a jog and I offered to run with him. "After all," I thought, "I am a marathon runner, I should be able to keep up and enjoy making a new running buddy." Neville was immediately one of my favorite people on the team; he was positive, funny, and extremely lively to put it mildly. But I could only keep up with him for a few hundred meters during his jog. Even though I could not complete the run with him, his personality and the warmth of the rest of the team along with Coach Mac sold me on wanting to be a part of this team. After the meet, I told Coach Mac I wanted to join as the manager the following fall. We shook hands and he told me he was looking forward to having me around to help him.

The rest of my visit to the University of Missouri, or Mizzou, went well. I felt like it would be fun to experience a large university and I was looking forward to becoming a small part of the track team. By the time I had driven back to Poplar Bluff, I had decided that Mizzou was where I wanted to be the following fall.

As I finished up my last few classes at the community college in town, I started daydreaming about the new friends I would make and what it would be like to be on the track team. I could not help but explore the possibilities in my imagination.

By the time summer ended, I had my bags packed and was heading to Mizzou to learn how to coach track. I was also looking forward to being around a bunch of kids my own age since there were only a few people my age in Poplar Bluff who I considered my true friends.

Mizzou

When I first arrived in Columbia, my mom went with me to help me move into my house. One of my best childhood friends and former high school basketball teammate was going to be my roommate. Kyle was one of the few of my basketball teammates who did not pick on me in the locker room. He and his dad had bought a three-bedroom house and planned have it pay for itself by renting it to college students. The house looked like the typical middle- to upper-class house, with three bedrooms, two bathrooms, and a large living room. My mom and I decided that we would park my truck in the driveway, take her car to buy furniture, then return that evening to unload my stuff.

As we pulled up to the house and parked my truck in the driveway, she commented on the beautiful flowers in the front yard. I thought it was a bit odd that Kyle and a couple college students would have flowers in their yard, but I was so excited about getting furniture for my room that I jumped in my mom's car and hurriedly went with her to furniture stores around town.

When we got back from shopping that night, we discovered my truck had been parked in the wrong driveway all day. My new neighbor said he understood but all I could think about was how upset he must have been having a truck at his house the whole day. My mom and I moved my truck, laughing, then finished unpacking my stuff. Once I had unpacked, my mom left and I felt relieved to have had her help me with my furniture.

The next day, I went to the bookstore to buy my books and could not believe the mad scramble I saw, with students running all over the place trying to find books for their classes. After finding my books, I went home to get ready for track practice.

As the manager of the track team, I thought I would be too busy to train for another marathon and had resolved to focus on school and helping the track team. I understood that this was my big shot at learning how to coach track and be around elite athletes.

The night before my first track practice, I conjured up images of sports psychological training going on during practice. I envisioned stations where athletes were meditating in strange psychology drills. I also pictured an unbelievable and continuous display of athletic greatness everywhere I looked. I expected to discover the secrets of being a great athlete. I also expected all the athletes to look down on me because I was the lowly manager. I envisioned getting jock straps thrown in my face and egotistical athletes laughing at me from every angle. Past experiences with my basketball team had taught me that most good athletes were rude and disrespectful. As these images whirled through my head, I mentally prepared myself to endure another bout of abuse at the hands of rude athletes.

Once I arrived at practice, I was greeted by Coach Mac and anxiously asked what I could do to help him. I was eager to jump in feet first as manager. He told me to follow him around practice and pay attention to the drills he was setting up for the team. I followed his every movement with intense concentration, thinking every drill needed to be set up with the utmost precision. I took mental measurements and tried to remember each drill that we set up. Once the athletes began arriving, I expected it to be just like high school: a huge show of egos and people who looked down on me. All that was destroyed by the first athlete I saw ride his bike up to the track. Neville greeted me with one of the biggest smiles I have ever seen. I was immediately drawn to the indescribable charisma that was beaming from his friendly persona. As more athletes arrived, the conversations and smiles grew until I was standing with a large group of athletes who were all talking with more glee and joy than I had ever seen in my life. I was submerged

in conversations and almost overwhelmed with intro-
ductions from each new team member who arrived at
practice. I immediately realized that these people were
much different than the athletes on my high school basketball team. I felt immediately accepted by the team.

Practice started slowly as everyone gathered themselves
for a warm-up eight-hundred-meter jog. I stood next to
Coach Mac as the team took their two warm-up laps.
It was then that I became worried about doing something wrong that might disrupt practice. I saw the team
get in lines and go through plyometric drills. I stood
back, afraid that I might say something that would
ruin the harmony of the team in practice. I watched
with extreme focus, trying to learn and commit each
plyometric drill to memory. As practice moved from
the warm-up to the regular practice, I continued my
extreme focus, trying to take precise mental notes
about each move in every drill. I saw the athletes split
into different groups according to their events. Coach
Mac coached the heptathletes, the female athletes who
competed in multiple events to earn overall points in
the heptathlon competition. I noticed that the hep-
tathlete women were working extremely hard, but
never seemed upset or unhappy. They completed their
drills with a hidden pleasure that I had never seen in
the sports world. I thought sports were supposed to be
hard and that only after successfully and perfectly completing a hard task was an athlete supposed to derive
joy from their labor. These athletes seemed to enjoy
every minute of working hard, even during their drills.
During each drill I watched Coach Mac telling them

great job and praising their efforts. When one of them would do something wrong in a drill, he would tell me what it was. He would always praise their hard work, then put his arm around them and kindly explain what they could do to improve their performance on a drill. This absolutely blew my mind. Every practice I had ever been to in my life entailed a coach screaming when an athlete did something wrong. At the end of practice, I talked with many of the athletes from the team, enjoyed conversations filled with joy, and went home filled with happiness that I had been accepted by such a wonderful group of people. As I left the track walking with Coach Mac, I asked him if he wanted me to call him Coach or Doctor. He told me, "Doctor is a title, coach is a compliment." I decided that I would only call him Coach because I was already starting to think the world of him and had only been the first practice.

That first week of school, I went to practice and school. I believed that I was done running and was going to focus on coaching. Besides, on this team, my role was an assistant to the coach, not an athlete. During the second week of practice, after setting up the drills for practice and learning each drill, I told Coach Mac that I was finished running and was going to just help him with the team. He responded by jokingly telling me that I should run and lift weights because he did not want a sloppy, fat track assistant.

The next day, after setting up the drills for the team, I went for a run, determined to stay with the team as long as I could. I was after all, a marathoner. I stayed with them less than one hundred yards and then continued the six-mile run on my own. By the time I returned to the track, Coach Mac was helping his athletes do drills. I walked over and continued learning the drills. It was fun to see all the drills and I even jumped in to instruct some of the athletes. As I watched the drills and practice, it seemed to me that none of the athletes were ever tired. They were all working hard but made it look effortless.

By the time the first track meet rolled around, I had learned a huge number of drills and was completely engulfed in the track and field world. I was back to running my normal three days a week and lifting twice a week in the athletic weight room with the rest of the sports teams. As I watched them train, I became more and more interested in the training of the distance team. I had already decided I wanted to run another marathon, but now I wanted to train hard to run it. I learned all the different workouts the distance team did for practice and started to add them into my training. It was not until the middle of the indoor track season that I asked Coach Jana, the track and field strength coach, if she would give me a weight routine to help with my marathon training. She gave me a copy of the weight workout the team was doing that year. I completed my first weight workout the day we were leaving for a track meet at Notre Dame University. When I awoke the next day, I was incredibly sore and struggled to go run before the track meet.

I had gotten into a routine of running around the towns we visited in order to see each campus while the team was still asleep. Each week, we would go somewhere new and I would venture out to see the new places and the sights of the universities on my early morning runs. After the weight workout before Notre Dame, I could barely crawl out of bed. I painfully dressed, feeling the searing burn of sore muscles course through my nerves as I put on my shirt. But by the time I had put on my shoes, the soreness was starting to feel a little better. I stepped into the cold air outside the hotel and started my painful run onto the campus. I looped around campus and ran painfully back to the hotel. Each step felt a little better as I ran, so by the time I finished struggling with my three-mile run, I was no longer sore. I walked to the hotel lobby to eat the complimentary breakfast before getting ready for the track meet. As I felt the warmth of the lobby sooth my cold body, I saw the team eating breakfast. I sat with them and talked with everyone as I warmed back up after my run. As I talked, I realized it was time to bring my marathon into a new era and start training like a collegiate runner. This meant scrapping a lot of the training routines I had leftover from my first two marathons.

My running and training increased from running three days a week to running five days. I completed striders, a controlled sprint where the runner focuses on running form, with the distance team, watched the heptathletes become stronger and faster, and learned the proper ways to train athletes to attain peak performances. I began incorporating the drills and stretches the team did into my own training. I also noticed that Coach Mac never forced me to do anything, he simply asked me for help with things and told me things to improve the ways I set up the drills.

Every day, I would wake up early, run before my classes, go to class, track practice, lift weights, and study after I was done in the weight room. In the weight room, I could feel myself getting stronger with the weight program I had been given by Coach Jana. I would occasionally ask her questions about the workout and was prepared to hear an answer from her that showed she was annoyed with a lowly manager asking her questions about the weight program she had graciously given me. But every time I asked a question, she answered with great insights, as if I were one of her athletes. The athletic weight room at Mizzou was beautiful—it had two floors of weights, and the top floor consisted of a few treadmills, an open area for plyometrics, and large exercise balls against the wall. The first, main floor was filled with platforms, free weights, and the strength coaches' offices. With each week, I continued to get closer to the members of the track team as we lifted after practice, but I also became friends with athletes from the other sports teams. I saw the gymnasts, wrestlers, and volleyball players lifting and became friends with many of them as we trained near each other. After a few months of increasing my running mileage, I was completely on fire for running and felt my passion for it grow deep inside my being with every day.

I felt like a real athlete; I was running the same distances as many of the track team members and completing their weight workouts. I sometimes recalled Strum and his disapproval of me lifting weights. I remembered him telling me I should not be in the weight room, and I remembered getting the grade of C in his PE class. Now I was successfully completing a weight workout designed for top collegiate athletes. I could not help but think, "Take that Strum! Give me a C in athletic PE and call me a liability? Fine, now I'm lifting with the Missouri Tigers!"

As my training continued to ramp up, I decided it was time to decide which marathon to run. This time, I did not want to run a small marathon; it was time I put my new training to the test in a major marathon. I chose to run the Chicago marathon the following October. After signing up for the race, I continued my routine with track and field. It seemed as though the entire world consisted of my training, the track team, the track and field news across the country, and what little time I had left to study.

Every weekend, we went someplace new and I met athletes from other schools and made coaching connections. It seemed as though every person I met across the country talked with Coach Mac like he was a good friend. I was proud when he introduced me as the team's manager and enjoyed getting to know him. I noticed that he never spoke to anyone in an adverse tone or acted as though someone was not worth his time. The closer I became with him, the more I realized he was a great man. When asked a question, he waited until the person was finished talking, then responded by answering the question from every single angle it could possibly be interpreted. He seemed to genuinely care about every single person he spoke with and especially expressed his love for each athlete on his team. It became clear that he was a person who had an amazing impact on people by showing them that he cared about them.

My second semester at Mizzou was tougher and my grades began to suffer. I was now making grades equivalent to the grades I had made at my community college. I had learned that I did not need to read the whole chapter for my classes, but just study my notes as a quick and easy way to pass my classes. While my coursework was getting worse, I was running more than I had ever run in my life, along with keeping a great weight workout and traveling every weekend to a new track meet. I believed that track was the most important thing I was doing at Mizzou, even though Coach Mac told us every mindset meeting that sports should only be a small piece of who we were.

Mindset meetings were fifteen-minute meetings that happened once a week before practice. Each meeting had a central message, reviewed the past week, and the week ahead. I thought these meetings were great. I internalized each central message and incorporated them into my life. My favorite central messages were "Ignore the boo birds," and "The road to success is open and full of room, but few dare to step on it." These were my two favorites because ever since Strum and my high school basketball teammates, I had felt as though I had to prove people wrong. I still felt like I was the only one who believed I was a great athlete, and I had to prove everyone wrong. The messages of these two mindset meetings spoke to the internalized desire I felt to prove the "boo birds" wrong. I had been proving everyone wrong since I woke up from brain surgery. My experiences as an athlete in junior high and high school made me feel as though I did not deserve to be on a sports team. I could practically hear everyone telling me all the things I could not do. And it felt as though all the people making fun of me would be justified if I quit. A lot of my experiences in sports involved people trying to get me to quit something I was not supposed to be able to do. While at Mizzou, I was surrounded by positive people who called me their friend and treated me as an equal even though they were far better athletes than me. Even with this new, positive team, I still felt as though I had a lot of people to prove wrong. I took immense pride in knowing that I was completing workouts that were similar to those completed by collegiate and professional runners, and with this simple mindset message of ignoring boo birds, I slowly started to turn a deaf ear to negativity in my life. I realized that this change would bring me closer to being like the athletes on the track team, thus taking me to a higher level of achievement than I had previously experienced.

By the end of the outdoor season (and the school season), I once again felt as though I was a great and tough athlete. I loved seeing the athletes on the track team improve throughout the season and then be at their best near the end of the season. I had developed a close relationship with most of the people on the team and enjoyed their company every road trip. I had come to admire Coach Mac as one of the greatest people I had ever known.

My love for running burned more brightly than it ever had, and that summer, I went back to Poplar Bluff with a sense of being a better runner from training like a college athlete, a sense of belonging from the track team, and an incredible knowledge of track and field training from helping Coach Mac with the heptathletes. When I went home for the summer, I was excited to show off all my new skills, and to run with all my hometown friends. I could not wait to tell the Lewis brothers about all the amazing track meets I had seen throughout the collegiate track season.

Since the Lewis family had become my second family, it did not take me long to show up at their house that summer. They all asked about my meets, training, and stories. We talked into the night and I talked about the character of the Mizzou track team that I had experienced and things I had missed while I was gone. I learned that John-Mark was getting some looks as a runner from colleges around the state. He told me he wanted to run the 800-meter race in college because that was his favorite. I asked him his times and nodded in agreement that they were good times. I did not have the heart to tell him that every race I had seen that year had been run in much faster times than his current fastest race. While I was happy he was getting looks from colleges around the state, what I considered elite running had changed since going to Mizzou and I knew he was not running fast enough to be recruited by the Mizzou track team. But John-Mark was one of my good friends and I would support him. Jeremy, the middle Lewis brother, was quiet as usual and told me he had been running a decent amount while I was gone. Matt, the oldest brother, was not running, but had a great many life stories to tell me. By the end of that night, I was filled with contentment after catching up with people I considered nearly family. I drove home and went to sleep early, as I had to wake up and run the next morning before going into work.

I had retained my job as a lifeguard that summer and was excited to be back at the pool with the same people I had worked with the previous summer. This job was fun because I secretly had crushes on a couple of the girls who were also lifeguards at my pool. It also meant that I would not need to shower before coming to work because all I needed to do was jump in the pool. This would allow me additional time to train for the Chicago marathon, but probably was not the best way to get a date from one of my coworkers.

Jeremy was to be my main running buddy that summer while training for the Chicago marathon. As a lifeguard, I had to teach swimming lessons at the pool by 11:00 a.m. every morning, which meant I would need to start my run around 7:00 a.m. in order to finish my run, stretches, and drills before going to work. I would drive to Jeremy's house and wake him up and we would go running almost daily. Twice a week, after work, I continued the Mizzou team weight workout in

my basement and Jeremy would come lift with me. The
first few times, I was expecting to be amused watching
Jeremy struggle with the new lifts I had learned through
the Mizzou strength coaches. But every time I expected
to see him struggle, he completed the exercise as well as
I had and smiled at the toughness. Every morning, we
would cruise through the streets of Poplar Bluff on our
runs sharing stories from our time apart. I became an
even more prevalent guest at the Lewis house because
we started a lot of our runs there. I became closer
with the entire Lewis family than I had ever been with
another family. Jeremy, John-Mark, and Matt were
my entourage. I loved hanging out with them and we
became closer that summer. Jeremy and I ran together
most of the time. John-Mark would occasionally run
with us, but he usually ran on his own and told us stories after he was finished.

As the summer continued its amazing routine of running, lifeguarding, lifting, and hanging out with the
Lewis family, I began to include a second run into my
day twice a week. On hard speed and hill workout days,
I would also go for a short run in the evening to help get
rid of the lactic acid built up from muscle stress earlier.
It was after these runs that we always had crazy stories.
The areas of town we would run through were the less
attractive parts, to put it mildly. We thought we were hot
stuff, being the only people running down those streets
into the dusk. Upon arriving back at the Lewis house,
we would always laugh about people we had seen on
the run—the cute girls I awkwardly waved at as we ran
past their house or the heavy men who always honked

at us from their cars—and we would almost fall to the floor laughing as we talked in the living room.

While I was becoming the best runner I could be, my brothers were making quite the splash in basketball. Tyler was in the top ten high school players in the country and it was clear that Ben was continuing to become one of the best players in high school as well. Every so often, I would help my dad rebound for Tyler and watch Ben play basketball in a local gym. It seemed as though the living room at the Hansbrough house had become the place we would all relax and gain some much needed rest after our workouts. I loved getting to spend time with my two favorite people in the world every day. While the Lewis family was a great second family, they paled in comparison to the closeness I felt with my own family, especially my brothers. Since I had started college, we had grown incredibly close, and I no longer felt as though I needed to dump my social baggage on them. Tyler and Ben were both making their mark in the basketball world and I was making my mark as a runner. As we lay on the couches in our living room every day, we caught each other up on our days and occasionally argued about politics, the attractiveness of girls, or the best exercise for strengthening a muscle between naps. We were all tired from our training. Tyler was already completing University of North Carolina basketball team weight workouts in the basement. I saw him working extremely hard and straining in the same way I had in completing the Mizzou weight routine for the first time. And Ben was lifting with an intensity that had transformed him into a much stronger person. I now hated it when we would wrestle because I usually got my ass kicked.

Tyler and Ben's friends hung around our house just like I hung around the Lewis house. It seemed as though my other entourage was Tyler, Ben, and their friends Phillip and Lee.

Phillip was one of Ben's best friends and always had a smile and a joke. He also loved to be right in the middle of all the action; he loved going places with us and being social regardless of the location or crowd. Lee was Tyler and Ben's version of John-Mark; he was their crazy friend who had a good heart but always seemed to be doing wild things without thinking too much and occasionally getting in trouble.

As the summer continued, I was almost always with the Lewis boys, training, working, or with my brothers and their friends. By the time that summer ended, it was as if my brothers and I had all progressed even further in athletic prowess in our own sports, Tyler and Ben in basketball and me in running. Tyler left for North Carolina to join the Tar Heels basketball team and I wished him luck, knowing he would do well just as I was with my running. We were both alpha males off to complete our goals in the most masterful way we could, while Ben was going to be the best high school basketball player in the state that year. The three Hansbrough alpha males were starting to make our marks.

***

I left Poplar Bluff after that summer satisfied that I had built myself into a well-conditioned runner, spent quality time with my family, and improved my relationship with the Lewis family. I could not wait to get back to Mizzou track and tell the guys on the team about my summer, and hear their stories as well.

Once I arrived back at Mizzou, I went straight to the track to see who was working out. It was empty so I went for my normal run by myself hoping that by the time I finished there would be someone on the track. As I ran up the big hill to the track and finished my run, there was still no one, so I went to the weight room and lifted by myself. I had envisioned a huge gathering of people sharing summer stories at the track, but, the place was almost completely empty.

That first practice back, I walked onto the track and the scenario I had imagined played out: everyone on the team was sharing stories with each other and laughing in the first few minutes before practice began. It felt incredibly good to be accepted by the athletes and people on this team. By the time Coach Mac arrived, I was elated from seeing everyone. I gave him a huge hug as soon as I saw him. He was happy to see everyone back and we set up drills for the team as they went through their warm-ups. I was confident that I had the knowledge to set up the drills by myself. I put the carpet strips down for shuttle runs, placed the hurdles in the right spots, and returned to stand with Coach Mac as he watched the team complete the drills. It was fun to see the way the freshmen struggled to complete the drills with the same perfection as the upper-classmen on the team and it was great to see the older team members readily giving them instructions and encouragement. I helped the heptathletes go through their warm-ups then went to hang out with the distance runners. I decided to try to run with them after training all summer as a collegiate athlete. I was able to stay with them for the entire first mile before falling to the back of the group and finishing my run by myself. As I reached the track, I saw a few of the runners lingering and we talked as we completed a few running drills. It felt good to be back around the group that had shown me how to increase my training to be the best runner I could while also showing me the beauty of a team full of great people.

Once we migrated to the weight room, I completed my weight room routine that I had done since the previous year with ease and asked the strength coach for a new workout sheet. She gave me the weight program for the team and I immediately set out to complete the program.

I continued to increase my mileage and my friendships throughout the first couple of months and started feeling comfortable back in the world of track and field even before the season started. In the weight room, I was becoming closer to Christian, a professional shot putter who trained with the team, and soon considered him a good friend. Our conversations always traveled quickly from one subject to another, and I realized he reminded me of my uncle Sean in his mannerisms.

My uncle Sean, a professional long driver and world champion in golf, had tough-guy sense of humor and Christian had a similar demeanor. He was about an inch shorter than me but outweighed me by over one hundred pounds. He is to this day the strongest person I have ever seen in a weight room. As I lifted what I thought was a lot of weight, I would look up and see him lifting almost three times what I was lifting. He completed each set with a smile on his face. He would make fun of my chin-ups for not going all the way down and I would make fun of him for not going all the way up. As the weeks in the weight room turned into months, I found a new friend and looked forward to seeing him at practice and the weight room.

A couple weeks went by where I did not see Christian, and I went along with my routine as best as I could without my normal weight room buddy while quietly hoping he was ok. One morning I went to lift weights before practice so that I could write a paper for class and saw Christian lifting by himself with a bandage around his knee. He told me that he had had surgery and I said I hoped he got better and headed to the other side of the weight room. I stopped when he told me to stay near him and talk as he lifted his arms. I went through my workout on the weights near him carrying on conversation between lifts. Even after I finished my workout, I stayed with him, talking, until he had finished his workout as well. I adjusted my schedule so that he and I could lift together for the weeks he was recovering from surgery. I wanted to be there to help my weight room buddy as much as I could by keeping him company as he lifted weights.

About a month before the Chicago marathon, I was ready to start a huge mileage week and tried to figure out when I needed to start on Monday so I could finish my twenty-two-mile run before class. I decided to start at 3:30 in the morning and run from the athletic facility parking lot. On my drive to school, I could not help but notice the emptiness of the streets; it seemed I was the only one on the road. Once I arrived at the athletic facilities, I began my run into the dark. The first mile of this run went along the road and under the street lights, which felt safe enough. After easing my way into that first mile, I turned left onto a trail and realized I was going to be running in the pitch black for a long time. A girl on the cross-country team had been attacked by a man on a trail a few weeks earlier, and remembering that fact did nothing to help me relax as I ran into the darkness, frightened out of my mind. As I moved through the trail, I saw a faint light in the far distance and was relieved to see that the tunnel under one of the main roads had a light inside. I ran toward the light and once I went through the tunnel, I continued to cruise through the darkness, gaining a greater sense of security with each mile. However, by the time I reached the turning point on the trail, it was still dark and I felt the chill of fear start to creep up my spine until I was just as scared on the way back as I had been when I started a couple hours earlier.

Finally the sun began to rise and I gained a little more security with each glimmer of light that increased my view of the trail. As I ran past a large meadow, I was greeted by the sun illuminating the meadow so that it glowed with all the colors of each plant. It seemed as if each blade of straw grass and each wildflower was displaying itself in divine splendor. I smiled as I took a mental picture and realized I was the only person to see that sunrise over the meadow. And I would have never seen it if I had not run through the night in complete darkness and fear. By the time I reached the athletic facility parking lot, I was tired but happy that I had completed my run before school. All I had to do was recover the rest of that day in order to run on Tuesday.

***

After a few more weeks passed, it was time to leave for Chicago. I was excited because my dad was meeting me there and he was going to cheer for me during the run. As I drove to the airport, I felt like a big-shot runner. I knew I had trained well enough to beat the times on my previous two marathons. This was a big race and I felt I deserved to be there.

I met my dad for dinner and we talked about the race, and everything that had been going on in each other's lives. I think he could see in my eyes that I was completely ready for this race. I awoke early the next morning to go to the race start, my dad walking with me. On the walk, I read notes from the track practice mindset meetings in order to finish mentally preparing for the race. I jogged for a mile and stretched the same way the track team did before races. By the time I reached the starting line, I thought, "This is it, the moment I have trained for has arrived, and it's time to run my marathon to the best of my ability."

Boom, the gun went off and I walked anxiously until I crossed the starting line. I tried to relax and run the first miles easily so that I could finish strong, but I was excited, I was finally running the marathon like a college athlete, so about halfway through the race, I noticed I was running a lot faster than I expected. I forced myself to slow down, I was running past people all the time because there were so many runners everywhere. As I reached for water halfway into the race, the lady in front of me came to a complete stop and I accidentally bumped into her and knocked her to the ground. I felt bad that I had knocked her down, but I kept moving because I wanted to run to the best of my ability and beat my previous two times.

Once I reached the twenty-two-mile marker, I was expecting to hurt like I had in my last two marathons, but this time I flew through the next couple miles. It was not until I reached the twenty-six-mile marker that I hurt like I had for the last four miles of the Country Music Marathon. But with only two tenths of a mile to go, I decided to run as hard as I could all the way to the finish. I wove in and out of people, passing large masses of them as I moved toward the finish line.

As I reached the homestretch of the marathon, I thought of my journey to get to this race. I thought about the track team, runs with Jeremy, struggles I had endured on hours of training runs. As I remembered these things, I was nearly overwhelmed by a rush of emotion. I had come from struggling to finish my first cross-country practice to struggling to finish my first two marathons, and now here I was, trained like a collegiate athlete, about to finish my third marathon. I felt the tears stream down my face as I ran across the finish line. I crossed the line and grabbed a celebratory beer as I walked to meet my dad. He was waiting for me at the end of the finishing area to greet me with a congratulatory hug. It meant the world to me that he drove up to watch me run a race and I hugged him hard. I was bursting with joie de vivre and endorphins as I walked with my dad back to the hotel. We said our goodbyes and I boarded a plane and went back to school, back to my normal life and routine.

Once I arrived back in Columbia, I remembered that I had told Mike, one of my running buddies, that I would bike with him on Monday. Mike was a runner from Michigan who had experienced a number of injuries while at Mizzou. He had the figure of a runner, slim features, black hair, and a short stature. Mike was the first runner on the team I had offered to ride with because we were good friends. He always kept his comments mildly inappropriate and entertaining. As inappropriate as we both were in our personalities, I was eager to hear the next comical thing that would come out of his mouth. He was from a rough town, so I also enjoyed the stories he told from his high school, stories that seemed completely foreign to me, having grown up in a nice small town. When I had agreed to ride with him, I hadn't considered that I would be running the Chicago Marathon the day before. Needless to say, this was not going to be my best cycling performance. But since I liked him so much and never liked going back on my word, I loaded my bike into my truck and met him for a bike ride that Monday during track practice.

On that ride, I felt like a completely flat tire; I was empty of energy and my legs were simply exhausted from the marathon the day before. He led most of the ride and I told him about the marathon in intricate detail. By the time we finished that ride, I was completely spent and went straight to bed after I made it home from practice.

About a week later, my legs were back and there was a general chatter in practice about the upcoming college basketball season. I remember Matt asking me during practice how I thought Tyler would do in his first year at UNC. I told him that I thought he would do pretty well, which caused Neville to join the conversation in his usual animated manner, telling me to not be too upset if Tyler took a little time to adjust to the college game. I remained confident he would play well and be more than able to hold his own in the ACC.

A couple weeks later, I flew to Chapel Hill to watch the first home game against the University of Illinois. This was a big game because Illinois had lost to UNC the previous year in the national championship game, and, while they weren't exactly rivals, there were a lot of emotions (namely school pride) tied to the outcome.

Once we got to the UNC campus, Tyler took my dad and me to the Dean Dome, UNC's legendary basketball arena. While we were there, we looked around the basketball court. I looked at everything with a sense of awe. Here I was, walking through the gym of one of the most storied basketball programs in the world. My mind was blown even further when Coach Roy Williams came up to us and started talking casually about how much he enjoyed having Tyler on his team. My dad, Coach Williams, and I stood there on the court talking like we had been friends forever. Then, coaching legend Dean Smith walked up and put his arms around our shoulders as he joined the conversation! After that conversation, I immediately knew Tyler was in a great place and understood why UNC basketball was such a special program. Two legends in basketball had just become my friends.

Tyler played great in his first home game as a Tar Heel, getting to start, scoring a lot of points, and even getting some dunks. I was frenzied the entire game; every time the Tar Heels did something well, I went nuts, and when Tyler scored, I was even more excited because he was on one of the biggest stages in his sport. Then it occurred to me: Tyler was playing on one of basketball's biggest stages while I was in road running's biggest race, the marathon. We had watched each other struggle through disciplined training to get to the top of our sports. For years, Tyler had watched me walk into the house tired from road runs and weightlifting. I had watched him come in the house tired from shooting drills and weight workouts. I had seen the desire and discipline it took for him to get to a starting role at UNC and loved it because he was my brother.

At practice the following week, Neville told me how impressed he was with my brother's performance. Matt also chimed in with compliments about his play. I was brimming over with pride for my little brother as I told them about my trip to Chapel Hill. After the chatter about Tyler had died, we went back to talking about track and were once again surrounded by our bubble of track and field.

I had finally become the runner I had dreamed of as a high school kid; I was training with a major track program, running faster than I could ever imagine, and I had friends who were all immersed in the sport that we loved.

While my running had improved, my school work was not very competent. It was as though class was something I did on the side of my training program. I never missed a class while I was in Mizzou, but I was never really prepared for the lectures or tests. I received Cs in all my classes. Still, I was passing and thought I would be okay since I had received those grades in most of my classes in community college. When I went home for the summer after that second year with a 2.5 GPA, my only desire was to train harder for my next road race.

Before leaving for the summer, I discovered that the College of Education at Mizzou , my college, required a 2.75 GPA, but I figured switching majors would be a minor issue that I would deal with once I returned to school. I was mostly just excited to see my friends and be back in Poplar Bluff for the summer. Besides, I also had to prepare for the Hospital Hill Run half marathon that June.

***

Back in Poplar Bluff, I dragged Jeremy on runs almost every day. We both planned to run the Hospital Hill Run. We ran all over town and it was clear we had both become much better runners over the past year. I felt as though I were invincible. My training was exactly the same as the runners on the Mizzou team, except of course my times were slower. I was completely engaged in my training and we both expected to run well in Kansas City for the half marathon, which was ranked as one of the hardest half marathons in the country.

We ran in the hottest part of the day and immediately went to my basement to lift weights after our runs. We went to the track to run speed workouts. We were firing on all cylinders by the time we left for the race. The tough training gave me a bit of an ego because I had gained such a high level of fitness. I would size people up in public and almost always considered myself better than them because I knew they could not complete the training I was doing for my race.

My aunt lives in Kansas City and told us we could stay at her house while we were in town. Jeremy and I made the seven-hour drive to her house the day before the race and our minds were preoccupied the entire trip with thoughts about the race. The whole way up, we made chitchat, talked about stories we had accumulated in college, and made jokes, but we both had the race in the back of our minds. We pulled into the driveway at my aunt Ann's house and were shown where we would be staying. I had the couch while Jeremy opted to sleep on an air mattress. We put our bags down next to where we would sleep and joined my aunt, uncle, and cousins for dinner. During dinner, we caught up and my family got to know Jeremy. The dinner was full of constant discussion. Before falling asleep, we discussed race strategy and I told Jeremy I was going to wait until mile eight to make my move and press the pace. Jeremy asked me what time I wanted to run and I told him under 2:05. He told me that he thought I could break two hours, but I replied that I did not have the ability to run under a two-hour half marathon, especially on such a hilly course.

We both drifted off to sleep and awoke the next morning with an instant bustle to get ready for the race. I thought we needed to leave really early so we could get a good parking spot and warm up before the race started. My aunt told us she would drive us to the race and pick us up. I was grateful to have such an amazing aunt who was willing to make the race as stress free as she could for us. We loaded into her car and left for the race an hour before it was to start. On the ride there, I had my aunt play a song that pumped me up. She dropped us off a mile from the starting line so we could do a warm-up jog to the starting line. She told us she would be at the finish line waiting for us. Jeremy and I jogged to the starting line talking about how amazed we were to be treated so well by my aunt.

Once we reached the starting line after warming up, it was clear that this was going to be a rainy race. A storm was quickly approaching and there was a flash of lightning as the starting gun exploded. I immediately found a person close to my pace and followed him through the first eight miles. I was close enough behind him that he blocked the wind for me and I was able to cruise through those miles with less effort than the people running into the wind. Once I hit mile eight, I told myself, "Greg, you've trained to run hard and planned to make a move here. Let's do it." I started running faster and quickly passed the guy who had pulled me through the first eight miles. Once I started running faster, I expected to get tired and slow down after a couple miles. I reached mile ten flying, as if my legs could not slow down even if I'd wanted them to. I continued my blistering pace through the course, up the big hills and then up the huge hill that gave the race its name. It was a mile-long hill at mile eleven and I was flying up it when I saw a huge downhill slope and decided to try to run even faster down the hill. I increased my speed until I was moving faster than I thought possible. I thought I had better slow down so I could still unleash a strong finishing kick and pass people near the finish line. I tried to slow down, but my legs would not let me; it seemed that every time I increased my speed, my legs became comfortable at the new pace. I passed the twelve-and-a-half-mile marker and started passing everybody in sight. I was picking them off one by one on my way to the finish line, I must have passed at least fifty people in the last half mile. As I crossed the line, I looked at the clock and realized I had broken two hours! I was so proud and surprised to have finished the run in under two hours. I wore an exhausted smile when I saw Jeremy and my aunt at the finish line.

On the drive back to Poplar Bluff, Jeremy and I told each other our different experiences during the race, what we each felt like at certain points, and talked about how much fun it had been staying with my aunt. Once we passed St. Louis and headed south, we were a little giddy with joy and belted out country songs the rest of the trip home. We were singing in celebration of running a difficult race better than we ever had before. We were making our mark on the athletic world through our running and our delight manifested as jovial singing in my truck for two hours.

After a week off, Jeremy and I started running again and it was clear that after this race we had again reached a new height in our running and closeness. We were able to cruise through town with ease and always chose to express our toughness publicly by running in the heat of the day. The new pace I found during the race propelled my normal runs to faster speeds than I had been able to achieve before the race in Kansas City. After running up the hills in that race, the hills around town seemed smaller and I pushed myself to run faster up them. As Jeremy and I ran faster around town, our conversations during the run became more energized and elaborate. I felt more like talking during our runs than when we were hanging out at one of our houses.

After my morning runs and work as a lifeguard, I would come home and lay on the couch with my brothers as we had every summer since we began working toward becoming great athletes. We all three had our own spots to unwind in that living room. I lay in the recliner, Tyler on one couch, and Ben on the other couch. We lay there talking and telling each other stories, but when a good music video came on TV, the whole living room would break out into us performing the greatest dance moves the world will never see. After the song, we went back to our post-workout resting positions in the room. When my dad came home from work, we all started talking at once and preparing for dinner. When dinner was over, all four of us would relax watching sports on TV and talking about sports. I loved being with my brothers and was happiest when we were all lying in the living room worn out from the day.

Near the end of the summer, I began to get anxious to see the guys from the track team once again. My thoughts started drifting toward what their reactions would be to the stories I had accumulated throughout the summer. I pictured Neville, fully animated and embellishing stories from his summer as well as hearing his stories told through his animated expressions. I could see Derrick, the team's expressionless comedian, calmly making comical remarks with his dry sense of humor that always left you wondering if he was joking or serious about something I claimed to have done over the summer. And I could not wait to get back to standing next to one of the greatest people I had ever met and watch Coach Mac lead the team.

***

Once back in Columbia, I felt at ease as I went to lift weights a few days before school started in the athletic weight room. Since the season had not started, I found an empty weight room, something I had hardly ever seen at Mizzou. I began to lift and noticed Coach Jana walking into her office. I greeted her and we caught up briefly before I asked her for an old copy of the team's weight routine. Once she gave me a copy, I began lifting and was pleasantly surprised to find that the workout was not as grueling as I remembered; I was doing the same type of workout, but my body was responding to each lift with ease. The first two years I had trudged through the workouts and dreaded having to step up to the next workout. But now I was able to cruise through the workout with an unexpected comfort. I pushed myself hard through the workout and finished with a lot of strength still left in my body.

My runs were the same way. I would do the normal running routes from the track and was able to push through each run with vigor and strength. It was as if my body had transformed so that I was never tired and capable of doing anything I wanted to do.

As I was walking into the weight room one day, I caught a glimpse of myself in the reflective glass doors and noticed something that made me smile. My legs had returned to the muscle tone I remembered carrying me to athletic victories before my brain surgeries, and I was beginning to see myself as the successful person I had been before my surgeries. I thought to myself, "It's been a long time, but you're finally back." I felt as though I had finally and completely overcome the trauma of my brain tumor to become the quality athlete I had been before surgery. I could do anything.

Once school and practice started, I set up drills for the team, helped coach them through drills, then went for a run and lifted weights. If last year I had been on an amazing level with my running, this year I felt immortal. I started doing a few sprints with the middle distance runners and was able to keep up with them for their first two or three intervals. I was lifting a lot also and felt comfortable in the weight room.

When I heard the news that Columbia was going to hold a half marathon that would run through campus and along a lot of my usual running routes, I signed up immediately and showed up at the starting line ready to race. One of my running buddies, who was also my friend Ross's sister-in-law, claimed that she and I would be in different sections because she was a lot faster than me. I tried to not let it affect me, but could not keep myself from thinking, "That's a lie, I'm ready to race."

When the race started, I slowly increased my speed, moving from one comfortable pace to the next. Half way through the race, I could not hold it back anymore—it was time to gun the engines. I started moving up and passing people one by one. I was trying to catch a pack of runners in front of me on a downhill, and a guy bigger than me tried to pass me at the same time. I immediately ran in front of this guy, cutting him off. We zigzagged down most of the hill, then he hit me with his elbow and moved past me. I burned with rage when I realized he had hit me intentionally. Soon after, I entered a short trail section that I knew well, so I flew through it and caught up to the elbower about a mile down the trail. As I approached him, I noticed that he had stopped running and was standing beside the trail with his hands over his head, a gesture of exhaustion. As I passed him, still chasing the group in front, I could not resist calling him a pansy.

As I reached campus, I pursued runner after runner. As I moved through the quad on the backside of campus, I was trying to catch one last person, but realized they were out of reach. I ran with everything I had and crossed the finish line with a new personal record for the half marathon. After the race, I eagerly awaited the awards and discovered that my time was 1:44:08, faster than I had ever dreamed of being able to run. As I put my sweats on, I noticed there was a guy printing out race results, so I hurried to the wall where the results were being posted. I had placed forty-third, finishing in the top fifty for the first time in my life. I walked back to sit on the grass with a smile of accomplishment.

The rest of that year went well. I was able to continue crushing runs and getting stronger and stronger each month. By the time summer rolled around, I was excited to go home and see Jeremy and my family. I wanted to show them the great athlete I had become that year. The problem was that I had neglected studying for my chemistry class in order to train for my race and was failing. This meant I was going to the first month of summer school to improve my grade.

During that month, I decided to study hard and often, but was unable to concentrate on the days I did not run. I started running again and studied between workouts. By the end of the month, I had improved my grade to a C and went back to Poplar Bluff to spend a little over a month with my brothers and hometown friends.

***

Like all my previous summers home from college, my brothers and I trained hard every day. Our entourage consisted of Lee and Phillip, friends from Tyler and Ben's high school days who were former athletes and lifted weights and hung out with the three of us. Lee had gotten in a bit of trouble throughout the town, but was a close friend who would always take his friends' side regardless of circumstances. I always knew Lee would never do anything to hurt me or my brothers and he would always stand up for us in any situation. Lee would lift weights with Ben, rebound for Tyler, and was always lying around the house with us during our lazy afternoons between workouts. Phillip was the gregarious one of the group; he had an infectious smile and warm demeanor that made everyone around him feel comfortable. Phillip could walk through a door, smile, and immediately put everyone at ease. He would also lay around the house with us in the afternoon.

I had two entourages, the Lewis family (my running family in the Bluff), and my brothers, Phillip, and Lee. That summer, it seemed as though everywhere one of us went, we all went. I usually just hung out with the Lewis family before my morning runs and after my evening runs, but the rest of the time I spent with the other group. The weight room in the basement was constantly buzzing with activity; between ping-pong and weightlifting, the basement was always in use by the three of us or our friends. Occasionally my two friend groups would meet and everyone immediately melded into one group. It was not until the end of that summer that I realized that it had been the best summer of my life. Not only had I increased my running ability, I had also spent the summer with my wonderful brothers and friends.

As I headed back to Mizzou, I was excited to get plugged back into the track team. I immediately fell back in line with the athletic world at the school, lifting weights, running, and preparing for classes. This year, I needed to make school a bigger priority in my life so that I could finish my degree in education as well as maintain my running program and work with the track team.

The previous year, I had been forced out of the College of Education because my GPA was too low. I had switched my major to general studies in an effort to bring my grades up and get back into the College of Education and finish my degree. Once I received my grades from my first semester, I called my dad and proudly told him I was going to be back in the College of Education. I was looking forward to achieving my professional goal of becoming a coach.

But the next semester, I started increasing my running mileage again. I was flying through campus on runs but my grades began to plummet. By the end of that semester, I was back out of the College of Education and looking for a different option to finish my degree. I thought I might as well finish my general studies degree and find a job, even if it wasn't my dream job of coaching. My dad told me I should try going to Columbia College for a semester to improve my GPA and get back into the College of Education to earn the degree I truly wanted. It was then that I understood I would have to leave the University of Missouri for a semester in order to achieve my long-term goal of getting an education degree from the university I had come to love.

With this little compromise, a little voice crept into my head. The voice told me that I was not good enough to be at Mizzou, I did not deserve greatness, and was lucky to have been with any major sports team for any period of time. I began to believe that I might not be as great a person as I thought. I was afraid that Coach Mac would not let me stay around the track team since I was no longer at Mizzou. But once I told him I was going to be at Columbia College, he told me he still wanted me to be around the track team and help as much as I could. This eased the feeling that I would lose my connection with the team and that my time with the Mizzou track team would be over.

Even though I still was at practice, was in Mizzou athletic facilities, and saw the team every day, I felt different than when I was a student at Mizzou. Setting foot on Columbia College as a student confirmed my feelings that I was small stuff and that my time at Mizzou had been a fortunate mistake. I felt that I had been fooling myself with false bravado about being an athlete at a major university. I started to think I was not worthy of being at a major school or getting a degree from a big-time school. I started to think I was lower quality than the people I was around on the track. I no longer felt as though I was an equal.

Running became stale for me. The routes I loved running and pushing myself through seemed easy and I was bored with the training. None of it was hard anymore. I could run a ten-mile route around town without having to work hard and became burned out on the sport. I put all my running clothes in one corner of my closet and decided not to wear them again—I was finished as a runner. My body responded quickly to the change of activity. I gained about twenty pounds in the first month away from running.

I went back to playing basketball a lot. I started shooting baskets every day and playing in games for at least an hour a day. I discovered the skills that I used to have on the basketball court came back quickly and I was certain I was the best player on the court every game. The gym at Columbia College consisted of a one-court space that was usually empty. There was never anyone who could give me competition, so I started sneaking into the gym at Mizzou and playing games on the best court they had in the rec center. I still felt as though I was the best player on the court.

While I enjoyed playing basketball every day, I felt I was missing a connection with the track team. I saw them continuing to train the way I used to and enjoying their daily routine of their training regime. I went on a few runs to try to get back to running, but each time, my heart was not in it.

I continued playing lots of basketball and still studied sparingly. My grades at Columbia College were actually worse than the grades I had made at Mizzou, even though I had cut running out of my life. I often took naps instead of reading for classes. I was incredibly unproductive in the library, and was not making good use of the extra four hours I had in my day from not training. I no longer felt as though I were an alpha male; I felt like a normal man, no longer capable of greatness. I resigned myself to living a mediocre life.

Midway through my semester at Columbia College, I started dating a girl who lived in Poplar Bluff and immediately fell in love. Every few weekends I would drive down or she would drive up and we would spend time together. She blew me away and I enjoyed spending time with her more than any other girl I had ever met. We could have a political argument for almost an hour, dance in our seats to goofy songs while driving down the road, and fall asleep together watching movies. After dating for a couple months, I was more in love with her than any girl I had ever met. She made me feel like I was a talented person. When we were together, I felt as though I were capable of greatness again. Any time I mentioned a thought about a current issue or my goals as an athlete, she always responded with support, even if she did not agree with me.

By the end of my second semester at Columbia College, my grades had not improved and I was no longer able to stay in Columbia and work toward a degree. I felt I had wasted an incredible opportunity by not graduating from Mizzou. I had lost my connection to the track team and was heading back to Poplar Bluff without achieving my goal of getting a degree. I felt like such a failure that I did not want to move back home with my dad because I had wasted a lot of his money and no longer felt like a son he could be proud of. I moved in with my girlfriend Amanda and decided that I was going to find a job in town.

Moving in with Amanda was great. I didn't feel like such a failure when we were together. She was working toward getting her nursing degree and was almost finished. Every day, she would come home and tell me about her day and how much she was enjoying school. I was struggling to find a job and tried to mask my own frustrations and show my support of her completing her degree. While she was at school, I started sinking deeper in depression over not getting my degree. I considered myself unworthy of having a job. I continued looking for work, but the only time I felt happy was when we were together.

One day I walked into Sterling Bank and was about to ask about job openings when the vice president of the bank called me into his office before I even had a chance. He introduced himself as Steve and told me he was good friends with my uncle Danny. I thought maybe I could get a job from this guy. Steve was one of the friendliest and most welcoming people I had ever met. By the end of our conversation, I felt as though I did not deserve to work for such an amazing person. He then asked if I was interested in being a cashier at the bank. My heart jumped for joy; I may not have thought I deserved it, but I'd sure take it. I was going to get to work at a bank— my job search was over. I was going to try to work my way up as a banker.

I learned I would be working part time and have to take a lot of online classes before I could start as a cashier. That did not bother me, I had my foot in the door and soon I would be walking through it.

Money was extremely tight while I worked at the bank. While Amanda was always able to use some of her school money to eat dinner while she studied for nursing school, there were many nights I simply did not have enough money to eat. During this time, the Lewis family was a gift from God. I had long since stopped running, but did not want to lose the good friends I had developed during my running career. I started hanging out at the Lewis family house after work; at first, it was to rekindle my relationship with them. I felt awkward asking them if I could stay for dinner, so I never did. One night, Mrs. Lewis asked if I wanted to stay for dinner. I immediately said yes, as I had not had dinner in a couple days and was salivating as the food was put on the table. I started to eat slowly, but eventually started tearing through the meal with the bliss of feeling my stomach fill with food. By the end of the meal, I was full of food and sat back reveling in the feeling of satiation. Every couple of nights, I would hang out at the Lewis house. I felt as though I were hanging out at a family member's house and loved getting close to them again. And of course being able to eat dinner was a huge bonus.

I guess Mrs. Lewis could see my soul through my eyes and could tell I felt ashamed of being back in Poplar Bluff. She understood I did not feel as though I could hang out with my own family. Every night I came to visit, she welcomed me with open arms and tried her best to make me feel less ashamed of who I had become after leaving Columbia.

***

Working at the bank was fun because I was able to interact with a lot of different people throughout the day, but I still felt I was not myself. It was as if I had worn the costume of something else so long I was starting to become it. I no longer felt I was capable of success and thought myself undeserving of greatness.

I decided to start playing basketball again. When I was about thirteen, I had played basketball with the guys in the morning at 6:00 inside the Three Rivers Community College gymnasium. The same group of guys had played there since I was a teenager, and they were the same guys that I had known almost my whole life. As I stepped back onto the court, I quickly jumped right back into talking trash, sharing stories, and playing basketball as if I had never left town. Playing that first morning felt like home to me. I went to work with a big smile on my face and was happy the rest of the day. I started playing every day the gym was open. I fell back in love with the game. I was less stressed about where I was in life and looked forward to feeling at home the three days a week I was on the basketball floor.

Slowly that feeling started to fade. As soon as I left the court, all my depression rushed back to me. It got to where I was only happy on the basketball court. I felt proud that I had renewed my relationship with the Lewis family, but they were still not my family. I did everything with Amanda and her family, mostly because the relatives on my dad's side of the family were all accomplished doctors and lawyers and I felt like the family failure, certain that everyone was ashamed of me.

One day while I was walking around the bank, my leg muscles started twingeing, making small contractions even when I was standing still. I felt this small desire to start running again. Each day, the voice telling me to start running again grew louder and louder in my head until one morning I went for a short run from my apartment. When I got back, I felt a little better and then worried about how I was going to eat that night, because I always had a huge appetite from running. I went to the Lewis house and hung out with them for hours and ate dinner. The next day after work, I ran a loop from the Lewis house and hung out afterward, eating and talking with them.

I continued playing basketball and running for a few weeks before my depression caught back up to me. My depression became something I could not shake. I no longer cared what food I put in my body, I only wanted to feel full because I was unsure of being able to eat my next meal. I started going into my Dad's house and eating when he was not home so that I could continue eating meals. I wanted to stay and talk with him, but I felt ashamed of who I had become—I was no longer an alpha male. I was a scavenger who had a very small job and no degree.

While my depression deepened, my love for Amanda deepened as well. She had been nothing but support-ive of me as I struggled with my perceived shortcom-ings. She was my rock, keeping me from slipping into a more desperate state of depression. I always felt happy when we were together. But every time we were apart, I got depressed about the direction my life was taking.

I formed positive relationships at the bank through hiding my depression with the cloak of a positive attitude. Even with my dissatisfaction in myself, I was happy I had gained the friendship of such great people. While I enjoyed their friendship, seeing their success deepened my depression by holding up a mirror to my own life and lack of success.

Amanda finished nursing school and obtained a job in Sikeston, Missouri. I was so proud of her for becoming a nurse, but I also felt I would be a burden to her because I was such a loser. We moved into a townhouse in Sikeston, which was a step up from the small apartment we shared in Poplar Bluff. Once we had unpacked everything in our new place, I began to look for a job. I had resigned myself to never finishing my degree and decided that I needed to get any job I could find. I interviewed for a job at a local power company and was asked back for a second interview. I was excited to have the opportunity to work a full-time job that would mean I could make enough money to pull my own weight. After my second interview, I was asked to take a test to see if they could hire me. I pumped myself up for the test with false security. I told myself I was intelligent and had made it into a major university. Despite that, I received a test score too low for the company to hire me. All my confidence crumbled and I felt even lower. A thought was emerging in my mind: "I am not valuable to anybody."

After a couple weeks of searching for a job, I needed money. I filled out the paperwork and started substitute teaching in the Sikeston schools. Again, in the school, I covered my deepening depression with a mask of happiness. I sat and laughed with the teachers at lunch, while every night I went home and cried while I waited for Amanda to get off work.

When she was home, I still felt like a normal person and not a lowly college dropout. We would watch TV, laugh, and talk about our days. I began to think I might want to marry Amanda because without her I would always feel worthless.

Part of the reason I felt this way was because my dad's side of the family had always been a source of strength for me and I could not visit them anymore because I felt like a worthless person next to them. I mean, they were all accomplished lawyers and doctors or phenomenal students. I was a college dropout, worked part-time in schools, and could barely afford to eat. I stopped having a connection with them because I did not feel they could be proud of a lowly person such as me.

While my relationship with my dad's side of the family was weakened, my mom's side of the family was there for me. My mom's side of the family is full of successful businessmen, athletes, and military officials. They accepted me regardless of my social status. They became a source of strength for me, but I felt it was a tenuous source. For some reason, I felt like turning to them meant I had to turn my back on my dad and his side of the family, which was my most significant source of strength and remained close even though they had no idea I was so unhappy.

My brothers had also always been a source of strength for me and I valued their opinions above anyone else's. They had always been the most important people in my life. When I talked with them on the phone, I did my best to hide my depression through listening to stories and laughter. But, there were times after talking with one of them I would break down and cry because they were achieving a lot more than me and I feared that they would start to think of me as their insignificant, failure brother. They never made me feel that way on purpose. But each day I began to feel worse.

I decided that since the only time I felt happy was when I was with Amanda, I should marry her. My mom helped me get a ring for her, I asked her dad for her hand, and I proposed to her at work. I gave her a beautiful three-stone ring and we were both in high spirits for a few days with the excitement of our engagement.

***

Once the excitement wore off, I began to slip deeper and faster into the darkest point of my life. I was no longer happy when I saw Amanda, I just saw her success as another source of depression because I knew I would never do anything as worthwhile as what she was doing. I decided my life was not worth living anymore. I was on a path to nowhere and would never achieve success. My family saw me as a failure. I began to think their lives would be better without me in it. They would no longer feel they had a worthless relative and I wouldn't have to feel bad about the person I had become. One day after getting home from school, I took a short piece of rope and decided to end my life by hanging myself in the closet. I would no longer be a burden to anybody. I secured the rope around the wooden hanging rod and placed the other end of the rope around my neck. I decided the best way to do it was to simply bend my knees. I was too tall to jump and hang myself. As I bent my knees, I closed my eyes and prepared for death. I leaned forward and heard a snap. The wooden rod in the closet had broken and rope slipped off the wood. I untied my neck and thought, "I'm such a loser I can't even kill myself!" I cried myself to sleep that night. As I cried, I wanted to tell my dad and brothers how terrible I felt, but did not want to be any more of a burden to them than I had already become.

The next weekend, Amanda told me she was going home for a weekend with her friends. I decided to go back to Poplar Bluff for the weekend with my dad and friends. During that weekend, I relaxed at my dad's house, saw a few of my buddies, and felt a small sparkle of happiness emerge from under my depressive darkness.

Back in Sikeston the following Monday, the depressive darkness began to tint my world once again. I decided to make a change so that I could lift the veil of darkness. Amanda and I had shared laughter, tears, and everything in each other's worlds. I had never felt love for a woman as I had for Amanda, but I wanted my own happiness more than I wanted to have her in my life. I told myself that if I broke up with Amanda, I could move back in with my dad and be happy again.

While Amanda was the most amazing partner I had ever had, I knew I needed to make a change if I wanted to regain happiness in my life. In the meantime, I also discovered that Amanda had lost our engagement ring during the weekend she went home. I broke up with her a week later and we both cried in each other's arms once we decided to split. As we embraced, all I could think about was how it felt being home without having to worry about anything. I was desperate to feel any happiness, even if it was just a small twinge. After we hugged, I decided to ask some friends to help me move back to Poplar Bluff. All the people I thought were my true friends had something better to do that day. I finally called two friends—twins—who dropped everything to help me move out of Sikeston. We got all my stuff back to my dad's house. That morning my friends did their best to cheer me up. I had always thought of the twins as just average friends, but the way they helped me that day solidified them as good friends in my eyes for the rest of my life.

The other obstacle was asking my dad if I could move back in with him. Since I had not talked to him in a long while, I was afraid he would just tell me to leave him alone. I thought he probably wanted nothing to do with his loser son. But when I called, he sounded almost happy that I would be moving back into the house. It was good to hear my dad's voice again and realize he did not want to forget about me.

I began substitute teaching in Poplar Bluff and noticed little flickers of light coming through my darkness. I began sleeping a lot and escaping into an alternate reality in my naps and dreams. I would envision myself happy and rich in these dreams. Every day after work I went upstairs to my room and escaped to my own dream world until the next morning. It was through these dreams that I began to want to be happy instead of malingering in my depression. I slowly began going to sleep earlier along with sleeping later into the day. I began reading books and playing basketball again. I loved playing basketball with my morning basketball group and saw more frequent flickers of happiness from that.

Out of nowhere I was contacted by the Paralympic soccer team. They had heard about my athletic career through articles written about my brothers that mentioned me. The Paralympic National Soccer team thought I might be athletic enough to pick up the sport and invited me to a training camp. I did not tell them that I had not exercised in a long time, but they sent me a training routine to complete in preparation for camp.

While I prepared to go to camp, I saw more and more light breaking through the darkness. I was excited to represent my country in an international setting. While I was training, my mind often wandered toward thoughts of gaining international acclaim as a soccer player. This might actually be my sport.

When my dad discovered I was going to California to try out for the soccer team, he thought it was a mistake and told me to find a job and not trying to chase a foolish sport. I couldn't believe what he was saying! All my life my dad supported my sports endeavors and now he was telling me to not pursue something that would allow me to represent my country on the athletic field. My mom also thought it would be a waste of time. I resolved to train hard without the support of my family.

As I completed the workouts, I noticed the depressive cloak being lifted from me and my heart started to fill with gratification again after each drill. By the time I left for the Olympic Training Center in California, I was no longer depressed. I had kept a disciplined training routine for a couple months to get ready for the camp and felt confident in my abilities. I was becoming an athlete again. As I boarded my plane, I was excited to show the training center its first glimpse of the alpha male—something I hadn't called myself in a long time.

Once my flight landed, I met up with the other group of Paralympic soccer players. I immediately sized them up and felt that I was easily the best athlete in the group. There were a bunch of small, skinny, frail-looking kids dressed in USA soccer gear, which was also what I had on, and after we introduced ourselves, we were told we needed to run to the other side of the parking garage to meet the van that would take us to the training facility. I thought this would be the perfect time to show these little people that I was a far superior athlete compared to any of them. As we began running, I was running at full speed and everyone in the group was right there with me. As we reached the team van, I realized I was not the fastest guy in the group. But I was certain I could show them my athletic prowess on the soccer field.

Once we arrived at the training center, I was beaming. I was enthralled with the possibility of being an Olympic athlete, so having a room at the training facility to try out for the Paralympic soccer team was amazing to me. Even though I truly wanted to be at the training center and train as a Paralympic athlete, I thought that the Paralympic label meant these were easier workouts and the athletes were babied much more than "real" Olympic athletes.

That first night, I rapidly disabused of that notion. After putting our gear in our rooms, we went to the soccer field for a scrimmage. I was eager to show off my skills. I was put in as a defender in the back field. I quickly discovered that I actually did not have the greatest soccer skills, but I was the biggest guy on the field and anyone who came through was going to have to pay the price.

The first play, one of the forwards broke past the midfield. I ran up and lightly bumped him with my hip in an effort to get the ball from him. He went flying through the air and I immediately took the ball and dribbled it all the way down the field before realizing that I wasn't skilled enough to pass the ball. I reared back and tried a shot on the goal from about twenty yards away. As the ball flew over the goal, I ran back to the defensive end of the field, head down. I had blown an easy goal simply because I could not pass the ball. The rest of the hour scrimmage went well enough: every time someone came into my area, I ran right at them and gave them a hard bump in an effort to get the ball. It seemed that every pass I made was getting stolen by the other team. But by the end of the scrimmage, I felt I had established myself as a physical defender and was on my way to being one of the best defenders they had ever seen.

The next day, we had two three-hour practices scheduled after our morning weightlifting session. Lifting weights had always been my strong point and I was able to excel in the weight room. But midway through the workout, my left foot started to hurt in an area that had never bothered me before. I thought it was nothing to worry about, so I went out to practice. By the end of that practice session, I realized something was really wrong with my foot. Every time I pushed off to run on it I felt pain shooting through my foot and I limped for the first few drills trying to run the pain out of my foot. In my marathon training, I learned that sharp pain goes away after a few minutes, so I continued struggling through practice while my foot griped in pain. After practice, I went to the training room and received treatment for my foot before lunch.

In training for marathons, I experienced periods of pain and struggle, pain that would fade away and come back again in waves. These pains were usually not permanent pains. I remembered running my first marathon with a pulled hamstring, how after a few miles, the pain would fade away, then return with a vengeance. This happened every few miles. I used these memories to understand the pain in my foot at this soccer camp. While I would be hurting terribly during the first few drills in practice, I noticed that halfway through each session, the pain in my foot felt less intense. I was able to run without much pain for a few minutes, but then the pain would return in a shooting fit. My entire left leg would almost collapse from trying to run during these fits. I told myself that it was not permanent pain, I could push through it to gain a few minutes of pain-free action. By the end of that first practice, I just wanted to get off my foot so I could escape the shooting pain I had endured for the four-hour session.

After each practice session, I went to the training room and received treatment to try to make my foot feel better. But each practice, my foot got worse and the shooting pain began to be a constant feeling in my foot. I couldn't help but want to get off my feet. My focus on the soccer field was less about defending my area and more about managing my pain.

I went to the last practice and played as well as I could on my foot. The next morning, I returned to Missouri—having made the United States Paralympic Soccer team. I was a part of the team but the camp had taken its toll on my foot. On the short walk through the airport, I tried to walk normally, but the pain in my foot was too great to allow a normal walk. I winced every time it hit the ground. I thought it would probably take a week for my foot to heal before I could get back to preparing for my next training camp. As I limped my way back to my truck to drive home, I was more motivated than ever to represent my country and make myself into an amazing soccer player.

Once back in Poplar Bluff, I was excited to get better at soccer and train to show the world my skills as a member of the US Paralympic team. But, I needed to rest until my foot got better in order to train the way I wanted for the next camp. In my mind, I knew that once I was healthy, I could be one of the best players on the team, because I was the alpha male, tougher than anyone they had ever seen before in their lives.

I rested for a couple weeks and noticed that my foot was not getting any better; in fact, it actually felt worse than it had when I was at camp. Now, every morning, I dreaded the first step out of bed because I knew it meant shooting pain. Each successive step caused my foot to explode with pain. I managed to suck it up and walk to the school each day to substitute teach. I then decided to start training on my foot in an effort to loosen the inflamed tendons and continue getting better. I was still an alpha male, tolerating pain was what I did; my foot would have to heal while I got better at a new game that I was planning to dominate on the international level.

I started lifting weights in my basement again, going to the track to run and do agility drills, and driving to soccer fields to work on handling the soccer ball. I expected the fire in my heart to flame up for soccer and the chance to play for my country, but I began to feel hollow inside. The flame I felt for running was not transferring to a passion for soccer.

Each day, I went home and my dad would tell me I did not need to play soccer. He told me it was a foolish venture and I needed to focus on finding a better job than substitute teaching. He began to tell me that training for soccer was keeping me from having a job that could sustain me.

I could not believe he was telling me that a sport was a foolish thing to do. The man that stood beside me and supported all the running I did at Mizzou was now telling me I should find a job and give up a passion that he had helped instill in me. I began to realize that one of the reasons I was able to be so passionate with my running was that I was surrounded by people who had similar goals. While at Mizzou, I was surrounded by college athletes and Olympians; in the summers at home, I was surrounded by top college basketball players, and now it seemed I was the only one trying to train for a sport. And each time I went to the field to kick the ball, it felt foreign to me. I was not used to using my feet to control something, and I thought I would eventually grow to love it since I needed to get comfortable with it before I liked it. Each time I started to run, pain radiated through my entire left leg as I limped my way through each drill.

Even though I was not excited about the sport of soccer, I was thrilled about the opportunity to represent my country. But my foot continued to get worse as I attempted to train on it. I began to dread my workouts because I was scared of the searing pain that I would feel course through my body each time I ran. While this one thing seemed to be coming together, I saw everything else in my life falling apart.

I was still ashamed of my place in the world and embarrassed to see my dad's side of the family. I did not want to talk with my dad because I felt he was ashamed to have such a failure as a son. I was a substitute teacher that could not afford to live on his own, had no college degree, and was still living with him. One night, as I lay in bed, I decided I needed a change.

I was either going to move to San Diego or Chapel Hill so that I would no longer be stuck in a life that promised little satisfaction. If I chose to live in San Diego, I would find a mediocre job and train to be the best soccer player I possibly could for the US team. If I chose Chapel Hill, I would be living in the same town as my mom and brother, and near the captain of the US Paralympic team (I respected Josh, the team captain, a lot for being an effective leader). After talking it over with my brother and mom, I decided that Chapel Hill was where I was going to move.

My mom told me I could live with her, and Tyler seemed excited for me to be in the same town, but as a substitute teacher, there was one issue that was a struggle: I did not have enough money to drive to North Carolina. I decided to hold a yard sale.

When I told my dad I would be having a yard sale that Saturday in his front yard, he was not happy to say the least. I still had not told him I was going to move to Chapel Hill because I knew he would be against it. I could hear him saying, "You'll have nothing out there. The smart decision would be to stay here and work."

He believed I was holding the yard sale to make a little spending money. I estimated three hundred dollars to be the amount I needed to make the move without being broke once I arrived in town. The night before the yard sale, I loaded my truck with the clothes I would need to make the move so my dad would not see me preparing to move. The next morning, I held the yard sale, and it was a huge success. In three short hours, I had sold all my stuff and held three hundred fifty dollars in my hand. After filling up my gas tank, I hit the road, bound for Chapel Hill and a better life.

***

Once I reached Tennessee, my dad called and asked where I was. I told him I was moving to North Carolina. He screamed at me over the phone for making this move without telling him and lectured me on how I would struggle with no college degree. By the time I hung up the phone, I started to pick out the pearls of wisdom from his outburst. One thing having high school basketball coaches yell at me for four years taught me was to listen closely when someone yells at you so you can gain knowledge from what they are saying and ignore their anger. The rest of the drive was spent in thought about things my dad had said to me and the goals I needed to attain in order to survive in North Carolina.

First, I needed to continue training and develop a love for soccer so I could best represent my country on the Paralympic team. Second, I needed to find a job that would be low stress and allow me to train for soccer. Third, I wanted to eventually finish my degree. Finishing my degree was one of my lower priorities; if I became the kind of soccer player I knew I could be, I could probably get endorsements and become a professional.

During the first week of being in Chapel Hill, I was still limping around on my foot and trying to train on the soccer fields every day. Each time I would push off to run, the pain in my foot would erupt. I did my best to muscle through the pain to improve my soccer skills, but something was missing; in the past, especially with running, I had felt my love for the sport well from deep within my being. Every time I tried to play soccer, I felt empty inside and could not even get a dim glow from the embers of my soul. And my foot continued with its incessant pain. Near the end of that first week, I started thinking about why I had been so passionate and realized that I was happiest pursuing the runner's lifestyle. I was conflicted, as I was still excited about representing my country on the international stage.

It was then that I heard Coach Mac's words ring through my head; he always spoke in a manner that showed objectivity and I always knew he had my best interest in mind with his advice. His voice told me, "No matter what accolades you'll receive, you have to love it first." That made sense to me. I flashed forward in my mind and saw myself unhappy as a soccer player: Everyone around me was proud of my skills and play, but I was miserable because I hated the sport. All I really wanted was to get back to running.

After this thought, I called the coach of the soccer team and told him I did not want to play soccer. He seemed a little upset, but understood when I told him I wanted to get back to running. Once I hung up the phone, I felt relieved that I didn't have to prepare for a sport. After trying for months to fall in love with soccer, I felt a weight lift off my shoulders at not have to force myself to like it.

The week following that phone call, I went out to bars and made friends with a lot of people in town. While I enjoyed meeting new people, most of the people I met knew me as Tyler's brother and were not interested in getting to know me; they only wanted to know more about my brother through me. I learned to shy away from those people because I wanted to be known for who I was and not for who my brother was as a basketball player.

I also began looking for a job. My mom told me to look at all the shops on Franklin Street (the main street in Chapel Hill, where people often purchase UNC clothing) to see if they were hiring for any positions. I went to every shop on Franklin Street and returned home fairly tired and ready for dinner and bed. The next day, I received a call from one store telling me they liked to partner closely with the basketball team and felt that hiring me would strengthen their relationship with the team because of my closeness with Tyler. I told them I was interested in working part time and could do anything they needed me to do. I wanted to work part time because I wanted to start running again and a part-time job would allow me to get back to running.

However, while my mind was ready to get back in the game, my foot would not stop hurting and the pain had changed from occasional intense pain to being a constant sharp pain. I did not like walking anywhere and wanted to sit down at any opportunity. I decided to rest a lot while I let my foot heal.

The next Monday, I started working at Chapel Hill Sportswear and quickly realized it was not going to be the easy and relaxed job that I had built in my mind. I had to bring shirts up from the basement and place price tags on items, and was constantly on my feet, which caused my left foot to scream in more pain than it had ever given me. Every time I got a break during the day, I would sit down and feel the pain in my foot slowly ebb. I relished those breaks because they were the few minutes that I did not have to endure sharp pain from my foot.

After a couple weeks of rest, I decided enough was enough, I wanted to get back to running and my foot was going to have to get better as I ran. During my off days from work, I started lifting weights in the Dean Dome with the basketball players and the people who would become my weight room buddies.

I came to know my weight room group through going to the Dean Dome with my brother Tyler. It consisted of Jay, the UNC strength and conditioning coach for the men's basketball team; Michelle, a diver for the UNC dive team who had a passion for lifting weights; Donnie, a dedicated cyclist who trained with us; and the current and former UNC basketball players.

Jay was a strength coach who loved his job and seemed to be an incessant student of athletic training. Every time I went to the weight room, he would show me some new training idea or a new piece of research he had found about ways that athletes train. Standing six feet tall and weighing about two hundred pounds, he had the build of a former body builder, while his glasses revealed his studious nature. His passion for training athletes exuded itself into a charisma that made people around him want to take his advice and incorporate the new things he found in his research into their everyday lives to gain approval from him. He had a way of getting his athletes, along with the rest of the weight room group, to improve their nutrition and lives through charismatic ridicule of their bodily flaws. To share a weight room with him was to feel his charisma work its magic on his athletes. He gained an in with people through his humor, teasing them, which lead them to desire to improve themselves athletically to gain his approval. The key to understanding Jay is that he wanted the best for everyone he encountered and this ribbing was intentional to push people to accomplish their goals.

Michelle was a beautiful woman who loved to push herself. It was clear that she reveled in doing exercises that seemed ludicrously difficult to most athletes and absolutely insane to non-athletes. She always laughed in a way that showed she understood that what she did in the weight room was considered crazy by most. That same laugh also showed an understanding that she enjoyed a position as one of the extremely tough people in the world; in other words, her smile showed that she knew she was an alpha female.

Donnie, or D-Train, appeared to be the closest thing to a normal person in the weight room group, until you began to analyze what he loved to do as an athlete. Standing at about six feet one inch with salt and pepper hair, he looked like a normal athlete, but he did extremely long bike races, sometimes over one hundred miles in length. In the weight room, he would make his way through his workouts and perform exercises that were difficult, but he always laughed every time he finished a tough lift. You could hear behind his laugh that he was quietly proud of himself for getting to a point where he could perform such exercises, but he also laughed at the exercises' absurdity. Donnie loved being around the athletes and lifting with Jay, as he was drawn in by Jay's charisma along with the rest of us. He enjoyed laughing about his shortcomings. He was usually talking about crazy things he had seen on bike rides or an incredibly greasy meal he ate, which he did because he knew it would draw a remark from Jay about how it was a poor decision to choose such a meal.

I began seeing these three along with my brother in the weight room about three days a week. I fed off their desire to improve themselves in the weight room and off Jay's teasing that caused us all to want to improve athletically through his pointing out of our downfalls. I felt that these were my first group of friends in North Carolina.

I began running twice a week on the trails through Umstead State Park. I loved running through the woods, but my foot pain was still unrelenting as I ran. I came to understand the first mile was going to cause me a lot of sharp pain in my foot, but after that first mile, my foot would hurt with a slightly more dull pain that was more tolerable. One morning as I ran along the Company Mill Trail, I passed the point where I usually felt my foot loosen up and ease into less sharp pain and I felt the pain shoot more violently through my entire foot in a burst that caused my left foot to lock up. I decided to walk for a few meters to let it get better, but it took almost a quarter mile of hobbling on the trail in the most painful limping I had ever experienced to get my foot to unlock. I then started running again and boom! It locked up again as I made my way up a hill. I again hobbled down the trail and tried to unlock my foot as it exploded with pain each time it hit the ground. I felt my foot bone was jamming into my shin each step. I finally got it to unlock and started to run again down a hill. I made it about a mile before it locked again on the next uphill. I decided to walk the rest of the run. As I felt my foot lock in pain this time, I tried to flex my foot forward in an effort to keep my foot bone from slamming into my shin. It worked! I started running again with a focus on trying to flex my foot as much as possible each time I strode. This time I made it almost to the end of the trail before I started my hobbling stagger, which was now more painful than when I started my run. I quickly jumped into my truck and immediately felt the fiery pain in my foot begin to subside as I sat down. On the drive home, I decided that I needed to stop running until my foot healed because the pain was worse than any foot injury I had ever experienced and I was probably doing permanent damage to my foot. I thought that I could still lift weights, ride a bike, and stay in shape while my foot healed.

My weight room circle had grown to include a few of the former UNC players who played professionally. Marvin, Sean, and Jackie were three professional players who trained hard, shared jokes, and seamlessly became members of the normal entourage. I would ride a bike in the weight room watching the guys and Michelle lift and participating in conversations that ranged from girls to training, and everything in between. I was getting to know these people, and also gaining another layer of closeness with my brother. I loved getting to watch him around his basketball friends and was incredibly happy that we could add weightlifting to the list of things we did together. Hanging out with Tyler whether with the weight room entourage or outside of that crowd made me feel closer to my brother than ever before, which made me incredibly happy.

***

While I was gaining a new group of friends, it was clear that I needed to find a job that would allow me to make more money than a part-time job at a T-shirt store. I started looking for job postings anywhere I could find them for full-time positions. I then came across a job with the YMCA as a camp counselor. It was advertised as a full-time job and I submitted my application to the

Chapel Hill YMCA. The next day, they wanted to give me an interview for the position. I was excited at the opportunity to have my first full-time job. I was unsure of how to dress for the interview and put on a pair of khakis and a golf shirt. My mom stopped me at the door and told me to put on a button-up shirt and dress shoes for the interview. I groaned, then walked back upstairs and put on my nice button-up shirt and dress shoes. I drove to the YMCA and walked into the building for my interview.

As I walked into the building, I smelled the familiar smell of a public gym, the faint, dank of sweat from quasi-athletes lifting weights on lifting machines just beyond the front desk. I asked the worker at the front desk where Ryan's office was and I was directed down a slim hallway that smelled of body odor more than the rest of the building, I walked into his office, which was a large room filled with a huge compilation of coloring books, crayons, and toys for children. I shook hands with Ryan and told him I was here for the interview for his camp counselor position. Ryan was a short man with a slightly bulging belly who I initially thought was a serious man wound tighter than he wanted anyone to know and trying to hide it with his smile. I tried to relax as we began our conversation about camp. I told him about my work with the Mizzou track team and how I loved being outside and working with kids. As the conversation continued, I thought I may have misjudged him as an extreme tight-ass. I started to relax as the conversation continued, and he told me I should come to the group interview that afternoon and wear comfortable clothes. I was excited by the proposition of being invited back for a second interview and drove home to prepare for the group interview.

 As soon as I got home, I saw Tyler and my mom sitting in the kitchen and I told them about my interview and that I needed to get ready for the group interview. I told my mom I needed to wear comfortable clothes but after an argument, which she won, I agreed to wear khaki shorts and a golf shirt. I then rushed out the door in order to be on time for the group interview.

I arrived back at the YMCA ten minutes before the interview and was directed to a row of benches outside the building on the playground. I found a seat on the bench among a large group of people around my age who were all interviewing for counselor positions. We were all around the same age and everyone seemed excited at the prospect of being a camp counselor. Ryan came outside and addressed the group of us on the benches, telling us that we would be asked to do a lot of tasks that evening aimed toward seeing if we would make good counselors. I was extremely confident in my ability to complete the tasks throughout this interview, as they were tasks aimed at exhibiting leadership, team building, and creative qualities. I was pretty certain that I was going to be one of the camp counselors for the summer once the interview was over. The next day, I decided to drive to the YMCA to see what Ryan thought about my abilities as a counselor. On my application, I had left the section of which camp I was interested in working open so that I would have a better chance at obtaining a position. Ryan asked me what camp I wanted to work. Since I had done basketball camps in the summer while I was in high school, I decided working outside would be a nice change from being inside all day. Plus, the gym at the YMCA reeked of body odor and I did not want to have that smell in my nose all summer. I told him I wanted to work at Camp Clearwater, which was an outdoor camp. He told me that I would be outside every day I replied that that was why I wanted to work there. He told me that I would be a counselor there for the summer and that I should come back to the YMCA in two weeks for training. My heart jumped for joy and I left the YMCA excited to start my first full-time job in a couple weeks.

I drove straight home and told my mom and brother that I had a job that summer as a camp counselor for Camp Clearwater. My mom jumped up in excitement and Tyler congratulated me on my position. The next day, in the weight room, I told everyone about my new position and they all told me congrats. Then we went back to lifting weights and the normal ebb and flow of conversations. I realized that my new job meant I would not get to lift weights or see my weight room friends the rest of the summer. I told Chapel Hill Sportswear I would no longer be working for them and decided that in the two weeks leading up to my job, I would go to the weight room every day and enjoy my time there as much as possible before leaving for the summer.

Those two weeks flew by as I lifted weights and rode the bicycle every day. My left foot still exploded in pain anytime I had to do anything athletic on it, but it seemed I would have a couple of days that my pain did not cause me to limp as badly in pain. I tried to do more lifts on my feet and felt the constant sharp pain return to my foot. I decided that I was going to have to push through the pain in order to do my job.

As I arrived at the YMCA for camp training, I saw the counselors I would be working with for the summer. Each of us had co-counselors for the summer. My co-counselor and I were assigned to a group of incoming third-grade campers for the summer. Every two weeks, the camp started a new session, which meant that we would have a new set of kids in our group. My co-counselor was Ashley; she was an all-star counselor from the previous year. I immediately saw that she was a great counselor, as she was creative, loud, and fun. During training we learned a bunch of camp chants, played a lot of games, and went over emergency procedures. I realized that I would have to rely on Ashley a lot and she would need to be able to rely on me as well. By the end of that training week, I was excited to get to play these games with the kids and knew that Ashley would guide me in many of the things that I did not understand, since this was my first outdoor camp.

While I was excited about the camp and knew it would be fun, I also felt the pain in my foot shooting throughout the day, and each time we played a game, I had to grit my teeth and push through the pain. As much as I loved the games, I knew that participating in them meant managing intense pain throughout the day.

After the last day of training, a large group of the counselors were going to get drinks at a local bar in Chapel Hill. I did not want to miss out on getting to hang out with my new coworkers away from work. If they were as fun away from work as they were in training, I was going to love having them as a new group of friends. I discovered that most of the counselors loved to party and drink a lot. I wanted to be a part of the group, so I started drinking a lot while we were out. I heard a lot of stories about intense nights of drinking they had all experienced and I told them a few of my drinking stories as well.

The following Monday, camp began and I discovered how much fun it could be to work with kids. Ashley was incredible at making the day fun for the campers. I followed her lead from the start and began to do a little more each day as a counselor. Ashley led the chants as I followed behind the group watching and slowly came out of my shell more and more each day. Every night I would get home exhausted from the day. By the end of the first week, I was completely out of my shell and immersed in the camp. Each day was filled with fun and games Ashley and I created at the different locations around camp.

My foot still hurt worse than anything I had ever experienced, but I pushed the pain to the back of my mind in order to continue working with my group. Each break, I sat on the couch in the lounge and felt the sweet sensation of the pain easing as I sat down. I was still able to play all the games throughout the day, but my foot locked in pain frequently. I had learned to flex my foot and push through the pain. I wanted this job more than I wanted my foot to be healthy; besides, I thought running around all day at camp would eventually cause my foot to strengthen and not hurt. I could not have been more wrong, as my pain was constant, but it did not get worse. I did not want to be on my feet unless it was absolutely necessary, but I continued to force myself through the pain each day.

After the first camp session, a lot of the counselors would go to the bars and drink heavily once the day was finished. I started meeting them at least three days a week to party after camp. After the second week of this, I was hanging out late into the night with a party crowd and getting through the days at camp in a hungover stupor. I was becoming a good counselor and devising great games for the kids, but regularly wound up in the bar room scene after each day of camp was over. I knew that Ryan viewed me as a partier who struggled his way through the day at camp. He was right but I was enjoying being the life of the party each night.

By the end of that first summer, I had found an entirely new group of people I called my friends and they loved to go out to the bars. I was no longer lifting weights or running, as my foot hurt me too much to even think about trying to run.

But one day on my lunch break, I received a phone call from Denver, Colorado. It was the National Sports Center for the Disabled. They told me they had read about my running and wanted to fly me to Denver for their 10k road race in August. I could not believe my ears. Even though I still disliked thinking of myself as a disabled athlete, I wanted to go to Denver. My heart leapt with excitement at this opportunity to run as a professional athlete in Denver with all my expenses paid for one weekend. I then thought I'd see if I could talk my way into getting them to pay for Jeremy to go with me as well. I had not talked to him in a few months and a free trip to Denver would be the perfect excuse to catch up with him and continue our running careers together, this time as paid athletes. They told me they would fly Jeremy out as well and I said goodbye quickly so the schoolgirl scream that followed wouldn't be heard over the phone. After that scream of joy, I called Jeremy and told him. He agreed to fly out there with me and we both hung up the phone pumped to get to Denver and catch up. Running a 10k in a new city was going to feel like old times when we were both showing the world that we were amazing athletes.

I drove back to camp and got out of my truck. As soon as my feet touched the ground, I felt my left foot explode in pain again and I knew I was going to have a tough time enduring the pain of running on a hurt foot in order to do this race in Denver.

Once the last camp was finished, Ryan told me that working the after-school program for the YMCA would be great experience for working camp the next summer. I agreed to work as an after-school counselor once school started again in the middle of August.

There were a few weeks before I had to begin work as an after school counselor. I set my sights on training for the 10k in Denver. I returned to the weight room at the Dean Dome three days a week while struggling through foot pain four days a week on the trails around Umstead Park.

After a week of struggling through foot pain, I decided to stop running completely to let my foot heal. While my foot was healing, I decided to go out and meet my camp friends at the bars. I was out almost every night. But I still went into the weight room to lift even though I was hungover. My weight room friends would just shake their heads at my barroom adventures. And my foot refused to get better, but I was getting used to the frequent explosions of pain. By the time I boarded the plane for Denver, I was out of running shape and my foot still hurt. But I was going to find a way to push myself through the pain to run the race.

When my flight touched down in Denver, I found Jeremy in the airport and we found our way to Katy, a friend of mine who worked for the National Sports Center for the Disabled. She greeted me with a big hug and we were all three off to Jeremy and my hotel to drop off our stuff and go to dinner.

Jay had told me about a good sushi restaurant in Denver, Katy offered to take us there for dinner. On the drive there, Jeremy and I caught up, telling each other what we had been up to since we last hung out. Our conversations spilled over through dinner and Katy joined in with her own experiences. The next morning, Jeremy and I went to the pre-race packet pick-up area and helped the race volunteers hand out race packets for a few hours. Katy then dropped us off at the hotel with meal money and told us she would pick us up in the morning for the race. Loaded with pockets full of cash, Jeremy and I walked into downtown Denver to look around the city. Along the walk, Jeremy noticed I was limping a lot. I told him the story of my injured foot and how it would not get better no matter what I tried as rehab. I told him I was going to run through it the next day. He looked skeptically at me as I limped down the sidewalk.

The next morning, we both crawled out of our hotel to meet Katy for our ride to the race. We both tried our best to look like we were not hungover from drinking the night before in downtown Denver. We decided that a short warm-up jog would be a great idea to loosen ourselves for the race and shake off our hangovers. During that jog, I felt my foot explode in pain with each stride it would lock in pain as it felt as though my foot bone slammed into my shin. I pushed through the pain and limped my way to the starting line.

Once the race started, I pushed through the pain and tried to ignore it. Within the first mile, my foot had locked in pain and I pushed harder as if running faster would cause it to hurt less.

The race went through the professional sports stadiums in Denver. I loved running on the baseball field, and they even put mats on the NHL ice rink so we could run through. Somewhere around the fourth mile my foot became a dull pain and I was able to start racing instead of focusing on the pain in my foot. I was passing runners right and left and continued running past people all the way into the final stadium, the football stadium where the Broncos played. As I crossed the finish line, I almost felt like my old self again by crossing the finish line having passed a large number of runners in my last couple of miles. After the race, I found Jeremy and we both began drinking beers to celebrate our race. Jeremy had finished in the top thirty of runners while I had beaten all the other disabled athletes they had invited to the race. I still had the killer alpha male in my heart.

***

Katy took us to the airport and Jeremy and I flew home after a weekend of catching up, drinking, and racing. After getting off the plane, I noticed my foot was still hurting, but I did not care, I had run a race as a professional and could now do nothing until it healed.

The next morning, I stepped out of bed and felt the familiar pain return to my foot. It was a struggle to limp my way to breakfast with my mom and Tyler. After eating, I looked at my left foot and noticed it was swollen much larger than my other foot. I decided to not do anything athletic until it got better, no matter how long it would take to heal, I thought the reason it had not worked in the past was because I would not wait long enough to let it heal.

About a week before I started working as an after-school counselor, I was looking at a few online degree programs as I sat around the house. I decided I wanted to finish my degree in order to get a better job and gain some independence. As I sat at the dinner table with my mom and brother, they told me UNC had a program where I could take classes part-time in order to finish my degree. Immediately, my mind shifted into gear and I became excited about the prospect of getting my degree from UNC, a great academic institution. I was excited to learn that I could finish my degree and graduate as a Tar Heel.

Over the next few days, I filled out the necessary paperwork to be admitted as a part-time student. I filled out all the forms and waited eagerly to receive an acceptance letter. I decided that I could afford to pay for one class per semester until I graduated by working part time as an after-school counselor and summer camp counselor.

The next week, I started working as an after-school counselor and quickly discovered it was a much different job than working as a summer counselor. The YMCA had a constant smell of body odor, the kids did not want to be there, and they did not want to play any of the games I tried to organize for my group. But I needed the job so that I could make money. It only required about three hours a day and that meant I had most of the day free to lift weights in the Dean Dome and study once I started classes. And it would allow me to continue going to the bars in Chapel Hill and meeting new friends.

It was not long before I received a letter from UNC telling me that I could take part-time classes through the Friday Center. The Friday Center was a large building in town that hosted conferences and had an office for UNC part-time students to register for classes and speak to advisors. I showed them my letter and made an appointment to sign up for a night class. I then looked at the prices per class and realized I did not have enough money to take the class I wanted for that semester. I called my dad and he sent me a check to cover the class and felt ashamed of having to ask him for more help. I signed up for a night class that met once a week.

I was excited about going back to school, but also was pumped that my class would not be so time-consuming and would allow me to keep the same social routine I had kept with the other YMCA counselors. Every couple of days, I would meet my YMCA friends out at bars and we would tell stories and laugh at blunders we had made trying to talk to women in the bars. I had become the main one who tried to talk to women when we went out. Usually, I got turned down by the woman I tried to talk to, which lead to raucous laughter from my friends. I gained the reputation as the bold one among the counselors because I excelled at obtaining stories from our late nights. My reputation began to spread through my coworkers and I could tell that Ryan was a bit wary of having me work with kids. I began to feel like he was looking for a reason to fire me. Each day at work, I would feel self-conscious about the games I was playing with my group. I felt as though Ryan viewed me as an out-of-control person who lived for drinking stories, but

I continued to go meet the other counselors at the bars on a regular basis.

During the day, I had a lot of free time and went to the Dean Dome in the mornings to lift weights almost every day. I felt really close to my weight room entourage and after each wild night out with the camp counselors, I would share the stories with everybody in the weight room until they also began to see me as a bit of a party boy. Jay always made a comment that made me feel self-conscious, but also motivate me to improve myself. Michelle (or "Mudge" as we called her around the weight room) would always laugh to the point of falling down at my stories and the inevitable comment from Jay. Donnie would add a dry joke about my inability to gain any interest from girls in the bar.

While we joked around during our workouts, we all still took it very seriously; I had added a lot of exercises to my weightlifting routine. I watched Jay guiding the players through lifts during their workouts, asked him about each lift, then added it to my own routine. Mudge was also a master of lifts, showing me some incredible ones that challenged me. I knew many of the lifts would cause my foot pain. Each time I would do a coordination exercise, I felt it in my left foot, so I avoided many of those exercises.

Even though I went to the bars at least twice a week, I spent the afternoons reading and studying my notes for class. In the class, I had somehow gained the reputation as the chatty student who enjoyed talking about the topic of the day. I was intrigued in my popular culture class. I read every article assigned regardless of how hungover I was or how badly my foot hurt, because I understood that the one time I let my studies slide would become a quick downfall into consistently putting off my class. When I was in class, I understood that I was there to finish my degree. This was my last chance to finish my degree and I was going to give it my best shot.

One day, I was lifting weights when Mudge mentioned that her and her roommates were going to have a get-together at their house. I told her I would come by and say hi. I ended up staying with her and her friends the whole night. We partied a lot harder than my counselor friends. I was not the crazy one in the group with Mudge and her roommates; every single one of them was equally fun loving and adventurous. I had unintentionally found another group of friends I could go out to the bars with at night. I discovered through Jay that they called her house the Cave and I immediately adopted that term. After I visited the Cave a few times, it became a hangout spot where I would go to relax during the day before it transformed into our starting point for going out to the bars at night.

Living in the house with Mudge were four other girls who shared the same sense of humor and enjoyed going out on the town. Alex was a short and attractive blonde who knew Mudge through diving. She was an exuberant person who could more than hold her own with us when we were drinking. Caitlyn was the tall, quiet one of the group who was always studying and rarely went out with the rest of the Cave, but when she came out, she immediately fit in with the group as an easy-going person who would spring to life whenever there was action going on. I guess she understood that if she was going to go out, the Cave was the group to go out with because we had the best times and generated more stories than anybody. Kacie was a sensible athletic girl with brown hair. She was the one who tried to keep everyone from doing incredibly stupid things; one day, she was talking me out of a terribly bad idea—trying to talk to a football player's girlfriend—and after she succeeded, Mudge called her Mom. It stuck as her nickname. Kathryn was an extremely attractive girl with smooth olive skin and a hesitant demeanor—but once she decided on something to do, she went all in with the rest of the group on whatever craziness was brewing.

This group of spirited women became some of my best friends. We would constantly laugh about crazy happenings and we were all friends because we all saw ourselves as the hardest partiers there were in town. We also maintained a sense of ego in knowing that we were also tougher than most people in the world, we all saw ourselves as alphas. The group of spirited women became some of my best friends.

At the end of that first semester, I had an A in class, but had also gained the reputation as the out-of-control counselor, due to my bravado about my nights on the town, at the YMCA. Still, I was pleased with my transformation into a person who had a few different groups of friends and was happy spending a few days a week hung over and lazy.

As I signed up for my next class, I was a little scared because it was my first Spanish class. I needed to pass two Spanish classes in order to fulfill my foreign language requirement for my degree. I chose Spanish because I thought it would be a useful language. Tyler told me it was a hard class and that I was going to have a tough time to pass it. I told myself that I had made an A last semester, so I could handle this course.

I walked into the Spanish class and immediately felt behind everyone else in my knowledge of the course. Although I had taken a couple classes in Spanish during high school, those classes had not even come close to preparing me for the course I was taking at UNC. Other students were spouting out phrases and questions and I could not keep up. And this was the first day! I recognized that I was going to have to work extremely hard to pass this class.

I continued with my normal routine of lifting weights, studying, and going out to the bars. I was enjoying being the guy everyone knew at the bars. I hung out with my friends from the Cave a lot on the weekends and even lounged around their house during the day. I was comfortable in the weight room as I continued to push through my foot pain. I began to enjoy getting a rise from Jay aimed at improvement, and sometimes did things to intentionally get a reaction from him. I was enjoying lifting and being a "gym rat" but also felt as if something was missing inside me; I no longer felt the flame of passion that had once burned intensely inside my heart, I no longer considered myself a real athlete. Every few steps, my left foot would be gripped with pain and I could not think of anything except getting relief from it. I had also gained weight. In the afternoon, I studied, trying to understand the class, with little success. We had a quiz in a couple weeks.

While I loved being the life of the party and telling stories about the crazy nights we experienced, I could not help but feel like a piece of me was missing as I continued in my routine. I felt like a hollow shell of the person I had been at Mizzou. I felt emotionless and devoid of feelings. I had never felt this way before, even in the darkness of my earlier depression. I wasn't proud of the person I was, I was missing the passion that had ignited me in training and racing, the passion I had before I went to soccer camp. I was tired of limping around in pain and living a muted, empty life as a directionless person who was friendly to everyone I met with no sense of purpose.

My struggles with my Spanish class forced me to miss a few nights on the town so that I could receive tutoring from students who volunteered. No matter how hard I tried or how much I rehearsed the rules of the language, I still got most of them wrong. My grade in the class was passing (barely), but I felt like I was failing miserably. I knew I had to at least pass the class to move on and get my degree.

I then found a small, hole-in-the-wall burger shack called Joe's Joint in town that was infamous for greasy burgers that tasted great, but should have come with a recommendation to see a cardiologist upon finishing the greasy meal. I noticed that the restaurant was never busy during the day and that it was run by a family from Mexico. I told the boy at the counter I wanted help learning the language, and he told me that as long as I came in and bought a burger, he would help me understand Spanish, his native language.

I would go to the burger joint before every class and ask him what was going on with each of the lessons. He explained what they were trying to teach me and I would practice with the family as I ate my meal. Hearing them speak with correct pronunciation caused me to change the way I spoke words and I gained confidence in my grasp of the language while at the restaurant. But each day when I walked into the class, the teacher told me my pronunciation was not correct and told me to practice it. I went to that burger shack a lot trying to improve my dialect, but each time I was told from the teacher it was incorrect. One day, one of the workers at the restaurant told me my pronunciation was good and my teacher was not good. By the end of the class, I was able to bring my grade into a solid D. I felt exhausted from this course and then found out I needed the grade of a C or better to go on to the next level class. I decided I needed a break from Spanish and was going to save money during the summer to pay for another class the following fall.

My job as an after-school counselor at the YMCA was still taxing and I tried to keep my spirit up, because I knew I was going to have fun as a camp counselor that summer. As the school year came to a close and the after-school program was about to shut down for the summer, I was anticipating being able to dump this horrible part-time job and be the fun camp counselor I had been last year. However, my foot was still causing me a great deal of pain, and I worried it would affect my ability to play games with my campers. I decided it was time to get my left foot looked at by a doctor.

Since I had little or no money to pay to see a doctor in his office, I drove to my dad in Missouri and asked him to look at my foot. He told me I had inflamed the tendon that held up my arch. We went to the hospital and he had them take an MRI of my foot and burn it to a disc so I could take it a doctor in North Carolina and save money. My dad also looked at the MRI and confirmed that the tendon was inflamed but not torn.

After a little research on doctors in the area, my mom found a doctor who was supposed to be pretty good. She also told me he was a runner. I was sold, and I made an appointment to see him the following week in his office.

As I limped into the doctor's office, I had a stroke of luck: he told me that his kids loved seeing me as a counselor at camp. I replied that his kids were a joy to have at camp, pleased that we already had this good connection. I then told him about how I had hurt my foot at soccer camp and the constant pain I had been in for over a year. I gave him the CD with my MRI and he disappeared into his office to look at it. When he returned, he told me that my foot had been under a lot of pressure and the tendon holding my arch up was injured, but not torn, confirming my dad's earlier opinion. He told me the swelling was a response to the injury. He said that an injection into my arch would allow one injury to heal and relieve the swelling. The injection was going to allow an inflamed area to calm down enough to heal another section of my foot. He said that an injection would allow the fluid to move out of the joint and alleviate the pain temporarily, but that if the pain returned, we would need to figure something else out. I told him to inject me.

The next day, my foot was no longer in pain. I could move without worrying that a certain position would cause my foot to lock up. The shooting pain was gone. I immediately went for a short run, then lifted weights and loved that I was no longer held back by the excruciating pain in my foot.

I was working camp again and loved every minute of it, I could run, jump, and play without fear. I started being much more active at camp and enjoying life a lot more because I no longer had to struggle with pain. I even began running in the mornings before camp and went out to the bars less and less because I wanted to get to bed in time to wake up and run from camp before anyone arrived for the day.

***

Early that summer, I then received a phone call from one of my old running buddies, Natalie. She told me she was doing running programs for Fleet Feet, a running store in town, and asked if I wanted to mentor one of her programs. I thought it would be a great way for me to help people who had never been runners to learn how to enjoy the sport that I was rediscovering my love for. This meant I would be taxed for energy, which also meant this program would be a great way to get back to being a runner once again. I told her I was in, and she told me when the mentors' meeting was and that I should be there on time.

The other mentors were all experienced runners and I felt honored that I had been asked to help with this program, considering I had not been a real runner for over a year and a half. I decided I would make this program as fun as possible for the participants and give them the pearls of wisdom I had gained while running and coaching at Mizzou. During the meeting, Natalie explained that the people we would be mentoring were training for their first 10k race. After hearing this, I was pumped to help these people and started to see myself as a real alpha male for this program, though it had not started yet.

I was still running in the morning before camp. I was also running after camp as a mentor for the Fleet Feet program. I settled into a routine of running in the morning, working camp, then mentoring my group twice a week in the evenings. With my foot pain gone, I always looking forward to running the next day. I started getting close to the people in the group I was mentoring and made friends with everyone. I was particularly impressed with one of the guys in the group, Tim, who was legally blind, even carried a cane when he was not running (though he left it behind during our runs), and was always in a good mood during runs. I loved seeing his face light up after completing a run that was farther than he had run before joining this group. I was incredibly proud to see him set milestones. It seemed that he gained confidence each time he ran. I was so incredibly impressed by his constant optimism that I could not help but smile after each group run we did together. We became friends through the conversations we had on runs, and watching him gain a sense of accomplishment through running helped me to remember how I had felt when I crossed similar frontiers training for my first cross-country meet. I looked forward to each group run because I would get to talk with Tim, encourage him, and see his positive attitude carry through to the rest of the group.

During these group runs, I tried to run with as many people as I could throughout the route for that day. This meant I would carry on conversations with a number of people and I noticed that everyone was impressed with Tim—he seemed to be motivating the whole group to keep moving forward and no one ever had any excuses for not being tough enough when Tim was there. I became the clown of the group, telling jokes and singing camp songs during our runs on hot days in order to help everyone keep their mind off the intense heat.

Near the end of the summer, we had a trail run planned for the group and Natalie told us that the Trailheads would guide us through the woods so that nobody would get lost. As soon as the group heard that the Trailheads would be leading us on a run, they immediately began to chatter about this mysterious running group that ran through the woods all night and seemed to be more at home on the trail than in their own houses. By the time I finished hearing stories, I had an image in my mind of legendary runners who seemed to be untamed and rarely ventured outside the woods to socialize with other people. I learned they had a reputation as the most extreme group of runners in the area. I was excited to get to see them in their element.

On the morning they were supposed to guide us through the trails, my big toenail was almost detached from my toe, hanging by a piece of skin on my cuticle, which happened periodically due to repeated trauma from running. I knew that during the run, the nail would continually jab me in my toe, so I put a towel in my mouth so I could not scream, grabbed hold of the nail, and yanked it off my toe. Blood immediately started coming from the cuticle, but I wiped it up with the towel from my mouth. I then placed a small Band-Aid over the spot where the nail had formerly been and headed out the door to meet the group for our run led by these enigmatic runners.

We met the Trailheads in Wilson Park parking lot and I noticed they were all calling each other strange names. We started through the woods and I hit my sore toe on rocks every couple steps, which caused me to scream words I certainly couldn't say around my YMCA campers. With each profane outburst, the Trailheads howled with laughter. I would be mid-conversation, bump my foot, then scream "Fuck!" and hear everyone laugh. I could not help but feel awe watching the Trailheads move effortlessly through the woods, navigating over roots, rocks, and fallen trees with ease. I was tripping all over the place and so was the rest of my group. Yet the Trailheads just laughed, told us jokes, and maintained a light and positive attitude during the run.

Once I stumbled into the parking lot after the run with the rest of the group, I saw that the Trailheads had changed into kilts and were carrying on friendly conversations mixed with laughter and the occasional joke. They oozed a collective charisma like no other group I had ever seen, and they all seemed incredibly happy just to have been in the woods that morning. I asked one of the Trailheads when the group ran and he told me every Wednesday and Saturday morning from this lot. I filed that away and decided I needed to go run with this group one morning to see if I could learn to run on trails and meet some new people.

***

The following week at camp, we were in our final session and for some reason I just could not connect with the campers in my group. It was the last group of campers for the summer and I knew I needed the last paycheck to pay my tuition for my class the following semester. I also wanted to finish the summer completely engaged with camp games and having fun with my group. But this final group was a challenge and no matter what I did, I could never get the respect of the kids. After the second day, I was just going through the motions and was anxious to get a few weeks off before starting work as an after school counselor.

Each week at camp, there was a pool day where every group went to the pool on a bus for a couple hours. That was probably our most chaotic time as counselors. We had to make sure everyone was on the bus and show them where to sit. I was always frantically scrambling to get my campers to sit quickly so we could get to the pool. Once at the pool, our jobs were easy as we got to swim and relax with the kids in the pool, but returning to camp from the pool was just as frantic a time as coming had been. I had developed a system of pointing to each camper and telling them to sit in a specific seat. I was always speaking quickly and scrambling through the bus to make sure everyone was sitting down so the bus could leave the pool.

This particular day, I thought we had returned smoothly from the pool when I noticed my co-counselor Katie walking toward me with one of the campers. The boy holding her hand was a blond boy with glasses from my group who looked at me with fear in his eyes as soon as I met him and Katie. Katie told me I had terrified

Henry on the bus. I told him I was sorry and saw him look at me with terror in his eyes. I had no idea what I had done to scare the boy so badly, but immediately felt bad that I had caused him to have a poor experience on the bus. Katie took him to the camp director and Ryan called me into his office five minutes after Katie had brought the boy to him.

As I sat in the office, Ryan told me he was very upset that I had scared one of my campers. I then noticed the assistant director sitting in the office with him. Nick, the assistant camp director, seemed to be peering into my soul with his gaze but remained completely silent. Ryan then asked me what he should do if he received a complaint from Henry's parents. I told him that I would be happy to talk with them about my method of pointing to a seat and having the campers sit in that seat. Ryan told me he did not want to take that risk and fired me from my position as a camp counselor on the spot. I could not believe my ears! He was firing me for telling a kid to sit in a spot on the bus? I am still unsure what I could have done differently to have kept my job.

All the stresses of not receiving a paycheck rushed back into my mind. I would not be able to pay for my next class without my last paycheck. I was going to need to find another job. Even though I was no longer working at the Y, I still had my friends from there I could hang out with after work. Or so I thought.

I thought that I would still have the counselors as friends after losing my position, but that entire group of friends distanced themselves from me. In the week after I lost my position, I noticed that my counselor friends had disappeared into thin air. I was no longer being invited to dinners or to join them for drinks. They were silent and absent. One night I called Ashley, a counselor I thought I was close with, and although she told me she was sorry I was hurting, I could hear in her voice that she thought I was a lousy counselor. I hung up the phone and cried my eyes out from losing a group of people I thought would always be my friends.

The following weekend, my brother Tyler asked me if I wanted to live with him in Indianapolis during the basketball season, as he was now playing for the Pacers. Immediately, I agreed to go with him because I was anxious to live in a new city and have fun with my brother, and I would only be a short drive from my youngest brother Ben at Notre Dame. I told him I would move with him and began to pack my bags for Indy.

Me, Tyler, and Ben at the local pool

After Tyler and Ben won the high school
state championship in basketball

Greg and Rustin during a high school cross country meet

Greg playing with his high school teammates

Neville and Greg at Mizzou track practice

Greg, Tyler, and Ben while in college

Greg during Hospital Hill Run half marathon

Greg during Little Rock half marathon

Greg in UNC basketball weight room

Big Top, Greg, and Shifty after Cloudsplitter 50k

Kevin, Greg, and Remus before Virgil Crest

Remus, Uncus, Greg, and Kevin after a
trail run in Carolina North Forest

Greg's grandfather

Indy

As my mom drove me to the airport, I could tell she was going to have trouble without me there, as I had been living with her for a couple years and we had been strongholds for each other. During good and bad times, we had helped each other and had become very close. When we reached the airport, I hugged my mom, told her I loved her and held her as she cried in my arms. I was a little sad as well, but my mind was filled with wonder about what it would mean to live in a big city. I could meet lots of new people, get back to running, and indulge in a city lifestyle. I could see myself walking through the tall buildings, making a large number of friends, and moving to the faster pace of an urban environment.

While Tyler and I had always been close, I knew that living with somebody can cause strain on a relationship. I thought of the fights we had as kids and all the times we used to get mad at each other growing up. But I also remembered how much fun we had hanging out in Chapel Hill and how I felt more comfortable with him than anyone on the planet. As I left the airport with my brother, I felt relaxed and excited at the same time.

Tyler told me there was room in the garage for a ping-pong table. We looked at each other and grinned in agreement that we definitely needed one for the house. We went straight to Dick's Sporting Goods and found a ping-pong table, paddles, and balls. All the apprehensions I had about putting strain on our relationship by living together were put to ease with that purchase. We were not boys growing up together trying to establish ourselves as cooler or tougher than each other, we were simply brothers excited about living together and being able to enjoy being ourselves. On the drive home, we laughed at the ludicrousness of buying a table before unpacking, but that was us, we knew we loved playing ping-pong and could not wait to indulge in our brotherly passion for table tennis and other activities together. These passions had been built through years of playing games and being in each other's lives. They included ping-pong, chess, milkshakes and ice cream, and the same TV shows. We shared a long list of inside jokes and stories that we had accumulated through the years. As we drove home, I felt at ease.

My thoughts then began to wander to our new house. As we drove into the downtown, Tyler turned onto our street and drove toward a gated community that looked nothing like the rest of the downtown area. He pulled out a remote control and opened the gate. Once we passed through the gates, we entered a place that seemed to be a piece of upper class dropped in the middle of the downtown. Beyond the gates, the concrete sprawl ended and was replaced with manicured lawns and three-story houses that would be expected in a nice suburban neighborhood. As we pulled into the driveway of a three-story house, I thought we might be sharing it with another group of people. Tyler told me this was our house and no one else lived here. He found it through the Pacers' network. After parking in the driveway, we unloaded the box with the table in the garage and agreed that it would stay there so that we could turn the garage into a ping-pong battleground.

As I walked into the house, I went into a nice kitchen that contained a beautiful electric rangetop, black stone counters, a huge fridge, and a sink. The kitchen opened into a small dining room with a four-person table, chairs, and wooden floors. I looked right from the kitchen and saw a bedroom with a bathroom, small closet. The walls of the kitchen were a beautiful golden color with a door that opened into a small breezeway. Looking at the door, I began to imagine myself starting my runs from that door and sneaking back into the house without waking my brother.

I quickly unloaded my bags in my new bedroom and walked around looking at the house. The small dining room opened into a white-carpeted living room complete with a gas fireplace. Off to one side was a stairway leading to the two upper floors. As I walked upstairs, I noticed a loft area just past the staircase with a large couch, huge lazy chair, and a TV on a dark wood entertainment center. I lay on the couch and felt myself sink into the cushions. It was the most comfortable couch I had ever sat in and I knew this area was where I would spend most of my time.

Tyler walked out of his bedroom, which was down a short hallway from the loft, and asked what I thought of the place. I told him it was great and that I loved the couch. He immediately sank into the huge lazy chair, putting his feet up on the matching foot rest and we both slipped into a nap.

***

The next day, some guys from Dick's showed up to put together our ping-pong table. I decided to look around the city. Tyler told me there was a nice area just outside our subdivision called the Canal where a lot of people ran. I laced up my running shoes and decided to search out the Canal and explore a few running routes from the house.

I walked down the hill through the neighbor's yard and ended up on a concrete sidewalk that ran along a canal, which cut through the city and was originally supposed to connect to the Eerie Canal, but was never completed. I started running in one direction and decided to turn around when I felt tired. As I ran, I noticed there was a little coffee shop just past my subdivision with outdoor seating and sun umbrellas. I mused on what it would be like to eat there and made up my mind to try it before too long. I saw an old stone bridge and a large business building, passed the lower level of a hotel, and interrupted some ducks. I passed a really large, gold-colored clock outside a huge building that, upon further inspection, turned out to be a museum. The path started going up a small ramp. I felt my legs getting tight running up the small hill and decided I did not want to risk getting lost in the city. I turned around and ran back to the house. I reached the breezeway door, went into my room, and cleaned up after my first run in my new city.

Once Tyler made it home, we agreed it was time to throw down on some ping-pong. We entered the garage and saw the newly assembled ping-pong table folded in the corner. We moved the table to one side of the garage, unfolded it, then started battling each other game after game. While we were in a new city and we were both in different parts of our lives, playing ping-pong in that garage felt like home for me. It felt like I was back in the basement of our house in Poplar Bluff, battling my brother as children. Tyler would try his best to slam shots past me on the table and I would surprise him by returning a few shots he did not expect me to hit. We played for hours and as we played, I felt the stress and worries about my future, not finishing college, and being unemployed drift away.

The next few days, I played a lot of ping-pong and I was a little sore from battling in the garage. We played probably four or five hours of ping-pong each day. We were both getting better; Tyler was now slamming almost every shot and I was able to return the majority of the shots. We both seemed to realize we were getting pretty good playing each other.

A few days later, Tyler had to go to training camp for the upcoming season, which meant that during the morning hours, I would be left to my own devices and with no one to play ping-pong. I had the bright idea to walk into the downtown and take a look at my new city by myself. After about two hours of looking around the town, I found a mall and looked through it for a few minutes. I noticed that the people in Indianapolis were not as friendly as people in North Carolina. It seemed everyone was in a rush to get somewhere and I was the only person in town taking time to look around and enjoy things. After looking through the mall, I decided I should get home to meet my brother. That's when I realized I had no idea how to get back to the house. I did not even remember the street we lived on. I wandered in a general direction that I assumed was toward the house, venturing down one street after another until I finally ended up in front of the entrance to our neighborhood. I flopped on the couch for a few minutes before I heard the garage open.

As soon as Tyler walked in, I could tell he was tired even though he laughed when I told him about getting lost. We went to dinner, and once we were home, I challenged Tyler to a game of ping-pong. He was tired, but we had a few vicious rounds before heading back up to the loft area, which we had dubbed the "den," to relax and watch TV. After a couple shows, Tyler asked if I wanted to go get some Little Debbie cakes. Of course I was not going to say no to the greatest brand of snack cake ever invented, so we headed to the store for treats. I started throwing Zebra Cakes, my high-school favorite, into the cart, but Tyler looked at me like I was crazy and said, "Dude! Get swiss rolls." We loaded up with four boxes of swiss rolls and a half gallon of milk. When we got home, we ate a box of swiss rolls each and drank most of the milk. As we lay there in a sugar coma with grins on our faces, I knew that living with my brother was going to be a lot of fun.

After a few days filled with ping-pong, swiss rolls, and me finding my way around the city, we began to incorporate chess into our list of games. These chess matches would usually happen after we had played a lot of ping-pong and were making the transition from dinner to our swiss roll dessert in the den. These were the most intense chess matches the world had ever seen as we both drew upon our competitive natures to try to win each match. They took a turn for the slightly strange when I discovered Tyler and I both had extra-large bathrobes with hoods on them. I was sure that I had seen a cover on a chess game featuring hooded chess grandmasters pitted in competition. This meant we had to wear our robes when we played chess. Every time we sat at the dinner table to play our games, we walked down the stairs with our hoods up over our heads and I was certain we looked like majestic chess grandmasters.

I was having a blast with this new routine. But it would all be put on hold, because the basketball season was beginning. It started off slowly. Tyler would leave for pre-season road trips and I would be left to handle the city of Indianapolis by myself. I was also quietly scheming about how to gain an advantage against my brother in ping-pong. At this point, my morning routine included hitting a ping -pong ball against the wall of the half-folded table two hundred times before breakfast. But I was still having trouble winning games in the garage. I discovered there was a table tennis facility across town that opened every evening for a few hours. I planned to go to the facility, improve my skills by playing there regularly, and establish myself as a top player at the facility. With this practice, I planned to dominate the garage ping-pong table.

With Tyler on a road trip, I could go to this facility and beat the other players to improve my skills. Since I had been playing for hours in the garage against my brother, I expected to be one of the best players in the facility as soon as I walked through the doors. I mean, Tyler and I were at the point now that we were hitting it almost as hard as we could each time we swung the paddle. Our games were so intense that it was rare we were not covered with sweat by the end of our daily battles. These guys at the table tennis facility were about to be introduced to a ping-pong force they had never seen in their lives.

After driving across town, I walked into the table tennis facility and noticed it smelled a lot like the boxing gym from Poplar Bluff. It had a dank smell of dried sweat, concrete floors, and a row of about ten ping-pong tables with dividers between each table. There was enough room behind and beside each table to allow the players to move as much as they needed in order to return a shot. After paying my admission fee, I challenged a woman who I thought would be an easy first match to gain a little respect from the other players in the facility. I noticed the game on the table beside me had two guys hitting incredibly hard shots and they were both standing about six feet away from the table. The game on the other tables were equally intense, but I had confidence that they had not played in matches as intense as the garage battles that I had with my brother. I was looking forward to gaining the respect of the people at this facility.

The first game lasted almost half an hour. I was hitting my shots as hard as I could to her and she was returning them confidently as we battled for each point. I finally won by a very narrow margin. The next person I played beat me by more than ten points, so I played a different person and won by one point. The last game I played was against a different woman and she beat me pretty badly. I was exhausted by the end of these games. I had been there for three hours and was covered with sweat.

Tyler called me after his game and I told him all about the facility. He was excited to check it out with me as soon as he got back from his pre-season game. I could tell from his voice that he expected to win every game the same way I had when I first walked in the door, only to find myself humbled by the table tennis players in the facility.

As we entered the table tennis facility the next night, I noticed that the women I had beaten were not there and the players at the tables all looked even more intense than the previous night. I challenged a lady I thought I might beat, but was quickly and succinctly beaten, badly, without even coming close to gaining a victory. I looked over and saw Tyler jumping all over the table and losing point after point. It seemed each game I played was against the best player I had ever seen. I did not win a single game.

Our battles in the garage became even more intense, as we were now focusing these games to prepare for the facility. We hit the ball as hard as we could each time and after a few days, we thought we were ready to go back and win a few games.

We returned to the table tennis facility and played with extreme focus and intensity. I was now scrambling to return every shot. I scored even less this time than my last visit. After three hours and the toughest games I had ever played, I saw Tyler walking toward me ready to leave. As I walked out of the facility, I was pissed that I had not won a single game. Tyler had the same look on his face. As soon as we got in the truck, he asked me how many games I won. I told him I did not win a single game. I asked him how many he won and he replied, "Not a one," in a tone that evidenced the same frustration I experienced that night. Neither one of us said another word on the drive home. This was the last time we went to the ping-pong facility, as we realized we did not want to devote a large amount of our time to becoming table tennis players.

***

Once the regular season started, I went to the games and was treated like a king. I received a special pass and was able to go to a room reserved for family members. This room had a catered dinner, waiters serving drinks and desserts, and cushy couches. I was loving this life-style and meeting family members of the players with whom I enjoyed talking.

During the day, I was bored and walked through the town looking for a place to hang out. I slept late, ate well, and became accustomed to napping in the after-noon. I was becoming closer to my brother than I ever had before and it felt good. He and I had already been close and our living together made it incredibly fun.

Since I had a lot of time during the day, I decided that I should continue my attempt to get my degree. I signed up to retake the Spanish course I had taken a year ear-lier at UNC, this time online. This meant that during the day, I would walk around town looking for Hispanic people I could practice with for my class. I found con-struction workers who spoke Spanish and talked with them as I walked throughout the city. I would take the new concepts we learned in the online class and immediately practice them with the construction workers. I was even able to incorporate my studying into my lavish family-of-the-NBA spoiling during games, as I discovered that a player's wife spoke fluent Spanish. Every time I saw her in the family room, we would speak a little bit in Spanish and she would correct me on issues I was having with the language. Between the construction workers and the family room, I was experiencing a lot of success with my online Spanish class.

Even with my class and studying, I still had a lot of free time on my hands and was starting to suffer from a weak bank account.

There was a gym I had been going to for a few weeks. It was about a mile-and-a-half walk from our house. I would walk there, sneak into the weight room, and work out three times a week. The second week I was caught by the people at the front desk. As I attempted to talk my way out of trouble (or into a free membership, depending on my luck), the membership consultant came over from her office and introduced herself. She told me her name was Lisa. I thought I was in huge trouble and would not be able to come back to the gym. During our conversation, she asked if I was related to Tyler. When I said yes, she told me that I could get a day pass from her anytime I wanted. I then went to the gym almost every day and enjoyed lifting weights there. I also became friends with Lisa, and stopped and talked with her almost every time I came to the gym. At first, I talked with her so I could get into the gym for free, but the more we talked, the more I came to consider her a friend. When my birthday rolled around, Tyler got me a membership to NIFS, the gym I had been sneaking into, as a present. It was the best present I could ask for, because now I did not have to time my gym visits to the times Lisa was working. I also would not have to feel like I was taking advantage of her kindness.

I discovered there was an early morning basketball group that met to play on Monday and Wednesday mornings. This group of morning basketball players reminded me of the group I had loved playing with in Poplar Bluff. It was obvious that they had all played against each other for years and had developed friendships through their morning basketball sessions, much like the group in Poplar Bluff. I was the new guy on the court, but considered them to be my friends after a couple weeks. The only reason I ever missed playing with this group was if there was a home game the night before because I was usually out late those nights. My basketball skills were coming back quickly. Within a week, I was able to play better than I had in high school. I was shooting jump shots, making hook shots, and establishing myself as one of the better players in that group. After these games, I usually walked back home. A few times, the weather was so poor that I would bum a ride from one of the guys I had played against. He would drop me off in front of the gate to the neighborhood on his way to work.

By now I knew all the gym workers by name, and was enjoying becoming an athlete again. For all of these reasons, NIFS was the first place I applied when I started looking for work. Heather, the lady who worked with the Pacers' families, told me she would talk to them about a job. I was happy about that and waited to hear back from her or NIFS. During one of the games, she told me that she had talked to the NIFS people and they did not have a position for me, but she asked if I was interested in working security. I thought security would be fun, since I could pretend to be a badass all day.

A couple days later, I met Joe, the owner of the security company, at one of the games. Joe had the look of a professional security guy. He was about my height, but he was a very thick and meaty guy with a shaved head, small goatee, and an all-business demeanor with just a hint of humor behind his serious eyes. After he introduced himself, he told me to swing by the office the next afternoon to talk about the job.

His office was just down the street from the house, so I walked a few blocks to his office. As I entered his office, I expected our talk to be an incredibly formal interview, and walked into his office expecting stuffiness. I was pleasantly surprised when we held a lighthearted conversation about our lives. He told me about his kids and I told him about my life with running and living with my brother, among other topics. This interview felt more like talking with an old friend than a future boss. After talking a few minutes, he told me I should go to training that night and then invited me to eat lunch with him. We ate lunch in the diner on the first floor of the building. I met some of his coworkers and was amazed how much fun I had talking with the other guys who worked security. They all seemed to have the same no-nonsense attitude, but they all used that demeanor to create great deadpan jokes, showing that there was a humorous side to their hard exteriors.

That night, I went to training and learned techniques to properly handle people who were behaving poorly in a crowd. There was a former prison guard who taught us how to tell if a person were about to attack, how to defend ourselves, and ways to combat violent tempers effectively without letting the situation escalate into a fight. Near the end of the training, we practiced a few of the techniques on other guards in training. I accidently threw one of the moves too hard and bruised my partner's shoulder. But he took it like a champ. He was the brother of the guard positioned in front of the Pacers locker room. He told me his brother was going to make a lot of fun of him for that bruise.

The way the job worked was simple: The security company had a list of events at different venues around town. These venues hosted events and the administration decided how many guards each event needed to effectively provide security. Once that number was established, they started calling a list of possible guards for each event until they had all the guard positions filled for the week's events. If I did not feel like working an event, I simply told them I could not be there and waited for them to call me for another event. This gave me the freedom to work when I needed to and go to games when I wanted without worrying about missing work.

I discovered that event security was a feast or famine business. Some weeks I worked three nights a week, others I did not have any work. One week there were very few events, so I decided to make the drive to visit my brother Ben in South Bend.

Driving from Indianapolis was a short hour-and-a-half drive that passed quickly because of my anticipation. I was going to get to hang out with Ben for a few days! I had not been able to visit my youngest brother much since I had moved to North Carolina and was looking forward to being around him. I'd missed his sense of humor, tough guy persona, and Type-A personality. While Tyler and I are extremely alike, Ben and I were also quite similar and I loved that he was one of the most intense people I had ever met.

As soon as I walked in the door, Ben wrapped me up in a huge hug and told me he was glad I was up to visit for a few days. I noticed immediately that his apartment looked like the typical college apartment. There was a large cushioned couch, a door with a hole in it, a kitchen that looked to have never been used, and a TV in the living room.

Over the next few days, Ben and I went to a haunted house, shot baskets, and hung out with his teammates. I felt as though I was back in college again, without the rigors of taking any classes. Ben had a much more active social life than I did in Indianapolis. After that first visit, I felt like I knew his friends and Notre Dame teammates decently well. I was happy that my youngest brother was enjoying his last year in college. He was making good grades, was friends with almost everybody, and always seemed to have something going on.

The last day of that visit, Ben had a game. I had grown accustomed to taking naps on the couch in the locker room during their practices. After many practices, I would rebound for Ben and was amazed how quickly and intensely he worked during these post-practice shooting sessions. It was as if nothing in the world existed to him except these workouts. Needless to say, I loved watching him in these workouts on the practice gym.

About an hour before the game, Ben asked if I wanted to play him in a game of horse. Horse is a classic shooting game where one person shoots the ball while the other watches. If the first player makes the shot, the watching player must duplicate the shot or they get a letter. If the first player does not make the shot, the second player starts shooting, and if the second player makes a shot first, the first player gets a letter. Every missed shot earns the player a letter until the word "horse" is spelled and the player loses. This was one of my favorite games, as I had learned certain trick shots that most people could not do. So, when Ben asked if I wanted to play, I was excited because I knew I had a good chance to win. I do not think Ben knew I had been playing basketball in Indianapolis. I shot the ball extremely well and almost won the game. Near the end of the game, Ben jokingly threw the ball hard against the backboard making it bounce back to him at the free throw line without the ball touching the rim. We both laughed and the pressure of the game seemed to lift from his shoulders in his joking shot attempt.

The rest of his teammates were trickling onto the court for a pregame shoot around. I sat in a chair on the side of the court and watched Ben shoot with his teammates. He was laughing and smiling more than I had ever seen him before a game. It seemed that joking throw had allowed him to relax a little and not be as intensely focused on the game. He looked at me and continued his lighthearted goofiness by throwing another shot off the backboard. As soon as the ball left his fingers, the head coach walked out of the locker room and saw him joking around. He called the team into the locker room for pregame. As soon as Ben saw the coach walk out, I saw his demeanor instantly change from his goofiness back to his intense game focus. I could tell he did not want his coach to think he was taking the game lightly. I could not help but laugh at him getting caught goofing off.

Ben played great that game and I sat in the front row watching and loving every moment. It was obvious he was playing better basketball than he ever had in his life. Near the end of the second half, he got on a fast break and jumped to throw down a windmill dunk. As he brought the ball in a full circle around his body, he cocked his arm back to throw down a hard dunk and hit the front of the rim with the ball, completely missing the dunk. All of his teammates immediately erupted in laughter. After missing that dunk, Ben started laughing and walked to the bench shaking his head in laughter. As he sat in his chair, I saw him look at me and shake his head. That look told me that Ben was happy and enjoyed being around his teammates, which made me smile.

After the game, we both laughed about him getting caught goofing off and his missed dunk as we drove to meet his teammates to celebrate winning the game. The next morning, I drove back to Indianapolis after breakfast with a huge smile on my face from spending time with my brother and seeing him with his friends.

***

Once back in Indy, I eased into a routine of playing basketball, lifting weights, studying, and going to watch Tyler play. While this may seem like a good routine, there were a lot of hours where I had nothing to do and sat around the house bored and looking for some fun. On the days I did not play basketball, these were long hours when I needed an outlet. I looked forward to going to watch Tyler play every night, but the more I went to the games, the more I felt out of place among the NBA crowd.

I began to feel as though I were living in a solar system that revolved around my brother Tyler. When he was in college, I had received some publicity about him, but always had a life that was completely separate from what he was doing. I had been working with the track team at Mizzou and training for marathons. When we were together, we were brothers and it was great, we allowed our brotherly instincts to run wild with each other by playing chess, binge-eating on swiss rolls, and playing ping-pong. But once we were apart, it seemed like everyone in the community was only talking with me in order to get to know Tyler. I felt no one was really my genuine friend, but instead just sports fanatics trying to gain a glimpse of my brother's personality through interacting with me.

While this was the way I felt most places, there were a few exceptions and those people became my good friends in Indy. There were a few neighbors who treated me like a real friend and seemed uninterested in getting to Tyler through me. Rob, an attorney, was a strongly built man with heavy features and a body that showed he was an athlete. He always came over and hung out with us, playing ping-pong, joking around, and drinking beer, and he became a real friend to me. He even took me to play basketball with him once.

The other neighbors lived across the street and they were the nicest elderly couple I had ever met. They walked their dog, and would stop and talk to me almost every day. They loved the city and seemed to have a new story for me about the town every time we talked. They also brought me a giant cupcake for my birthday.

But once I stepped past the gate to our subdivision, I would introduce myself to people and during conversation, I would mention something about Tyler and they immediately wanted to know all about him. I felt as if I were only significant because I was Tyler's brother. While Tyler was on road trips, I stayed in the house most of the time. I slowly felt more and more as though I were no longer living in my own world, but was simply a figure in my brother's.

But when Tyler and I were together, we were just two normal brothers and I could relax. I wasn't just another figure in his world, we were brothers having fun together. As soon as he left on a road trip, I was once again alone in his world. Until a friend from my Mizzou days contacted me.

Michael, the teammate who had first gone cycling with me, sent me a message telling me he was coming through Indianapolis for a few days with his job and asked if he could stay at my place. I was pumped that one of my Mizzou friends was going to be hanging out with me for a few days.

In conversation, Mike told me his job was based in Indy and he would be in town a lot with work. I told him he was welcome to stay at our house whenever he came through. Every time he came into town, my spirits lifted and I had my own world back. I enjoyed hanging out with an old friend and we became closer. He had a charisma that attracted more friends, so we would go to a bar in town and by the end of our beers, he and I would have flirted with a large number of women. He was also still a runner, and every time he shared a story about running, I felt a little tug at the running strings of my heart. After his influence, I would feel a renewed flame for running fire up and go for a run through town.

Every time Mike came to town, it felt nostalgic. He was one of the few people who had seen me during my passionate running days. He had been there when I was completely engulfed in the world of track and field and training hard for my marathons. He had been training to be the best runner he could during that time also. I had a piece of my former life as a runner back and all the old memories came back with it. Every time he came to town, I felt myself reverting to the person I had been at Mizzou. Small flickers of passion would flare to life then fade. I would wake up, go for a run through town, then not run the rest of the week. One morning, I ran through the snow for ten miles, then met Mike for dinner. With Mike around, I I had my own world instead of just being a piece of my brother's.

The more Mike visited, the more he got to know Tyler. Before long, a piece of my Mizzou world had met my family. Mike went to a few basketball games with me. We yelled together when Tyler got in the games. Mike met some of the NBA family members I knew and it seemed my good friend was permeating two of my current social groups. This made me want to get back to my old running days even more.

I tried to run every day for a week and felt my old foot injury flare back up. I was reduced to my old limping ways. I tried to push through the pain, but found myself hurt more and more until my foot refused to work because of the pain. No longer could I play basketball in the mornings, no longer could I go for runs through the city, and now even walking caused me to hurt again. I realized the injection I had to my foot had worn off and all the pain from my foot injury was on its way back. I would still drive up to visit my brother Ben and hang out with his friends, pushing myself through the pain to keep this sense of closeness with him. I now knew most of his teammates and felt comfortable with them socially. I was also relaxed with the friends I had made with the other NBA families, and was still hanging with Mike every time he came into town.

***

One week, I flew back to Chapel Hill to visit my mom for a few days. While I was in town, I went back to the foot doctor who had saved me from foot pain for months. Unfortunately, he was not available, but his wife, who was also a doctor, told me she would see me. After giving her a rundown of things I was experiencing with my foot, she told me she would inject it, but that once again, it would be a temporary fix. She then advised me to stop running so far. She told me I was going to have terrible arthritis when I was older and that I needed orthotics. She offered to refer me to someone that could make orthotics for me in Indianapolis, but I balked at that suggestion, believing I could strengthen my foot on my own. Plus, there was no way I could afford orthotics.

Boy, was that assumption ever wrong. The injection I had just received in Chapel Hill wore off in about three weeks. I tried to do everything I could think of to strengthen my foot. I did whatever drills my dad suggested and hobbled around in barefoot shoes. My foot pain just continued to get worse.

At this time, another old friend contacted me.

Kyle had been my best friend through grade school and being roommates in college only strengthened our friendship. Through the years, our banter always kept me in a relaxed mood and made me laugh. So when he contacted me and told me he was coming through town, I insisted he stay with me.

Kyle, his brother Kevin, and a work friend of his pulled into the driveway and I showed them the house, telling them they would have the basement to themselves that night. I immediately relaxed and told jokes. I made an incredibly inappropriate remark about strippers and binge drinking to Kyle, Kevin, and the third guy. Kyle and Kevin erupted with laughter and proceeded to tell me that James, the third member in their group, was a preacher. This only elicited more laughter from everybody.

I took them to a bar and we caught up over beer and dinner. With Kyle there, I was myself again, hitting on women, listening to his remarks, and hearing about what they had been up to since the last time we hung out. After dinner we went to the store and loaded up on junk food so we could watch the Super Bowl together in the house. While the game was a bit of a letdown, hanging out with my friends was incredibly uplifting for me. We told old stories and new stories about our lives the whole night.

The next morning Kyle left early and as he drove away, I felt my insecurities rush back about not having my own life. When Tyler was in town, I had a blast hanging out with him. We were still up to our normal shenanigans of ping-pong, chess, and bowling, a game we'd just added to our repertoires. I knew Tyler was not the reason I felt I did not have my own life, so I did not want him to know that I felt insecure about living with him. We had become so close living together in Indy that he had become my best friend on top of being my brother. I knew telling him I felt as though I were just a planet in his orbit would make him feel awkward by opening his eyes to my insecurities. He had become the person I cared about more than anyone in the world. And each time I visited Ben, I felt myself growing closer to him in the same type of way. I had an incredible closeness to both of my brothers, but I could not tell them how I felt.

Near the end of the regular season, not having a life of my own finally became too much to handle. I told Tyler I wanted to move back to Chapel Hill. He wanted me to stay, and there was no one in the world I liked hanging out with more than him, but I felt the need to get my own life.

No matter where I go or what I do, he will always be a piece of me. But I wanted to create my own solar system instead of completely orbiting around him. As I drove back to North Carolina, I felt my soul lift as I reflected on the good times I had with my brothers. My heart filled with joy as I realized that I was closer to my brothers than anyone else in the world and was proud to have gained such a close relationship with them.

Trailheads

Once back in Chapel Hill, I made a few new goals for myself. First, I needed to find a job, and second, I needed to find my own place. I wanted to get some independence from living with my mom. Once this was done, I wanted to slowly finish my degree through an online degree program. I also wanted to get back to being a runner.

I found a part-time job working as the front desk attendant for a local gym. The manager of the gym told me there would be opportunities for a full-time position in the future if I worked part-time. As a full-time employee, I would be able to afford my own place, and begin to settle into a nice lifestyle.

Working part-time allowed me to ease back into my old lifestyle of lifting weights in the UNC weight room. I fell in with the UNC basketball weight room crowd again. This time, I was trying to heal my foot so I could start back to running regularly. I asked Jay and other people in the weight room for advice to get my foot better. It seemed no matter what exercises they tried to get me to do, my foot stayed the same. I began lifting with increased vigor and tried a lot of the new exercises the basketball players were doing as I gained a type of tough-love friendship with the weightlifting group once again.

I began running again as well, but it was difficult because my foot would scream in pain each step. I then tried riding my bike again only to find that after a little while, even riding it caused my foot to hurt. Then, one day, Chris, the trainer for the basketball team, told me to stop by his office so he could fit me for an orthotic.

Orthotics are customized supports for people with joint problems. They can be inserted into a shoe to support the foot of the wearer in the manner they need in order to walk. I felt like a pansy. I thought orthotics were for weaklings or at best normal people, not alpha males. But I was beyond desperate to get my foot better, so I told Chris I would see him in the morning.

That next morning, I walked into the basement of the student health building to find Chris waiting for me with a cheerful smile on his face. I explained to him how I had hurt my foot years ago at soccer camp. He placed my foot on a warm mold and began fashioning a mold for my foot that would support my arch. Once he got my foot molding, he disappeared into a back room. I sat on a chair in the open area of the physical therapy department and heard noises coming from the small room Chris had disappeared into. I heard a hair dryer, then a belt sander. It seemed as though Chris had hopped into his laboratory. When he came out of the room with the orthotic and I slid it into my shoe, I immediately felt my foot pain begin to lessen. I walked around the open air space and felt a welling of emotion as the foot pain that had plagued me for years began subsiding with every step. Except, the more I walked, the more I felt my foot being pushed too far out of place. I told Chris what I felt and he nodded, took the orthotic out of my shoe, and disappeared into his laboratory once again. I heard more belt sanding, and then he reappeared with the orthotic and asked me to try it. That first step in the revised orthotic felt like heaven. My foot felt amazing as I took my first pain-free steps in years. I continued to walk around the area and felt my heart swell with joy as each step yielded a painless stride. I walked all the way outside and still experience the same easy, natural stride. As I walked back in the door to Chris's office, I was beaming from ear to ear. I was finally free from foot pain! After years of foot pain, I realized the best way to improve myself was to admit to my own mortality and ask for help when I needed it.

After a couple days of testing out the orthotic to see if it were too good to be true, it was time to go for a run and give it a real test. As I began my run from the Dean

Dome up the hill, I expected my pain to return on one of my strides, but I was pain free the entire two miles. I finished my run with a huge smile on my face. I could finally get back to being a runner. After I finished my run, I went into the weight room to lift weights and was simply beaming with joy. I felt the embers of passion begin to slowly glow in my soul again. Now that my foot pain was gone, I could get back to my former lifestyle. In short, I was back. After finishing my workout, I saw Chris in the training room. I shook his hand and expressed my gratitude for him building my orthotic from the bottom of my heart.

***

After a few weeks of running, I was slowly starting to rebuild my endurance. I built up to six miles comfortably before thinking it was time to go check up on the group I had run with before moving to Indiana.

A bunch of the mentors from my Fleet Feet group had created a running group called the Blazing Soles and I was going to try to start running with them once I found time. I started tossing around the idea of running with the group that had guided my Fleet Feet group through the woods. The group that seemed to have a personality and mythology all its own that drew me to show up one morning for a run.

After looking on the Trailhead website, I learned that the group met every Wednesday morning at 7:00 and Saturday morning 7:30 in Wilson Park. Thinking this

group would be exactly like every other group of runners I had ever known, I loaded up on running gear
and dusted off my knowledge of past runs to try to
dazzle the group with my knowledge. I also thought
that, given the group's reputation for being incredible
ultra-runners, there would be a lot of people show up
early to prepare for the Saturday run.

I gleefully jumped out of my truck as soon as I got to
the parking lot a half hour early and saw no one. A few
people ran through the parking lot and I asked if they
were Trailheads. They laughed and shook their heads
as they went by into the woods. I was about to give up,
but decided to wait until 7:30 before going home. As
soon as my clock turned over to 7:30, the parking lot
was suddenly full of cars zooming into parking spots.
Everybody jumped out of their cars, smiling and greeting one another. We talked in a circle for about twenty
seconds before venturing into the woods for a run.

In that twenty-second introduction, I met guys with
names like Grub, Hodag, Kerndog, and Galoot.
Everyone was cheerful and there was no shortage of
hearty laughter. Once we ran into the woods, this same
hearty sense of humor continued as we went down a
trail. While everyone else was laughing, telling stories,
and having a grand ol' time, I was scrambling behind
them to keep up. Hodag slowed to run with me.

Hodag was an older man with gray hair, a white mus-
tache, the stocky yet muscular build of an athlete, and
a boyish gleam in his eye. As we ran, he told me stories

about the group, how it started, why we were running to the Improv, what the Improv was, and how he got his trail name (it came from a book of fearsome creatures, as was customary in the beginning of the Trailheads running group).

He explained that the Improv was the outlet of a trail about two miles into the woods, where all the trailheads met during the group runs. I absorbed all this information while scrambling up and over roots and rocks and through mud trying to keep up with the older man. After running for what seemed like hours, we arrived at the Improv.

Once I reached it, I saw a large group of trailheads standing in a circle laughing and telling stories. Curiously, the small group from Wilson Park had grown to a much larger group since arriving at the Improv, but it still consisted of people with bright eyes and smiling faces, glowing with life. While these radiant features were welcoming to me as I gasped to catch my breath, I could not help but also notice that all the runners were in incredible athletic shape. Their well-shaped, muscular legs and thin builds loudly proclaimed them serious athletes beneath their lighthearted banter and goofing around. In accordance with Trailhead rules, I introduced myself to the group and told a pretty poor joke. As I spoke, I felt happy to be with such a great group of people. Once I finished my joke, I looked at the group nervously to see how my inappropriate punch line would be received. As the group erupted in laughter, I relaxed a little and was glad I had not offended anyone.

It was time to run back to the Wilson Park parking lot. Hodag told me he would run back with me and as I turned to follow in his footsteps, I saw that the majority of the group was heading out to run other trails that ventured further into the woods. I could not help but smile watching them all trot back into the woods like the mythical beings I had initially imagined them to be.

On the run back, Hodag treated me to hilarious stories and even more Trailhead lore. I heard his legendary "Onion joke"—which requires running at least two miles of trail to be told and involves a grocer using profanity with an elderly lady—as well as the names for the different trails. Once we crossed the bridge, I decided to try to run hard up the last hill to impress Hodag and gain a little respect from him and the group. As soon as I started to sprint, my lungs screamed for air and I could do nothing more than struggle up the hill way behind Hodag. That sprint took a lot out of me and I struggled to make it the last quarter mile to the parking lot.

Once Hodag and I reached our vehicles, he told me I should get coffee with the group at the Open Eye Café. He explained that the group always met there after group runs. After seeing their pleasant personalities in the woods, I was overjoyed to have another chance to hang out with the group I had just met. I changed shoes and followed Hodag's car to Open Eye.

I parked my truck in the dirt parking lot across the street from the Open Eye coffee shop and felt my imagination run wild with the things I might discover about the group. I was also happy to have found a group to hang out with that consisted of runners. The Open Eye Café is a large brick building with large windows making up most of the storefront, so people can see outside from the tables. As I opened the door to the coffee shop, I saw that the interior was an open area with small tables and a mismatched assortment of chairs scattered throughout with plenty of space for walking through the shop. There was a line of customers eager for coffee standing patiently in line. The baristas behind the counter were busy making coffee but still smiled at each other as they worked. I saw Hodag standing in line inviting me to join him. I stood with him in line and he pointed to the group at the far end of the shop sitting on three couches and chairs fashioned into a haphazard square. The Trailhead conversation was an underlying buzz in the coffee shop, occasionally broken up by laughs that bellowed from the circle. Hodag and I got our coffees and went to sit with the group.

Everyone in the group had a zest for life and cheery personality and seemed to be on the verge of laughter all the time. They introduced themselves to me by their trail names. I met Goofus, an older thin guy in sweatpants and a shirt with a hole, with a warm smile and a loud laugh. There was Spinz, a woman who told stories about hilarious situations and things she had seen in her life and as a social worker. Yellow Dog, a larger man who had a personality as charismatic as anyone I had ever met. Half-Dome was a man with a hearty laugh, an anecdote for every situation, and a mischievous grin that showed an affinity for creating controversy. Remus was another guy with an inviting personality that made me want to hear every word of his stories so I would not miss something funny. Everyone in the group all had their individual niches in the conversational flow. By the time I looked at my watch, I realized I had been immersed in conversation with the group for three hours. As I walked out of Open Eye, I felt my heart swelling with happiness.

Every day, I would leave work and head to the trails to run by myself; if I wanted to be a part of this new group and become a real trail runner, I needed to learn the trails. I also showed up for the group run on Wednesday morning.

The group on Wednesday morning had the same jovial disposition, but they ran much faster than the group on Saturday. I ended up just trying to keep some of the group in sight so I would not get lost in the woods. I finally struggled back to my truck after the run and drove to the coffee shop to hang out with the group. I found the same personalities drinking coffee and laughing that morning as well. I left the coffee shop again with a smile on my face. It was only my second time hanging out with the group, but I was 100 percent sold on becoming a Trailhead.

When I ran the trails solo after work, I would park my truck in the same parking lot and head out onto the trails. The first few days, I was lost and unsure of where to go, but enjoyed it thoroughly anyway. Every night all I could think about was the trails. I dreamed of dirt then woke up the next day and headed right back for another run. I ran with the Trailheads on Saturdays and Wednesdays and found that the more familiar I became with the group, the happier I was. I realized that the group was less about running and more about the friendships gained through a common love of the sport. This became clear to me on the first happy hour I attended with the group.

The Trailheads' happy hour took place every Friday in the summer, in the yard in front of Weaver Street Market. Weaver Street is a local store that serves as a cornerstone of the Carrboro community. The town of Carrboro is best described as Chapel Hill's hippie sister, and has a certain character that makes for great people-watching, particularly the hipsters walking around in their vintage garb. The granola lifestyle is everywhere. Weaver Street is one of the town's central meeting places, with picnic tables in the front lawn, open spaces between the tables, and no shortage of people meeting in front of the store. I showed up to the happy hour and was greeted by the laidback atmosphere I'd learned was the normal behavior of the group. No one was trying to one-up anyone else's accomplishments, they were just sharing common experiences from running adventures. I realized this group was not focused on a hierarchy of achievements, but simply enjoyed spending time together. It was at that happy hour I stopped trying to gain respect from the group and simply enjoyed being there. I watched Willow juggle her kids while attempting to maintain conversation with the group at the picnic table before eventually leaving to take her kids home. I sat at the table drinking beer from a communal jug being passed around the table. Chaser and Remus kept encouraging me to drink more beer and before I knew it, the entire jug was gone and the conversations had become incredibly inappropriate and riotous. I could not stop laughing. I made a few comments, but mostly smiled and enjoyed conversations with the group regardless of which direction the discussion led us.

Talks with Pawpaw

As my trail running began to pick up, my family was going through some new stages. My youngest brother Ben had graduated college and was getting ready for NBA training camps. Ben came out to Chapel Hill to work out with Tyler, prepare himself for camps, and spend time with our mom, Tyler, and me. Tyler had finished his second season in the NBA and was back in town for the offseason. After leaving my job at the gym, I started working as a cashier at a local grocery store, The Fresh Market.

Both of my brothers graduating from college made me feel self-conscious about my life. I once again felt as if I were the loser of the family, the brother who worked as a cashier and had not gotten a degree from college. I began to think, "Maybe this is all I can achieve, so I might as well begin trying to work my way up in the grocery store." I was disappointed about where I was in life, but began to think that this was where I belonged. I became used to the life as a cashier, I got used to being on my feet all day and helping customers out in the store. A few of the regular customers even became friends of mine.

Once I started running with the Trailheads, however, I found my identity in being a trail runner who only worked as a cashier as a way to support running on the trails. That became my mentality: I might not have my degree, but I was able to run in the woods, and that was good enough for me. At work, all I could think about was getting back to the trails and hanging out with the Trailheads again. When I was not at work or spending time with the Trailheads, I was with my brothers goofing off. It is always amazing to me how easily we slip back into our brotherly behaviors when we're all together. We have so many inside jokes and ridiculous conversations that there seems to be no end to our shenanigans. These jokes and conversations come from our shared experiences through the years, from laughing about family to referencing things experienced as kids, like playing intense games in the basement or inside jokes that we remember. There was the story about Tyler and Ben scaring me with a paintball gun and strobe light while I was asleep, and the boxing matches we held in the basement.

Being with my brothers is one of the joys of my life. We revert back to the way we behaved in college or at home in Poplar Bluff. We all three revel in competition and doing things just for the stories. We are so similar and yet so different at the same time. The bond I share with my brothers is something that means more to me than anything else in the world.

As we cruised through the summer, Ben was going to NBA training camps. We were all excited to see where he was going to play next season. A few days before the big NBA camp in Chicago, Ben went back to Kentucky to visit my dad. I called him a couple days before he went to Chicago to wish him luck and he told me he had sprained his ankle badly playing beach volleyball. My heart immediately sank. I felt sorry for him because he had trained so hard to do well at this camp. I wished him good luck and we hung up the phone.

On his sprained ankle, Ben had a tough time at camp. About a week later, the NBA draft was on TV. Ben did not get drafted by an NBA team. We all sat in silent disappointment, and I felt my heart sink deeper for Ben's misfortune. Just then, Ben received a phone call from Europe—he had been offered a deal to play in Germany! I heard his voice brighten as he told us he was going to Germany to play basketball. I was excited for my brother because he was going to go to Europe and it was nice to see him so happy after such a disappointing evening. We all smiled as we talked about his upcoming adventure to Germany.

A few days after the draft, Ben went to Poplar Bluff to hang out with his friends and train at home before heading to Germany. While he was in Poplar Bluff, he stayed with my grandpa. Ben told me he and Pawpaw, as we called him, were having a lot of fun talking and enjoyed each other's company. Pawpaw would later tell me how much he enjoyed having Ben around, but also how funny he was as a person. He would tell me how every day Ben asked him to make an omelet, and no matter how many times Pawpaw showed him how to make one, Pawpaw always found himself cooking an omelet for Ben. A few days before going to Germany, Ben came back to North Carolina for one last visit.

We hung out a lot during this visit since, as I said before, there is nowhere I would rather be than hanging out with my brothers. We all had a blast being together before Ben's new adventure. I wanted to spend a lot of time with him because I knew that I would not get to see him for a while. And when the time came, Ben left in his typical fashion.

We scrambled to get him to the airport in time for his flight. I had to throw his clothes in a gym bag for him before he and I rushed out the door to race him to the airport. Once we were cruising to on our way to the terminal, we talked about Pawpaw. Ben told me how much it meant to Pawpaw to have someone to talk to and that we should call him more often. Ben did not know it, but I then made a small commitment to myself to call Pawpaw everyday on my lunch break to keep him company. Once we arrived at the airport, I dropped him off at the departures section of the curb beside the entrance. I wanted to give Ben a hug and tell him how much I was going to miss him. But as I walked around to hug him, he told me he hated goodbyes, so instead of a heartfelt embrace, he playfully jabbed me in the chest and just said "Bye," as if I would see him in a few hours. I sat in my truck and watched him until I could no longer see him anymore. I was going to miss Ben.

***

The next day, I called Pawpaw on my lunch break from the grocery store. We talked for my entire break. I told him about the Trailheads and how much fun it was finding a new group of friends and he told me stories about times when he had found new groups of friends. We laughed, then talked seriously, and by the time I hung up the phone, I felt much closer to my grandpa. I never remembered my grandpa being so funny, but the conversation was entertaining and fulfilling. I was looking forward to calling him the next day on my lunch break.

That next day it was the same thing: I called Pawpaw, began talking, and away we went with our conversation. He would tell me stories about things he had done and seen, and I would tell him about similar situations in my life. I discovered that hidden in these stories were jewels of wisdom. One story he told me that day was about his time as an army doctor in Alaska. He was the only doctor who grabbed his rifle and stood with the enlisted men during air raid drills. He went on to explain that he was continually voted best doctor by the soldiers simply because he stood with them during these drills. I loved this story and filed it away in my mind. By the time I hung up the phone, I was again amazed at how much closer I felt to my grandpa as well as at the wisdom I'd gained from his experiences in Alaska.

I incorporated a lunchtime conversation with my grandpa into my daily routine. In the morning, I would go for a run, then get ready for work, call Pawpaw on my lunch break, then go home after work. Each day, I discovered a few new things about my grandpa that I did not know and I shared things with him he did not know. Every day I grew closer to him and discovered that my grandpa was quickly becoming my best friend.

The conversations I had with my grandpa always left me wiser than before we talked. I learned about how hard he had worked and the obstacles he had overcome to get to the position he was in life. I heard the funny stories he had gained along his journey as well. Through our talks, I came to understand that my grandpa was one of the most amazing men on the earth. I would ask him for advice occasionally during our talks and he always gave me incredibly objective advice about whatever I asked. Every time I followed his advice, things got better for me, I came to realize that the stories my grandpa shared showed an incredible use of intellect and discipline. I understood the things he valued most were the things he worked hard to obtain. My grandpa had worked incredibly hard to become a doctor. Along his journey, he discovered that he loved to learn, which is why one of his life passions was working with the local junior college in my hometown. I discovered he was the chairman of the board for Three Rivers Community College, the school I had attended after high school. I told him I'd had no idea he was the chairman of the board while I was there. He told me that was because he did not want me to know. He did not want me to think I would get special privileges because I was his grandson. Which was a good thing too, as when I was younger I would have probably tried to use that to get better grades.

One day, he told me he had asked some of the teachers at TRCC how well they thought I could do at a four-year university. They told him they thought I was capable of getting my degree. When I heard him say that, I explained to him my GPA troubles at Mizzou. I thought the TRCC teachers might be wrong. But then Pawpaw explained to me that the reason I did not finish my degree at Mizzou was because I was running too much to effectively study. I immediately fought those words in my mind, but after a couple hours of consideration, I realized he was right. I had been spending my time running instead of reading textbooks and writing papers. With his words, I realized running had been my priority and school was my hobby. This was an incredibly tough realization for me, because I remembered fondly my days at Mizzou and working with the track team. But each memory seemed to focus around running.

My routine of running, work, and talking to my grandpa went on for months. One lunch I was surprised by a question he asked me. I knew by now that anytime my grandpa needed to ask or say something to me, he began the conversation with his serious topic first. As I called Pawpaw that afternoon, like I had for months, he began the conversation by telling me that he and my aunt Ann had been talking and he wanted to pay for me to finish my degree. He told me that I could choose anywhere I wanted to go, I would have a monthly budget, and I would be going to school to study above all else. Getting my degree was going to be my job. He then asked what I thought of that deal. I told him I would love the opportunity and that I would let him know where I wanted to go the next day.

The rest of the day at work, my thoughts drifted through the prospect of going back to Mizzou and finishing my degree at the school I had started years ago. But each time I pictured going back to Mizzou, I envisioned the track team and my familiar running routes around Columbia; I could almost smell the mulch pit at an intersection of one of my favorite trails. Just as my thoughts of my Mizzou running days would dance through my head, I would hear my grandpa's words: "You will be going to school to study." I tried to think about studying in little nooks and corners of Ellis Library. I thought about the quiet reading room in the Life Sciences building with the loud air-conditioning system that made the room the quietest room on campus. Each time I saw myself in these locations, I would remember the feeling of trying to study for chemistry classes and getting poor grades for my efforts. After seeing myself in those study spots, my thoughts continually drifted toward rejoining the track team as the manager. As my daydream began to flow in my head, I again heard my grandpa's voice, cutting through my daydream of returning to Mizzou track: "You will be going to school to study." I realized returning to Mizzou would not be a wise decision because returning to the track team at Mizzou would be too big of a temptation for me to effectively study. I was going to make the most of this opportunity. I then started thinking about my success in the part-time classes I had taken at UNC and the great group I had found with the Trailheads.

I realized I was happy in North Carolina and I did not want to use more money than was necessary to finish my degree. I wanted to finish my degree at UNC. In Chapel Hill, I could live with my mom, instead of having to pay rent at an apartment complex that housed mostly college students who were motivated to party. While it was difficult at times to live with my mom, I had grown to enjoy her company and knew she was always on my side and wanted the best for me. That would not be the case with a college roommate in Columbia. The next day, I was not working. I called my grandpa on my way home from a run. Pawpaw answered the phone and I told him I wanted to finish my degree at UNC. I told him I liked it here. He told me to start figuring out what I needed to do to reenroll and finish my degree, then let him know what I needed him to do. As I hung up the phone, I began figuring out what I needed to do to get back in classes at UNC. I sent the Dean of admissions an email asking if I could sit down and talk with him about what I needed to do to become a full-time student.

Meeting with the Dean did not intimidate me because I had met him before when I started taking classes as a part-time student. He was a nice man who seemed happy to be in his position and whose love for his job came through when he talked. He understood that the things he does in admissions helps people to become successful while at the same time benefitting the university. He seemed very eager to help me in my goal to finish my degree. As we talked, the conversation felt more like a discussion among friends than a dean handing down strict provisions to the aspiring student under him. During the course of our conversation, he explained to me that I needed to take one more class as a part-time student in order to be considered for status as a full-time student. He then explained I would need to fill out a number of applications and meet with a few academic advisors after my last class as a part-time student. He told me that as long as my GPA was above a 2.5, I should not have any problem getting into UNC as a full-time student.

I set out the next day to sign up for the one class that summer in order to be ready to start as a full-time student in the fall. I met with an academic advisor and decided to take a drama course that summer. After learning all this information, I called my grandpa the next day and told him what I would need to finish my degree.

He asked me what I thought my budget per month should be and told me he was going to cover the tuition and books for me as long as I let him know how much they were going to cost. A few days later, I paid for my summer class, picked up my textbook, and began daydreaming about my return to student life.

Every day, I continued to call my grandpa on my lunch break. He told me to tell my manager at The Fresh Market my intentions to return to school. He also told me I should give them my two weeks' notice because I was going to start back to school shortly. I noticed that everyone I worked with at the grocery store seemed sad that I was going to leave. In the last two weeks with the store, I noticed a bunch of my coworkers would come to me wishing me good luck and telling me how much they enjoyed having me around. On my last day, they gave me a large gift basket filled with food as a goodbye present.

As the beginning of my summer class grew nearer, I began to shift my thinking to a student mindset. I wanted to make the most of the opportunity my grandpa was giving me, so I resolved to read every page assigned to the class, attend every class, and really give my best effort.

In my daily talks with Pawpaw he told me stories about his own collegiate experiences and the motivations he had had to excel in his coursework. He told me how the northern students considered him and his southern friends stupid because of their southern accents. He also described the looks on their faces when he continually received better grades in their classes. With each story of his success, he continued explaining the hard work he had put into receiving those grades. It was through these stories that I strengthened my resolve to study incredibly hard so that if I did not get my degree this time, it would not be from lack of effort. I was going to work hard just like my grandpa had when he was in college.

Back to School

With school getting ready to start in a few weeks, my mom kept pressuring me to take a test to see if I had any learning disabilities. I thought it would be a waste of time and told her there was no way I would take that test. In my mind, getting diagnosed with a learning disability would be the same as being told I was a mentally challenged person. Every time she told me to take the test, I envisioned my life after a diagnosis.

My mental image of a person with a learning disability was someone incapable of completing any academic work. I pictured someone kept in cold dark basements who spoke incoherently and scared people in social settings. I thought about the mentally handicapped people I had seen in public, working low-level jobs and making other people feel uncomfortable. It was my fear that taking this test was not a waste of my time. But I repeated to myself that I was not mentally handicapped; the reason I had not seen success in the classroom was because of my running, not because I was mentally incompetent. I had received a C average during my time at Mizzou, which proved to me that I was smart. In my mind, taking that test would be an admission that I might have a problem with my intellect.

But my mom kept pressuring me about the test. Finally, I was fed up with her hounding me. I decided to take the test and show her what a monumental waste of my time it would be. I was mad I had to take it, and I was going to show this psychiatrist I was the alpha male by crushing this test.

When I arrived in the psychologist's office, I was already pissed off about being there, so when he asked if I was ready to take the tests, I replied with a quick and slightly sarcastic "Yeah! Let's take it." I was determined to show this guy, along with my mom, that I was the alpha male and did not have a learning disability.

Over the next few hours, I took reading, writing, and math tests in the psychologist's office. I attacked each section with fury. I could not believe my mom thought I had a mental handicap! As I reached the section of the test dealing with math, I noticed that my ability to answer questions was quickly faltering and I was struggling with a lot of the problems. The reading section also gave me problems; I was scrambling to finish each reading section in the allotted time. But I crushed the writing section. By the time I finished the tests, I was exhausted mentally and a little nervous about what the tests would reveal.

Taking the tests made me feel vulnerable but I made up my mind that whatever the results were, I was going to accept them as correct and figure out what to do with the information.

A couple days later, I walked into the doctor's office and he explained to me that I scored well above average in writing, but severely low in reading and math. I asked him if these tests meant I was not capable of completing collegiate coursework. And this smug guy responded with, "I am impressed that you have completed as many courses as you have." I could not believe my ears. Maybe I did need to take special classes. My heart sank a little as I thought I might not be able to finish my degree. He told me I had slow processing speed and had a slight disability with math.

Once I got home, I showed my mom the test results, and explained to her how I had slow reading speed and a math disability. She already had the next phase of her plan devised. She told me to use these test results to apply to the university's disability office. I immediately balked, telling her I did not want to do that. I was afraid they would not let me take the classes I needed to get my degree.

But that night, as I lay in my room reflecting on the day, I realized that I wanted my degree no matter what

I had to go through to get it. If I had to be in special classes for disabled students for a while, I would—all I wanted was to get my degree.

The next day, I contacted a lady in the university's disability offices. Tiffany, the lady at the office, sent me an application and told me I needed to fax her the tests I took. Then a committee would review my tests and let me know if I were eligible for the services provided by her office. I quickly filled out the application and faxed her the test results. After submitting my tests, I was worried that I would be placed in a special basement classroom designated for mentally handicapped students. I shook that image from my head and resolved to accept whatever help I might need to complete classes.

While I waited for the committee to make a decision, I received a letter confirming my admission as a full-time student at UNC. Reading that letter of admission, I felt my heart leap; I was going to get to finish my degree in a town that I had fallen in love with. My head raced with images of myself studying all over campus. I was going to get back to being a college student instead of working forty hours a week on my feet.

The following week, Tiffany invited me to meet with her in her office to go over the services I could use for classes. As I entered her office, I saw that Tiffany was a lady close to my age with dark brown hair. As I sat in front of her desk, I noticed that she had a very warm smile as she told me that after reviewing my tests, the committee approved for me to get extra time on tests and I would be eligible to take a math substitution course instead of a traditional math class. She explained I would take the same tests as everyone else in class, but get extra time to take the tests in a quiet room. She also told me I could use a smart pen to take notes in class. I asked her what that was, and received an explanation of probably the greatest study tool ever devised.

With this pen, I could take notes and record lectures at the same time. I could then upload my notes, review my notes, and listen to lectures again. I asked how much it would cost to use it. She told me it was free to a full-time student. With this new tool and the extra time, I was going to give this college thing my best shot.

That visit to Tiffany's office taught me that the world was full of people with learning disabilities who were incredibly intelligent. My previous notion of what it meant to be a person with a learning disability was completely changed in that one visit. I began to see myself once again as an intelligent person thus preserving my alpha identity.

After leaving her office, I called my grandpa and told him about all the accommodations I was going to use to finish my classes. He told me that was great and reminded me that I still had to do the work required to pass the classes. Those words landed on the ears of someone ready to do the best he possibly could academically.

As soon as I walked through the door, I told my mom all about the accommodations I was going to use for my classes. She told me how happy she was for me and that she now wanted me to go see an academic coach to help me create a plan for managing my study time. I told her I would make an appointment the next day. I was beginning to see that my mom had my best interest in mind no matter how much I fought her advice. So I decided to go with her suggestions.

The next day, I made an appointment with an academic coach and went into his office. The coach looked the way I envisioned a stuffy Harvard professor would look, sitting in a room full of books and stacks of papers, wearing academic-looking round glasses, and seeming roughly groomed. He spoke with the easiness of a professional interested in helping me with my academic goals. When we talked about my interests, I told him about my running and that I was willing to quit running altogether if it would take away from my academic success. He told me that it would be best if I had other interests outside school so that I would not get burned out. He said that doing these activities would be good ways to take breaks from studying and allow me to return to my books with a refreshed mind. I thought, "Thank God!" I was not going to have to give up my running, but could use it as a study tool to reward myself for finishing my studies each day. I could still be a Trailhead and go to college! We created a daily study schedule for the semester. This schedule broke up my classes into individual study sessions each day; we even put a break in a the middle of a couple days so that I could go for a mid-day run! I liked this coach.

After hearing from the academic coach that he wanted me to continue my running, my mind returned to those early morning runs at Mizzou, and I was tempted into thinking that I could do that again here at UNC. Before my imagination was too carried away with this thought, I heard Pawpaw's words ringing in the background of my thoughts: "You are going to school to get your degree." I realized that school needed to be my main focus and running was going to be a fun side thing. This would be my last chance to earn a degree, and I did not want to mess up this opportunity.

The study schedule that I had created with my academic coach kept me busy studying for most of the day but never had me studying past five o'clock in the evening. I decided that everything in my life was going to have to revolve around this schedule until I finished each semester. Sticking to this schedule was going to be everything to me. I was not going to let anything come between me and academic success.

Once classes began, I began to keep my study schedule from the beginning of the semester. As soon as I received the syllabus for each class, I immediately started on the readings for the class during its allotted study time. With the knowledge of my slow reading speed, I decided to listen to a few online readings instead of reading them. I sat in the front row of almost every class diligently engaged in the lectures and participating in the discussions. I listened to the lectures each day after each class as my schedule had outlined. I was completely dedicated to this schedule and eased into a disciplined study routine every day. I met with teaching assistants and wrote papers little by little, during time allotted for the class's spot in my daily study schedule. I quickly noticed that I was succeeding in all my classes. And I was able to go for a short one-hour run three days a week as a break from my books.

I thought that I would not have time to talk with my grandpa with my study schedule, but started incorporating him into my study breaks. We talked about topics from my classes and I was amazed at the wisdom he gave me on a lot of the topics from each class. He seemed to have knowledge about almost everything I was learning. He was a huge help in my understanding of the material because he was a wise person to whom I could voice my thoughts on topics. A few times we laughed because I would call a professor out on issues I felt were untrue because of my life experiences. Pawpaw thought it was pretty funny that I called the teacher out on something he had written in his book. He also loved hearing about the grades I was getting in each of my classes.

I discovered that taking my tests with extra time allowed me to think about questions and formulate responses without feeling the pressure of a time constraint. I no longer settled for getting Cs in my classes; I wanted to get As on everything and only settled for Bs on a few things. The smart pen was the most useful thing I had ever seen for class; I would listen to lectures again each evening on my computer. I was amazed at everything I was learning and able to comprehend in each of my classes by keeping my study schedule. In keeping my study schedule and using my test accommodations, I no longer felt apprehension about taking tests or writing papers. I had developed confidence in my ability to complete collegiate coursework.

I continued to hang out with the Trailheads on the weekends. Each Saturday, I would head out the door to meet my friends in the woods then hang out at the coffee shop. The group provided a release from studying and an escape from the academic world. I could shut my brain down and participate in the group discussions that always ended with hilarity. The Trailheads allowed the stress of the week to lift from my shoulders. They had shifted from providing me with a social group to hang out with to a group that allowed me to relax and de-stress after the week was over.

By the end of this first semester of full-time classes at UNC, I was achieving my goals and felt incredibly comfortable with my daily schedule of studying, talking to my grandpa, and running. I finished that first semester with the best GPA I had ever had in college. The discipline I had used to be a runner at Mizzou had been transferred to my studying and it was showing. I knew that I was smart and that if I stayed disciplined, I could finish my degree with good grades.

Following that semester, I went back to Poplar Bluff for Christmas at my grandpa's house. The whole trip there, I was excited to get to spend time with him. I could not wait to share stories with him in person and to tell him how much I appreciated him helping me finish my degree. Once I was back in town, I was less interested in going out to visit my familiar hometown hot spots and more interested with spending time with Pawpaw. All we really did was watch TV and talk about everything from school to girls. And since the rest of my family was there, we all spent time together. It made my soul smile to see my grandpa enjoying the company of everyone in his house. I saw him beaming almost all day in the house filled with his sons, daughter, and their families. Everyone was interested in how I was doing in school, and I jumped into conversations with confidence in myself, no longer feeling inadequate around my aunt, uncle, dad, and grandpa. By the end of Christmas that year, I felt a little closer to everyone in my family. Gone were the negative feelings I used to have about my place in the world. And I got to spend time with Pawpaw, the relative I was now closer to than anyone besides my brothers.

A few days before my second semester, I decided to take my new class schedule to my academic coach, check out my smart pen for another semester, and prepare to continue with my new study schedule. I felt confident that with my discipline channeled to studying and these new tools, I could achieve success in all of my classes.

But this semester presented itself with greater challenges. I discovered that one of my communications classes was a philosophy class with one of the toughest professors in the school. My second Spanish course also looked to be a challenge because it moved at an extremely rapid pace.

I stuck with the study schedule I had created with my academic coach and was successful in all my classes except my philosophy class. That course was giving me serious problems. No matter what I did, I could not make a grade above a C. So I devised new ways to absorb the material.

While on a run one day, I started relating the lessons from that class to things I saw on the trail. I compared rocks to philosophers, then mused about how each philosopher would understand things in the woods. And by the end of the run, I walked off the trail with a better understanding of the topics in class. I learned to read the articles for class by skimming, looking for the main points. But I still received Cs on all my papers and tests. Midway through the semester, I realized that the majority of the students who had started the class were no longer there. I began to take pride in knowing that at least I was sticking out the class. Pawpaw told me that one C was okay, it would still count toward my degree. He told me to keep working hard and try the best I could.

After a few runs spent thinking about course work, I had gained a better understanding of the material and received my first B in the class following a quiz. Encouraged, I took that lesson into overdrive and started relating every perspective covered in class to things in my everyday life as I ran, walked across campus, walked home from the bus stop, and watched TV. There was no off button in understanding the material in this philosophy class, and by studying so hard for my classes, I was gaining an understanding of the world through a much broader lens.

By the end of the semester, I had kept the study schedule for another entire semester and gained an enhanced confidence in my intelligence. Everything went smoothly, and I discovered I only needed one more class to graduate.

One of my favorite professors was going to be handing out diplomas for the end of that semester's graduates. I asked him if I could walk without finishing my last class so he could call my name as a graduate. He told me that would not be a problem. I felt a little guilty walking across the stage as they called my name, but I was confident that I could pass my last class that summer, so I walked confidently across the stage and shook his hand with a huge grin as my parents watched from the bleachers. I only wished my grandpa could be there to see it, but he had trouble traveling, so he missed my walking across the stage. But I called him and told him all about it the next morning. He made sure to tell me that I still needed to finish my last class before celebrating.

My last class at UNC was an entry-level communications course and I kept a disciplined study schedule the whole month even though it was mostly a review of classes I had already taken.

I finished my last class with an A and waited proudly to receive my diploma in the mail. In finishing my degree, I learned that my greatest strength was in my discipline. I discovered that I am just as smart if not smarter than anyone else once I discipline myself for a goal. My discipline for running had created a strength in my ability to work from that discipline to achieve goals in other areas. I could do anything I set my mind toward achieving.

Becoming an Ultra-Runner

With my degree framed and hung nicely above my desk, it was time to find a job. I was eager to find a job using my degree in communications. I looked for positions in marketing and other fields that required a knowledge of communications. Each time I interviewed, I was not chosen for the position.

My grandpa continued to help me with my finances while I looked for a job. But, after a couple months of me overdrafting our account, he took away the joint account we had been sharing for the past couple years.

I understood why he removed the account. I was upset with myself that I had chosen to take advantage of my grandfather's generosity in such a selfish manner.

I apologized to him over the phone, he knew that I felt bad for making such poor decisions. I was afraid my actions would cause us to have a poor relationship, but I was wrong in that assumption; each day, we talked and continued in our normal fashion as if nothing had happened. Once when we talked he suggested that I think about getting a job as a teacher. I thought about it for a few days, then told him I was going to find work as a substitute teacher.

I remembered that I had started at Mizzou with the goal to teach. Working with kids was something I was good at, it seemed to come naturally to me. But I quickly discovered the public schools had all the substitute teachers they wanted to use. I then thought I could work in the private schools as a substitute to get a little money in my pockets.

I went to a couple of Catholic schools in the area talking to them about substitute teaching. I received an email from the principal of Immaculata Catholic School asking me to come in for an interview. As I read the email, my heart jumped out of my chest. I was great at interviews. I was going to get to be a substitute teacher and make enough money to get by, I could do this job until I found something better for work.

As I walked into the school the next day, I was amazed at the small and cozy feel of it. It looked exactly as I would picture a small schoolhouse from years ago. It had a large open playground in the front, one large brick building, and old and chiseled lettering above the doorway that had the name of the school upon it. I found my way to the principal's office and sat in the room with Dana, the principal, and Jim, the assistant principal. Dana greeted me with a warm smile and asked me to have a seat. She introduced Jim, who was professional. Dana seemed to be happy talking with me, telling me how happy she would be to have me as a sub. Jim asked necessary questions about whether or not I was qualified to fulfill the position. After answering his questions, he seemed satisfied with me. Dana told me she would make sure I was placed on the sub list to be called in as a substitute teacher. She then asked if I could coach. I answered with a calm, "Yes," and Dana almost jumped out of her chair in joy. I felt the same way inside. This was a great day, as not only was I going to be able to have a job while I looked for something else, I was going to get to coach my own basketball team. This interview could not have gone better!

A couple days later, I received a call from Jim asking if I were available to sub on Friday. I told him I would be there and my mind raced with anticipation to what I would be like as a substitute teacher. I envisioned myself looking the part of Arnold Schwarzenegger in the movie Kindergarten Cop as I waited for Friday morning.

I ended up subbing for a kindergarten class as a teaching assistant for an entire week. I became attached to the kids in the classroom. I enjoyed getting to know each of them and could not help but smile when I saw one of them do something I had taught them.

After that week, it seemed I had a job as a sub almost every day. I got to know lots of the kids in the school and learned the names of the teachers. One day, I discovered that one of the kindergarten teaching assistants had quit her job. I was asked to sub for the class as the teaching assistant for the next couple weeks. Jim then told me that I should consider myself as the TA for that class.

The teacher of the kindergarten class was the best teacher I had ever seen in my life. She seemed to have a way of gaining the interest and respect of each of her students in a very effective and comforting manner. Mrs. Waz went seamlessly from lesson to lesson explaining the assignments and asking me to do increasingly more things throughout the day to help everything run smoothly. Over the next couple months, I became attached to each of the students in my class and enjoyed helping them in their learning. I also found a friend in Mrs. Waz, who had the respect of everyone in the school. I learned everything I could from her about the way she controlled her classroom.

While I was experiencing success at work, as soon as I walked away from the school, I had become fully immersed in the Trailhead world. I discovered there was a pint night every Tuesday that the Trailheads went to as a weekly hangout. I met the group every Saturday for a run and coffee, becoming even more deeply involved in this group of runners. I learned inside stories about the group, jokes they had played on each other, crazy things they had seen, and knew more people on the trails of Carolina North Forest than anywhere else in town. Almost every time I went for a run through the woods, I saw somebody I knew. I felt like I was on the top of the world.

My trailhead life was also seeping into my work as a teaching assistant. During down times, I told the class stories about the "magical animals of Carolina North Forest." They listened intently as I told them stories about talking foxes and owls. I had both of my worlds colliding for a beautiful meld.

I then began to coach the JV boys' basketball team at the school and my whole world changed a little bit. I was forced to figure out a way to balance my time between school and running. I knew there were a few Trailheads who occasionally went for night runs, but I was scared to go running at night in the woods.

One morning, Alex, a large Russian guy who I had found to be a fun person to run with, and I were running through the woods and carrying on with our normal conversations about the crazy things we had seen in Missouri and work. I mentioned to him that I feared I might have a tough time balancing running and coaching basketball at the school. Alex told me that he used to do a lot of night runs when he lived in Kansas City and that he would be up for running at night a few times a week. As we crashed up a couple hills and jumped over the ditches on the trail, I told him I was going to take him up on that and suggested that we go for a run Wednesday night at 6:00 from Wilson Park.

He told me he would be there, and I felt my nerves start acting up, even though the run was still a few days away.

At coffee after the run, Sputnik told me he too was planning to go for a night run, one Monday night after work. He told me to meet him for a run at 8:30. I was nervous because I had never run at night, never used a headlamp, and had only run with Sputnik one other time. Kerndog told me to start night running on the easy trails before venturing onto single track trails. I thought this sounded like a good game plan. Kerndog was full of wisdom gained from being a runner for many years.

When I got home from my normal Saturday routine of hanging with the Trailheads, my mom gave me the headlamp that she had used on her last trip to Africa, where she had been on a mission trip in Uganda. I had no idea how to use it, but I was pumped because now I could go for my night runs without spending what little money I had saved from work.

As I met Sputnik at the start of the trail, he told me that we would do a short little two-mile run so I could learn what it was like to run at night. I decided to leave my glasses in the truck to ensure that I did not break them during our run. Big mistake! As we ran through the woods, I could not distinguish the trail with my poor vision. I decided to use a strategy of simply following closely behind Sputnik. I think Sputnik thought my traveling so close meant he was running too slowly, because he kept going faster. Every time he had me lead, he would tell me I was off trail practically every thirty seconds. Seeing the trail through the light of my headlamp was incredibly difficult and after a little over an hour of arduous eye strain and stumbling through the thick of the woods, Sputnik and I arrived back at my truck. He told me he was going to continue running and thanked me for joining him. As I climbed into my truck, I was proud of having completed a night run with Sputnik and decided that Wednesday's run would be different because I would wear my glasses, since it was important to see the trail.

After coaching practice on Wednesday night, I drove to Wilson Park and changed clothes for the run. Alex pulled into the parking lot on time. We looked at each other and shrugged, thinking, "Here we go" and started out down the trail. Wearing glasses made a difference for me and I was able to follow the trail a little better, but still got off trail every so often. After our five-mile run, I was feeling a little better about night running, which was great because it meant I would be able to keep running while coaching basketball.

Alex and I continued running almost every Wednesday night for the next few weeks. Shifty, a muscular guy who always had an incredibly hilarious comment waiting any time we were on the trail, even came out with us on a bunch of the runs. Chad, one of Alex's friends, also joined us, and suddenly our night running duo had grown to a group of four runners. One night, Stumpwater joined us for our nightly jaunt. Stumpwater was a Trailhead who embodied everything you would imagine an ultra-runner would be, with his salt-and-pepper goatee, thin yet strong build, and demeanor that easily flows from joking to serious, a common trait in the ultra-running community. This was the biggest group I had seen on a night run.

After a few weeks of running in glasses, I switched to wearing contacts and my trail running improved by a lot with the addition of these pieces of medical plastic in my eyes. I was ready to improve my running. I no longer had to adjust my glasses toward the area I wanted to look, I simply looked in that direction and the contact lenses automatically adjusted to my eyes' new position. I could see everything on the trail and I stumbled a lot less than when I had glasses. Still, as I ran behind Stumpwater, I noticed his headlamp was a lot brighter than mine and seemed to illuminate the entire trail as he ran. I then saw Shifty shining with an even brighter headlamp and even less difficulty seeing the trail.

After that run, Shifty told me the type of headlamp he had bought, and I decided to buy one so that I could see the trail as well as him. The following week, I tried it out and the new headlamp worked like a dream; I could see the whole trail and it seemed to light up the woods with incredible clarity. I was able to lead through most of the run without needing help from the other runners in the group. I could now focus on conversations with Shifty, Chad, and Alex during our jaunts, instead of worrying about seeing the trail. As the weeks rolled by, I became more and more comfortable running through the woods at night. I also started inviting other Trailheads to meet for night runs. Remus and I once went for a run that ended at 11:00 p.m., making us laugh at the ludicrousness of what we had just done.

My middle school basketball players seemed to look up to me more after I told them stories about my running at night. They understood that I was not asking them to do anything in practice that I was not already doing myself. They looked up to me because I was an athlete and not just some nobody trying to coach them. In pre-game talks, I told them stories about my runs and how they related to our current situations. Again, I was able to bring my running world into my profession. By the end of the season, I was proud of my team because I had put a lot of myself into coaching them and saw positive results from sharing my experiences on the trail with them to help them become better basketball players.

That summer, I cruised through the warm months hanging with my brother Tyler and the Trailheads. I do not think I missed a single run with the Trailheads all summer. I also was able to hang out with my weight room group, which was more fun since I could not see them during the school year.

Once the school season came back around, I was back at the school, only this time I was on staff as a teaching assistant for third grade and would also be helping as a development officer part of the day. As I was told which class I would be assisting, I recalled the horror stories from the other teachers about the wild and unruly nature of the class I was going to assist with.

The teacher I would assist was a very calm and patient teacher who loved helping students learn. She related to each student with a smile and calmly showed that she cared in everything she did. I quickly learned that she was the quiet and strong leader of the class. I was amazed at the way she cared for each and every student in the manner that made them feel comfortable. Each week, I gained more and more responsibilities, and it was not long before I felt that we had a good working relationship.

I continued to run through the woods with the Trailheads each week. I became curious about these ultramarathons a number of the people in the group kept talking about during coffee and beer. Remus told me there were about six Trailheads traveling to upstate New York for a hundred-mile trail race called Virgil Crest. I told him I would love to go and crew for the race, but told him I was running low on funds. He said he would pay for my room as long as I crewed for him during the race. I told him I was in and requested off from work for the days we would be gone.

There were two cars traveling from North Carolina to upstate New York for the race. Both of them were filled with Trailheads. In all, there would be six running the hundred-miler and two of us to crew for the guys in the race. In my van Remus, Uncus, Kevin, and I rolled out of town in what would turn out to be an epic road trip.

Remus was known for his inappropriate remarks and ability to entice others to have another beer. That extra beer usually turns into hours of sidesplitting conversations and great stories. He and I became good friends through the number of trail runs and happy-hour forays I had attended since I joined the group.

Kevin was around my age and a former marine and I was gaining a good friend in him as well. We would go out and chase women on weekend nights, then laugh when it inevitably did not work out. He was also a fun person to run with due to his seemingly endless supply of interesting stories and his ability to laugh at his own blunders.

Uncus had a sense of humor that allowed for easy laughter and joking about the mishaps in life. He also has the unbelievable capacity to carry conversations about anything from trail runs to Broadway plays.

Then, there's me, the newbie trail runner with one ten-mile trail race under my belt, a reputation for inappropriate comments, and the ability to find humor in almost anything in life.

The entire trip to Virgil, New York, was filled with conversations found nowhere else in the world. We heard Uncus express his desire for a Russian beet and Kevin explain how the Tinder dating app worked, while Remus threw in comments at every direction our conversations took. I think we all enjoyed the road trip, as we had laughed almost the entire time. I did not want it to end, and would discover that the feeling of humorous camaraderie would last the entire weekend.

Before going to the hotel, we decided to walk out onto the start of the trail for a picture and a chance to stretch our legs. As I looked around the area of upstate New York, I was amazed at how different it was from the city. We looked out the car windows and saw rolling hills and lush green mountains that rose into the sky. All four of us scrambled out of the car and relished the feeling of stretching our legs after the twelve-hour trip. We stepped into the cool shade at the beginning of a trail and posed for pictures before heading to the hotel. As we posed for the pictures, my smile was genuine and huge, seeming to come from every part of my being, as I was thrilled to be on such a fun road trip.

We then pulled up to the hotel and I was pleasantly surprised to find that it was a beautiful place that looked like a giant hunting lodge instead of the roadside motel I thought to be normal for ultra-runner lodgings. The front lobby had tall log ceilings and taxidermied animals adorning the walls surrounding a large stone fireplace in the middle of the lobby. The hallway smelled of cedar as we walked to our room and we tossed our bags in before walking down to meet the Trailheads from the other car for dinner.

All eight of us were seated around a large table in the hotel restaurant, and everyone seemed quite pleased about having dinner together. I exuberantly ate dinner and became immersed in the roaring laughter and buzz of conversation as we ate. After dinner, we all went to our rooms to sleep. I shared a room with Remus, Kevin, and Uncus, and felt like I was a kid at my best friend's house for a sleepover. We told stories for about an hour before going to sleep.

The next day was the day before the race and most of the group opted to stay at the hotel and prepare. Since I was only crewing, I went with Wackus and Icarus to nearby Ithaca to look around. Before heading into town, I took a look outside the hotel and nearly lost my breath as I gaped at the beauty of the mountains. On the drive to Ithaca, we decided to go to an outdoor clothing store. I thought I had found one and plugged it into my GPS system only to find upon arriving that I had led us to an Urban Outfitters. I nervously looked around the car to see what Wackus and Icarus would think of my blunder, and they thought it was hilarious. We laughed about my misguidance all afternoon. This reaction further sealed my surety that I had found an incredible group of people to call friends. We spent the afternoon drinking local beers and exploring the streets of downtown Ithaca.

We arrived back at the hotel in time to meet the rest of the Trailhead group for dinner and an early bedtime. As the joyous conversations continued, I grew closer to each person in the group and had a blast. We all went to bed rather early that night as the race started at 6:00 in the morning, meaning we would all be awake at 4:30 to get ready to run.

By the time 4:30 rolled around, everyone was already up and getting ready for the race. Remus was jovially telling stories, Kevin was peppering them with comments, and Uncus was singing in the shower. I decided to pass on taking a shower, opting instead to put on my running pants, rain jacket, and everything I needed to crew for the six Trailheads attempting the hundred-mile course. Remus, Uncus, and Kevin packed their drop bags, loaded with things they were going to eat during the race: candy, trail mix, and all kinds of goodies. We all walked to the lobby to find the rest of the Trailhead contingency waiting for us. We loaded into the vehicles and drove a couple miles to the starting line.

As we drove through the morning darkness to the park where the race was starting, I was still amazed at the beauty of the mountains all around us. The mountains seemed to loom in dark majesty overhead and the pond reflected the glow of the moonlight to the right of the starting line. Once in the parking lot, it was clear there was an event about to begin. The small parking lot was bustling with activity, there were people wearing headlamps. Everyone had a wide-eyed enthusiasm for the race that was about to begin. The race director, wearing a smaller version of the typical mountain-man beard and with the gleam of trail runner's passion in his eye, was greeting everyone as they walked by him. The Trailheads racing buzzed with excitement, Uncus leading the group in discussions of the absurdity of the race they were about to run. They placed their drop bags, which would be transported to some of the aid stations along the course. Wisp, the other Trailhead crewing, and I stood beside the start, waiting to start crewing for our six friends attempting to run the race. A few minutes before the start, Kevin introduced me to his mom, who said she would crew with us. She was a sweet, short lady whose caring heart showed through her eyes. I could tell she was proud and happy to see Kevin. She had brought another person with her to help crew. Our two-person crew had become four.

As the race director fired the race-starting gun, the park looked as though it had been invaded by lightning bugs as the racers' headlamps burst to life. We watched as the lights slowly made their way around the small pond on the edge of the meadow near the starting line, then turned and began climbing the first mountain into the forest. Once we saw most of the lights disappear, Wisp and I loaded into Remus's Subaru and headed to one of the aid stations to wait for the runners.

Crewing for an ultra entails friends, family members, or significant others meeting the runner at aid stations along the course to help them however they can. It's usually as simple as refilling water bottles or grabbing candy from the food offered by the aid station while the ultra-runner changes socks or shoes, or puts on anti-chafe powder. Sometimes it requires helping your friend change clothes or pop blisters. So, here I was, about to crew for my Trailhead friends in the mountains of upstate New York, and I wanted to do my best.

As Wisp and I made our way to the aid station, we made small talk. We found our first aid station at the base of a ski lift that had been converted for the race. Under the platform of the lift, the racers' drop bags were laid out on a tarp for easy access for the runners as they came into the aid station. Rising directly beyond the aid station was a mountain that started the alpine loop section of the trail. The path went up for a little over a mile then turned into a series of mountain slopes that followed the trail below the ski lifts. It was the toughest hill I had ever seen and I began to feel a sense of awe that people could run up such a difficult hill only to climb a series of hills just as difficult as the previous one. I quickly began mingling with the crew members for the other racers; Wisp, Kevin's parents, and I sat in a circle with other crews sharing stories and talking about the different trail races we had run. Wisp kept talking on the phone and came back to the group to tell me Ringo was driving over to help crew for the six Trailheads on the course.

Ringo was an older trailhead with a muscular build and a tough and gruff personality. He was also the most experienced ultra-runner in a group that boasts more than its fair share of ultra-runners. He had completed more than twenty hundred-mile races in his life and loved sharing his hard-earned wisdom with Trailheads who might benefit from such knowledge. I had heard tales of him assisting another Trailhead to finish the Western States One-hundred-mile Endurance Run by pacing and motivating him to keep going, along with completing the toughest races in the country. Hearing that he was coming to the race peaked my interest. I was going to get to see this legendary runner in action helping other Trailheads achieve their goals. While I had talked with him quite regularly and knew of his feats, I thought he was a very gruff and almost unfriendly person. I often heard him joking with the rest of the Trailheads but I felt he did not like me very much, so I was a little nervous to have him join us.

As soon as he arrived, I saw that he was the same ol' Ringo. But as we waited for the trailheads running the race to come through each aid station, I discovered he really loved helping the guys. He enjoyed being able to pass on wisdom he had gained through his life. He also had a great sense of humor. He easily melded into the group crewing for the Trailheads. We had now grown to a group of five people assisting the racers.

Throughout the early morning, the next day, and the night we would help the Trailheads that came through one aid station, jump in Remus' car, then drive to another aid station and wait for all the Trailheads to come through that station.

It had been raining all day and as the night wore on, the rain continued to pour on the mountain. Icarus told me about a section of the race where he fell backward down a creek and had to climb out by grasping shrubs with his hands and pulling himself up over the bank. Wackus seemed to be moving steadily. I couldn't help but notice his lips seemed a little blue as he came out of the ski lift aid station at around mile forty-two. A few hours later, I discovered he had to drop out of the race at mile fifty due to hypothermia. Uncus was forced to drop out of the race as well due to a foot issue.

Once all the Trailheads were through that aid station for the first lap, I drove to the fifty-mile aid station to meet the remaining four racers. The fifty-mile aid station was at the end of the first lap, the location of the start line, and the location of the eventual finish line. Lynx, Kevin, and Icarus came through with normal strains and issues. They ate a bunch of food, quickly changed into some dry clothes, and then they were off, back up the mountain. I helped each of them get moving again by turning on my headlamp and running with them to the small pond they would round before heading up another mountain.

As the night went on, we drove to the aid station under the ski lift and waited there for most of the night. Lynx came through the aid station a second time running in third place, not far behind the second-place runner. Icarus came into the aid station with his head sunk into his shoulders. He looked miserable. I think being rained on all day had finally caused him to lose his muster. Remus seemed to be doing fine, steady and being his jovial self.

Icarus told us that he was not planning to go back out. He told me he was done. Ringo sprang into action and told Icarus he wanted him to show him the alpine loop along with Remus. Icarus looked up from underneath the hood of his rain jacket to find Remus standing beside Ringo looking down on him with lively eyes. Ringo again told him that he wanted to see the Alpine loop. Icarus slowly climbed out of his chair, steadied himself with his trekking poles, and told them he would head back out to run the alpine loop. As they began their trudge up the mountain, I realized that Ringo had found the perfect way to motivate Icarus to keep going on the race. A few hours later, I saw three head-lamps coming down the mountain to the aid station on the other side of the trail, signifying that they had completed the alpine loop. Icarus was bounding as he entered the aid station. Remus, Ringo, and Icarus were covered in mud, soaked from head to toe, and grinning from ear to ear. With this renewed energy, Remus and Icarus headed back out on the trail. I was amazed at the ability Ringo had to improve Icarus's mood simply by being himself. After seeing this transformation, I realized the best way to encourage someone is not through empty lines of reassurance, but through being yourself, which was how Ringo was able to improve moods through easy conversation and a good sense of humor. The sight of seeing the three of them smiling in the aid station was powerful. And seeing Icarus and Remus grinning as they went back out to the trail was a beautiful sight.

Once Icarus and Remus were on their way, we rushed to the next aid station to meet Lynx and Kevin. The rain had finally stopped pouring and faded into a light drizzle. The sun began to come up as we watched Lynx and Kevin cruise through that aid station. Lynx was in second place now and Kevin was in tenth. We realized there was a lot of time before Remus and Icarus would be coming through this aid station, so we hurried to the finish line to see Lynx come in second place and Kevin cruise in at tenth place. As Kevin approached the finish line, he threw his water bottle in the air and was grinning from ear to ear. He was beaming with the excitement of finishing his first hundred-miler. I could not help but smile as I saw him accomplish his goal.

After finishing, Lynx sat under a blanket next to the winner and sipped chicken broth. I heard them both talking to each other about the race. The winner, a thin guy who trained in the mountains and sported facial hair that made him resemble a mountain goat, recounted Lynx flying past him early in the race. They chatted too about their struggles with the course, from the mud to the rain. Both of them seemed to be chilled to the bone. Kevin then joined the circle around the fire pit, sipping a mug of hot chocolate. The three of them told stories about the race and I sat and listened as they discussed everything about the race.

A couple hours later, we headed to another aid station to help Remus and Icarus to finish the race. After waiting for a couple hours, Ringo and I took off on the trail to run with them into the aid station. I could not keep up with Ringo and decided to turn around and wait at the aid station for them to return. After about an hour of waiting, the aid station began to shut down. This meant that Remus and Icarus would have to run the last twenty-five miles without help from an aid station. I tried my best to talk the workers into staying a few more minutes. They agreed to leave the remaining food there, but they were going home. I then saw Icarus, Remus, and Ringo coming through the woods. Remus and Icarus were still moving strongly and looked as though they would be able to finish the race. I immediately gave them some food and was eager to see them finish the race, but upon hearing that they had missed the time cutoff for the aid station, they both agreed they were finished. They had been running for thirty-six hours straight.

We loaded into Remus's car and headed to the finish line to pick up the rest of the Trailheads and return to North Carolina. We all met at the finish line area and discussed what to do before leaving town. We agreed that everyone needed to shower before we did anything else. One of the race volunteers told us the indoor water park connected to the hotel was letting people from the race use their showers. As we all walked into the water park, we were back indoors for the first time in over thirty-six hours, and in the closed quarters it became apparent that we were all filthy and smelled horrible. While there were individual shower stalls in the locker room, I noticed with a pleased grin the steady streams of mud and dirt from being in the woods all night that were steadily running toward the drains.

I was amazed how rejuvenated I was after my shower and change of clothes. We all appeared from the locker rooms clean and happy. Ringo jumped in his car and left the group, as he was heading to New York City to visit his daughter. We all agreed we would be in the same vehicles on the return trip to North Carolina and planned to stay somewhere along the way to break up the road trip into two days.

We all loaded into Remus' car and began the road trip home. I offered to drive, but Remus insisted he was okay. I slept for a few hours, then awoke as we pulled into a gas station. It was here that Remus, Uncus, and Kevin lined up to race about thirty yards as a postrace competition that was more of a painful hobble for all three of them than an actual race. After filling up, we returned to our banter; Uncus was still talking about how much he wanted a beet. After a while, I noticed that we were not stopping for the night. Remus mentioned he wanted to get home and told me he thought he could make it, so he drove through the night and dropped me off at my place around five in the morning. I left the car tired physically, but smiled after realizing that I had had one of the best times of my life on the trip. As I climbed into bed, I realized Remus had just run seventy-five miles in thirty-six hours then drove thirteen hours back to Chapel Hill. "Holy shit!" was the only reaction that came to mind before I fell into a deep sleep.

***

After the trip to Virgil Crest, I was hooked. I wanted to run my first 50k. During a happy-hour evening with the Trailheads, I talked with Lynx, who told me that I should run the Carrboro 50k as my first ultra. I asked him when it was and he told me it was in the beginning of January. I told him that I would run it, then began to devise a training schedule in my mind for the event. For my marathons, I had trained for about a year before running one. I had less than three months to train for my first ultra! There was a difference of about five miles, and I hadn't done a marathon in a long time, and marathons were on roads while ultras were mostly on trails that required more effort to complete.

I decided the best way to train would be to increase my long run every weekend by a few miles until I reached twenty-four miles. I would run two other days throughout the week and keep those runs pretty easy. I was running with Alex, Shifty, Chad, Remus, and Stumpwater on my night runs, and I took little pieces of advice from each of my merry band of twilight runners. Chad, the newbie to trail running, modeled for me how to keep a steady and cautious head when in the woods. We would get lost and hike off trail for about half a mile before finding our way, but he maintained a laidback sense of humor. Alex had run a couple hundred-mile races and gave me insights about increasing mileage. Remus kept me laughing and always made me feel as though we were at happy hour drinking beer and telling stories with the ease of mild intoxication, even if we were running up a steep and muddy hill in the middle of the night. Shifty showed me toughness through humor as he continually dropped joking remarks of the ludicrousness of what we were doing. Shifty would show up to run with the same attitude regardless of the distance we were going to run. One night, I surprised him by telling him our five-mile run would actually be more like twelve miles. He finished that run pushing me to run faster and made me laugh the entire way.

I had also developed a friendship with Uncus and Kevin from our time at Virgil Crest. We would meet at bars, drink beers, and hang out on a regular basis. Kevin and Uncus joined me for a lot of runs during the day as well. I had found my pack of runners within the Trailheads. The more I ran, the closer I felt to each of my buddies, and the less I stressed about anything in my life. It seemed as though I spent my days accumulating stories to tell them as we merrily ran through the woods guided by our headlamps.

The night before the Carrboro 50k (which was in reality a local run through the woods and not an official ultra), Uncus and Remus told me they would meet me at the start to run the 50k with me. I told them I was starting at four in the morning. They both agreed to meet me.

The next morning, I pulled into the parking lot half-expecting to start the run by myself. As I drove to the top of the lot, I saw Remus sitting in his car waiting for me. I then received a text message from Uncus saying he was on his way. At 4:00 in the morning, the temperature was around thirteen degrees. The three of us made our way through the familiar trails of Carolina North Forest. The course had been marked on the ground with arrows made from flour. Remus took the lead and kept us moving at a pace faster than I normally ran. Uncus told me an inappropriate story about one of his wild nights from Colorado to start off the first few miles. Remus joined in, adding to the steady increase of unseemliness as we moved through the frozen woods.

As we continued our run, Remus informed us that he had not gone to bed the night before, but had instead stayed up all night drinking wine with friends. Uncus was still talking about beets. Near the end of the first lap, Uncus and I were engaged in a rap battle when Uncus tripped over a log and went sailing through the air, landing hard on his back on a frozen rock. Remus and I checked on him and saw him hop to his feet and keep going as if nothing had happened. As we finished our first lap, the other runners in the race had started coming through the woods.

There was a small number of runners, mostly Trailheads, attempting to run the full 50k. Most of the runners on the course were going to run one lap, with a few running two laps totaling a little over twenty-three miles. These were mostly runners new to trail running. I waved to all the Trailheads as they ran past me. They were full of encouragement and would occasionally slow to tell me a joke. Uncus stayed with me throughout the miles, and our conversations ebbed and flowed in a number of directions. After the second lap, I saw his foot was hurting him. I was also starting to get a little tired, but we went through the second lap in a routine manner. I was amazed at the help I received from Trailheads not running the race. They all crewed for me, just like I had crewed for them during Virgil Crest. They refilled my hydration pack, brought me soup, then kicked me out so I would not get stiff. Halfway through the second lap, Uncus decided his foot hurt too much to keep running. I said goodbye to him as I staggered into the last miles of the 50k.

As I increased my long run distance each Saturday, I had started eating more and more candy during the runs. My last long run before the 50k had included four bags of chips, three cokes, and a handful of chocolate espresso beans. I had discovered what it felt like to get a caffeine boost through these magical beans. But during those last miles of the 50k, I found myself disgusted with the jelly beans I had left to eat. I gagged at the thought of eating another one of them.

I could feel every rock through the sole of my shoes. My left toenail was slowly falling off and I was starting to hurt. I went from one trail marker to the next. Passed the tree with a sock hanging from it and painfully picked my way down the last rocky hill and turned to head up the parking lot to finish. I was the last runner on the course and as I staggered toward the top of the parking lot, Wackus yelled out, "Hurry up, Tiny! You're about to miss the time cut-off!" I mustered up every ounce of energy and ran to the top of the hill to finish with a time of thirteen and a half hours.

As I drove home from the race, I reflected on the way I had become a member of the Trailheads. I went back to the path I had taken to meet the group and how they had changed my perception of a long run by telling me about ultramarathons: my definition of a "long" race had changed to thinking that the marathon was the longest distance possible for a runner. I recalled how I gained a "trail name" as a member of the Trailheads. I had told a joke, bought coffee, and volunteered at races. During our spring race, Wackus told me it was ironic I was bigger than the other Trailheads and called me "Tiny" as a joke. The name stuck and a few days later, the naming committee put out an email giving me the official trail name Tiny. After being named, I began to compare my trail name to Snake Diesel and came to the conclusion that I liked Tiny better, because there was no way it could be twisted into a joke at my expense. And I knew the wonderful members of the group would never ridicule me about my arm, although I was sure the name "Tiny" was not going to get me a girlfriend. I remembered how I had found people willing to run with me through the night to prepare for this race and the guys who showed up to start my 50k early in the morning. I realized the Trailheads were a huge reason I had regained my passion for running and was able to take my passion to a level I never knew existed.

Cloudsplitter 50k

After running the Carrboro 50k, which I discovered was in fact a couple miles further than fifty kilometers, I felt invincible. I started going for runs through trails all over the area. I met my Trailhead buddies for runs all throughout the week. Almost every run, I saw a friend, usually a Trailhead, coming down the trails. Sometimes we ran a couple miles together and sometimes we simply said hello and continued on our way. I almost never felt alone in the woods. I now looked at a thirteen-mile run as a normal trot through the woods.

I was back in love with running and I felt nearly invincible. The only thing I did not understand was why I had not lost any weight during my training for the Carrboro 50k. I thought eating tons of candy and sweets was what you had to do to be an ultra-runner. I also thought chocolate milk was the best recovery drink for runners. I came to think that I was just always going to be big, which was okay with me; as long as I could do the things I loved, my weight did not bother me. I was having a blast running and drinking beer, and I prided myself on being tough enough to finish a 50k.

One hot Saturday morning in May, Kevin and I met for a run through Umstead State Park. We were going to run the big loop around the park. As we ran the first couple miles down single-track trails to get to the big loop, we were running pretty fast and I felt good. Once you hit the big loop, the trail becomes almost a dirt road, and we cruised through at a pace that was faster than I was used to running but kept up our normal chatter about women, crazy life stories, and hypothetical situations that made us laugh. Occasionally the conversation turned to serious subjects such as politics or hardships someone was enduring and we always ended those subjects with mutual respect for each other. We finished the run sooner than expected and we both agreed to finish the afternoon by heading to Weaver Street for chocolate milk.

Once seated comfortably outside the store in chairs primed for checking out women as they walked by, we sipped our chocolate milk and enjoyed relaxing after such a fun run. As I drank my second chocolate milk, I thought to myself, "This is what it's all about." I drove home to take a nap before meeting up with my brother Tyler.

Once I got to my apartment, the muscles right above my hips began pulsing in pain. I ended up laying on the floor sweating in pain. I thought it was a muscle spasm. I called Tyler to tell him I needed him to come over and put ice on my back so the spasm would stop. As I lay on the ground, I continued sweating as my back hurt worse and worse. Tyler walked in, saw me on the floor, put ice on my back, and told me he hoped I would feel better. While he was brief in his words, I could tell through his eyes he was worried about me. After he left to meet his shooting coach for a workout, he told his girlfriend to go back and check on me, which was a good thing, since after he left, I started vomiting from the pain that had moved into my right testicle. Tyler's girlfriend came in to find me hovered over the toilet in pain. She offered to drive me to the hospital and I quickly accepted her offer.

During the ride to the hospital, my right testicle felt like someone was squeezing it. We had to pull over on the side of the road so I could throw up. Once we pulled up to the hospital, my mom and brother met me in the emergency room. With them by my side, I tried to tell a few jokes, but could only wince in pain as my back and my right ball pulsed in immense pain. The doctor entered my room and asked about what had happened.

The doctor examining me was a blonde lady who radiated passion for her profession. She listened intently as I told her about where I was hurting and asked if I had done any rigorous activity. I told her I went for a run, but it was not particularly difficult. I asked her for some water, but she told me there was a chance I might need surgery, and so could not have water. Once the nurse gave me morphine, the pain began to lessen a little bit, but it was still significant. The doctor told me she thought I might have testicular torsion, which is essentially where one ball gets tangled. She explained this can happen from exercising in boxer shorts. Once she told me she suspected torsion, I saw my mom and brother immediately dive into their phones. A few seconds later, they both looked at each other gravely and put their phones away, which was not reassuring, to say the least.

After running a quick test, the doctor rushed back into my room and told me she had good and bad news. Good news was that I did not have torsion. Bad news was that I had a kidney stone. She went on to explain that she would prescribe pain medication for me and that I should drink lots of water to pass it through urination.

Once she left my room, Tyler and my mom breathed a quick sigh of relief. They told me that if I had torsion, there was an hour and a half window for them to perform surgery. Outside that window, they would have had to remove one of my testicles.

With the understanding that I would pass the stone, I drank as much water as I possibly could the next day. I did not notice a stone any time I went to the bathroom. Tyler insisted that I stay with him until I passed the stone. I agreed and lounged around his place all day.

He rented movies and we watched them together. He was doing everything he could to keep my spirits up. He went to the gym to work out and called me every hour to check on me. I felt bad that he was so worried about me, but it really made me feel good that he was there for me when I needed him. I went to bed expecting to pee out the stone soon, but I peed all night and did not see a stone.

Around three in the morning, I awoke with incredible pain in my back. The pulsing pain had returned with a vengeance. I rolled over and said Tyler's name. He immediately shot out of bed and rushed to my side. I told him I was hurting bad again and wanted to go to the hospital. We left his condo for the hospital. Even though I was in incredible pain, seeing my brother eager to help me made me feel good. Once in the elevator, I could not hold it back anymore, I started crying from the pain. Tyler gave me a hug and consoled me. By the time the elevator doors opened, I had pulled myself together. We drove back to the emergency room. Tyler stayed by my side the entire morning. He kept me company as I went from one test to another. It was these early morning hours that reminded me that my brother is an incredible person. Once my mom heard I was back in the hospital, she rushed to be by my side as well. My mom and I had fought tougher battles than this, and having her there gave me some reassurance about being in the hospital. She had sat in my hospital room and watched me learn to walk again. A kidney stone was a piece of cake compared to the things we had been through.

Zu, one of my Trailhead friends, was a doctor, and he stopped by to check on me. He cancelled a meeting and hung out with me as I awaited results from some kidney tests. I was amazed how well Zu was able to join in the conversation with my family. I felt as though he had joined my family at that point. The doctor returned and told me he thought I should have surgery to get the stone removed. Zu looked at the results and agreed that surgery looked like the right move. I was told that they would move me in for surgery in about three hours. Zu left to finish his rounds and Tyler left to lift weights, but told me he would be back after his workout. I could tell he was really worried as he walked out of the room. Once it was my mom and I, we looked at each other and laughed, saying, "Here we are again." My mom has always been great at making me laugh during tough times.

After a couple hours, Tyler was back by my bedside. He immediately asked how I was doing. The nurse then wheeled me back for surgery. Tyler and my mom told me they would see me once I was out. As I was wheeled into the pre-operating room, I teared up a little as I felt blessed to have a family that cared about me so much. A few minutes before being taken into the operating room, Balto, a Trailhead who was also an anesthesiologist, came to my bed to wish me luck. It made me feel good that my running family cared about me enough to stop by and wish me well. As I went back for surgery, the doctor told me he was going to retrieve the stone by going in through my favorite appendage. I watched him putting on gloves and the last thought I had before going under was, "His hands are huge!" Then the lights went out as the anesthesia worked its magic.

***

When I awoke, I saw Tyler and my mom right there by my side. The doctor told me I was too inflamed for him to remove the stone, so he put a ureter stint in to calm things down. In a couple weeks, the inflammation should have gone down enough to allow him to remove the stone.

A ureter stint is a device that is implanted through the urethra and placed in the ureter, right above my balls, to relieve the inflammation caused by the stone. It relieved the pulsing pain in my back, but was a little uncomfortable.

For the next two weeks, I was forced to lay low. I relaxed and read books, then became bored. I was really looking forward to having this thing out of me so I could go back to my old ways.

After two weeks, I went in for the surgery, saw the doctor with big hands, went under, then awoke to find out he thought it would be a good idea to put another stint in me for two more weeks to make sure everything healed correctly. My one thought was, "Fuck this guy!" I had been going nuts with this thing in me for two weeks. Now I had to have another one for two more weeks? I asked the doctor if I could run with the stint and he told me it might be uncomfortable, but running was okay.

Two days later, I hit the trail for my first trail run in three weeks. The doctor was right. After a mile, I was pretty uncomfortable, and by the time I reached a mile and a half, I was hurting pretty badly. I went to pee and saw that my penis was bleeding. I immediately turned around and walked back to my truck. Once in the coffee shop, the other Trailheads cringed when I told them about my bleeding. I went home and resigned myself to staying on the couch until I got this stint removed.

After two weeks I went into the doctor's office to have the stint and the kidney stone removed. It was a quick procedure and I left the doctor's office with my trail running shoes already on my feet. I drove straight to Wilson Park for a run.

That first run back, I had the feeling of an animal released back into the wild. I hopped roots, rocks, and cruised through the trails I had missed while dealing with this kidney stone. I decided that I wanted to run another 50k.

***

The Trailheads' listserv is a bit of a support network for the group. It is also the place to get advice, whine, joke, and basically entertain yourself by seeing all the responses you get from the group. To get emails from the listserv, you tell Kerndog to add you and boom! You'll be entertained and informed at the same time. Anytime someone sends out an email seeking practical advice or searching for fellow runners to join them on a race or run, there are guaranteed to be at least four emails filled with inside jokes and unbelievable stories. You are also guaranteed to get at least one informative email about the subject.

Sputnik sent out an email about a race called the Cloudsplitter in Kentucky. I looked it up to discover there was a 50k option for the race. I immediately decided that was the race I was going to train for the following October. During a night run, I told Shifty about the race and he told me he would run it with me.

The elevation chart for this race showed that it was a mountain race. I started slowly increasing my mileage the same as I had for the Carrboro 50k, but decided I needed to run a little more on the days between my long run so I could have increased stamina for the mountain climb.

One day, I planned to do a night run after work and sent out an email to see if anyone wanted to join me. I got a response from a Trailhead that I had only met once, and did not remember very well. Big Top told me he would meet me to run from the Seawell School parking lot at 9:00 that night. I saw him jump out of his jeep, a red-bearded fellow donning a headlamp and, I was pleased to see, a big smile. He told me he was Big Top and we both headed out into the woods for a run. I was pleasantly surprised to find that Big Top ran at about the same pace as me. Usually I'm forced to run at a pace faster than usual and it was nice to run at my normal pace with another Trailhead. We ran almost five miles and our conversations came naturally as we cruised through the trails. We shared stories and I thought he was incredibly interesting; it seemed he had something to say about every subject imaginable. I was laughing through a lot of the run. By the end, I had made a new friend and we decided to run again together the following week.

The next week, Big Top, Shifty, and I met for a night run and it was a blast. It seemed there was no end to the topics we could talk about as we crashed through the woods. Week after week, Big Top, Shifty, and I met for runs. We were becoming quite the pack. And as the months passed, I realized we were stress relievers for each other. One of us would talk about tough situations, then another person would vent. Once we had all three thoroughly vented our stressors, we returned to crazy stories and hypothetical situations. I then talked Big Top into signing up for the Cloudsplitter race. I was the only one who had not signed up for the race yet.

I saw an email on the liveserv that Sputnik and Replay were going to run the Cloudsplitter course over the weekend. I decided that I would wait to hear from Sputnik before signing up for the race. A couple weeks passed and I saw Sputnik on the trails. As we ran, I asked him about the course for Cloudsplitter. He told me it was a bunch of ATV trails with beer cans everywhere. He backed out of the race due to such poor trails. I began to look for a different race. I decided I would run the Whitewater Center 50k. It was in a park just outside Charlotte with easier trails than Cloudsplitter and no beer cans or four wheeler ruts along the trail.

After picking this race, I greeted my brother Tyler as he returned to town for the off-season. I love having my brother in the same town as me; he is my best friend and every year, after the NBA season, he returns to Chapel Hill. I look forward to his return all year because it means I will get to hang out with him regularly.

Once he had been in town for a couple weeks, he decided we needed to do a diet for the summer. He told me we should cut out candy. I agreed but found my definition of candy changing quickly so that I could still eat junk food while on this diet. A week later, Tyler revised the diet to include cookies, ice cream, and fried foods on the list of banned foods. He then wrote the diet on a piece of notebook paper and signed it. The diet allowed for one cheat meal every two weeks. I signed the piece of paper with the intention of keeping with the diet.

The first couple of weeks, I struggled to keep from eating the foods in the restricted section of our diet. I wanted fried food and candy so bad it hurt. My body was craving these foods throughout the day. But I kept from eating them. At first, I ate a bunch of protein bars and popcorn. Then I only ate popcorn to ease the pangs of having junk food completely removed from my diet.

As the summer wore on, I noticed I was losing some weight. I increased my weekly mileage from thirty to forty miles a week. I was now getting up and running on the trails every day at 5:30 in the morning, going to coffee with my brother and the Trailheads, and going to the Dean Dome to lift weights. I was back to hanging out with my brother and was gaining confidence in my ability to run fast at the Whitewater 50k.

During one of our night runs, I told Shifty and Big Top that I was going to run the Whitewater race instead of Cloudsplitter. They both agreed we should train together and do our races, then return and share race stories. During that same run, I noticed Big Top and Shifty talking about the Cloudsplitter race and saw the glimmer of excitement in their eyes as they discussed the race. I felt like an outsider for choosing to do a different race.

A few days later, I was running with Galoot and discovered the Whitewater race included a lot of paved trails on the course. That was not what I wanted for my race. I wanted a real trail 50k. With Big Top and Shifty already signed up, I went home after that run and signed up for the Cloudsplitter 50k. This would be my first mountain 50k. And with my weight loss and increased mileage, I was fairly confident in my ability to run a strong race.

When I told Big Top and Shifty I was signed up for the race, they were excited and told me we would have fun. The rest of that run consisted of talk about our upcoming race.

Starting my runs every morning from the Seawell School parking lot at 5:30, I discovered that Grub started his run at the same time from the same place. Day after day, we ran together into the morning light. He was training for the Leadville hundred miler. I got excited every time I pulled into the parking lot and found him ready to run. Grub always gave the most practically impractical advice. His laugh could be heard throughout the entire forest. And with my frequent dirty comments, he would unleash these huge laughs often. Each morning, I would finish my run at ten miles, then wave bye to him as he continued on his run.

Though my runs with Grub had anything but a serious tone, there was an underlying discipline to them. I noticed he was always happy while we were running. Even though we were joking and laughing, we kept moving, drank water when we needed it, walked a few of the harder uphills, and pushed each other when we needed to. I was running more miles than I had since leaving Mizzou and was able to laugh through them with Grub. It is through these morning runs that I learned that maintaining humor and the ability to smile as well as a disciplined running routine makes the miles a lot more fun. When Grub returned from Leadville, I could not help but smile as I remembered the early morning runs we shared in his preparation for the race.

***

After a couple months passed, Big Top, Shifty, and I used a run the week of the race to discuss our plans for Kentucky. I was going to ride with Shifty and Big Top would drive over on his own, and my dad had agreed to drive over to crew for us during the race. Once our plans were agreed upon, the rest of the run consisted of talk about the race.

The day before the race, I met Shifty at his house and loaded my stuff in his car. Big Top was going to meet us at the pre-race meeting after he left work. I parked my truck in Shifty's driveway where his car had been after he pulled it into the street and we were off on our road trip. As we pulled out of town, I felt my nerves working, but I recalled the early morning runs and night runs I had done preparing for this race. Thinking back on my training helped me to relax with a confidence in my ability to complete the mountain race.

I had envisioned the town around the race to be fairly similar to the small and quaint towns in upstate New York. The closer we got to the town, the more I noticed the communities were nothing like upstate New York. After the five-hour drive, we pulled into the town where the race was being held. It was a mining community with a blue-collar feel to it. Pulling into town, I saw the large coal mines situated on the sides and bases of the mountains. In a lot of ways, the town reminded me of my hometown with little presence of growth and the feel of everything being unchanged. There was a certain undertone of strength and toughness emitted by the town through its identity as a blue-collar community.

We pulled into the church where the pre-race meeting was to be held and saw it filling with runners. The people meeting at this church had two body types; many had the wispy, thin build of traditional runners but others looked like normal people until you saw their legs, which were incredibly muscular. And everyone had a flinty look in their eyes that reflected their inner determination.

I sat there completely confident in my ability to complete the run. As I waited for the meeting and meal to begin, I kept trying to give my dad directions to the church. A couple minutes before the meeting started, I saw my dad walk into the church. I was excited to introduce him to two of my friends who had become like family to me. We sat for a few minutes and saw Big Top walk in the door just as the meeting started. I waved him over to a chair next to me. We all four sat quietly whispering to each other as the race director gave us instructions. My dad fit in well and as he joined in our conversations, we discovered that we shared the same view of the town. None of us had ever seen a real mining community before and we joked about the differences between it and Chapel Hill. I was so excited about my dad joining me and the group that night, I almost forgot that I had to run a race the next morning. After the meeting, I grabbed my stuff and rode with my dad to the hotel.

As we pulled into the hotel parking lot at the base of the mountain, I could not help but feel my nerves act up with the realization that I was going to run up this mountain in the morning. I felt prepared and checked the weather before going to bed. Just as it had predicted all week, the forecast showed rain all day. I had packed two rain jackets for this occasion. My dad asked a couple questions about crewing and I told him it basically consisted of helping us with whatever we needed at the turnaround point. I could tell by his manner that he expected this to be similar to the marathons he saw me run where he simply cheered as I went by running the race.

The next morning, I awoke with plenty of time to meet Shifty and Big Top in the lobby for the race. We had all agreed to meet there by 6:00 to make sure we got to the starting line in time, and we were all in the lobby by 5:45 in the morning ready to race. We loaded into the cars and headed down the small winding road that led to the starting line.

The race began in the middle of a baseball field located in the center of the small town. My dad watched us tie our shoes and throw our drop bags in his truck. He was going to meet us at the aid station that marked our turnaround point on top of the mountain. Shifty, Big Top, and I thanked my dad for agreeing to crew for us and we walked toward the starting line. I could tell my dad still expected this to be similar to a marathon.

As we lined up behind the starting line with the other runners, I saw a boy dressed in brown suspenders and a big brown hat walk in front of the starting line carrying a musket. The director wished us all luck and told the boy to fire the gun to start the race.

As I watched the smoke explode from the end of the musket, I eased into the race. We were lucky because the rain had not started yet, but the looming clouds suggested it was on its way. As I ran out of the baseball field and made the turn into the local neighborhood, Shifty was running beside me. Shifty made a crass comment that immediately put me at ease. We turned with the other racers down a street through a neighborhood of small houses with elderly bearded men in overalls sitting on their front porches smiling lightly, watching us make our way through their small town, a scene that looked like something from the movie Deliverance. Shifty said, "Look, they're here to watch the annual parade of idiots." With that comment, I felt all my anxieties melt away in one uncontrollable burst of laughter. The only response I could muster was that we surely fit that description.

Once we had run past the town, the race turned onto a trail and began to head up the mountain. I knew this uphill was going to continue to go up for the next ten miles and told myself to just get used to it. My reassurance for the knowledge that I would be climbing for the next ten miles was my confidence in the miles I had run in my training. Shortly after we started the uphill, Big Top caught up to Shifty and me. We quickly fell into conversations about the race, the community, and when we thought the rain would start.

After a couple miles of running up a dirt road, the race went onto a trail that looked like an ATV trail. I thought, "This is what Sputnik was talking about." I could see the tire marks that caused deep ruts along the outside of the trails. The rain the past few days had made the mud along the trail thick and it seemed to stick to my shoes more with every step. Occasionally, there would be puddles in the trail caused by deep ruts that forced us to run through the brush in the woods to keep from submerging our shoes in the water.

The climb up the mountain changed in grades from very steep to relatively steep, and then to gradual inclines. But the climbing was incessant. Then the rain began and everything that had been just a little sloppy from the past rains became incredibly sloppy. In many sections of the trail, it was so slick we were forced to walk through the brush and leaves along the side of the trail to gain enough traction to continue going up the hill. I had adapted a method of grabbing the branches of bushes and trees along the side of the trail and pulling myself up the hill. These branches also kept me from falling, for the most part, but I was still slipping and falling all over the place.

In one section, the hill went from a short downhill to a steep incline covered with mud. I fell during this short downhill of about fifty meters, then sat in the mud waiting for the runners in front of me to clear out of my way, as I had decided the best option for getting down this hill was to slide on my butt. I used the trees on either side of the trail to launch myself down the hill and I did not stop until the bottom. The runners in front of me started laughing.

Shifty and Big Top took it upon themselves to make remarks that kept me laughing as we continued climbing up, up, and up the mountain. I had fallen so much that I no longer cared about wiping the mud off my face. The rain continued to pour. We arrived at the first aid station joyous to see an abundance of food. We had been climbing for five miles and I was happy to refuel. This aid station was a white tent on the side of the trail holding a couple tables of food and water jugs under the tent. As I looked at the selection of food on the table in the aid station tent, I noticed an abundance of junk food. Everything from Oreos to chips to Nutella were on this table. Unfortunately, I had made a promise to my brother that our diet did not end until after the race. Instead of indulging in the plethora of sugary delights, I grabbed a couple handfuls of pretzels and trudged on through the mud. Big Top, Shifty, and I were still together and I could not help but notice how incredible they looked as specimens of endurance athletics.

From the start of the race, I had noticed our body language, but it was incredibly prevalent the further we climbed up the mountain. Shifty was consistently strong with a bounce in his step, smile on his face, and strength in his demeanor. Big Top was also consistent and seemed to draw upon his experience from running past ultras to maintain his consistent pace. He was using his trekking poles for balance and maintained a poise that showed strength and confidence in his abilities. I on the other hand felt like a sprawling duck, slipping frequently, and growing comfortable with the understanding that I would fall. I fell, picked myself up, ran a few steps, then slipped and fell again. It was not until around mile eight that I discovered a way to point my right foot so that I could maintain a sense of balance and traction as I climbed the hill. Then, about mile nine, I felt a sharp cramp in my inner thigh. I pointed my foot forward in its normal position and felt the cramp lessen a bit. As soon as I felt the cramp begin to lessen, I fell flat on my face. As I lay in the mud, I decided I would have to get used to the cramp if I wanted to be able to climb the rest of the mountain.

As I steadied myself under my feet, I pointed my right foot outward again and continued climbing the incline with the cramp in my right quad pulsing with each step. I pushed the pain to the back of my mind with disassociation and continued to follow Shifty up the mountain. Big Top was behind me and was having great success keeping on his feet by using his poles. Shifty fell a few times, but his falls were few and far in between. One section, I slipped, face planted in the mud, and slid fifty feet backward down the hill. I reached to the side of the trail to use the branches for stability only to feel thorns dig into my hand as I pulled myself up the hill. I gritted my teeth and continued climbing the hill with my hand grasping onto thorny bushes. I could feel small drops of blood trickling down my arm as we moved uphill, but I did not care, my only goal was to get to the top of the mountain. According to the race map, once we reached the eleven mile mark, it was going to be flat for the next six miles before turning around and heading back down the mountain.

Once we finally made it to the top of the mountain, it had quit raining because we had climbed slightly above the clouds. Shifty discovered a ledge with a viewpoint and we all took turns standing on the ledge and looking out over the mountains.

We then continued our slog through the mud. I quickly discovered the map was not telling the truth, as the ridgeline was riddled with continual up- and down-hill sections for the next six miles. Along the way, there were two rocky ridge crossings that showed views of the surrounding mountains. These views were enough to raise my spirits as we continued our way up the trail. After the second ridge crossing, the clouds rose and the rain began again. As we neared the aid station marking the turnaround, I began looking forward to putting on dry clothes from the bag in my dad's truck. As we approached the final uphill into the aid station, I saw my dad standing on the side of the trail, aghast at the difficulty of this race. As soon as I saw his face, I was rejuvenated. He was standing in the rain cheering me on as I ran through the mud. Once in the aid station, it was clear my dad understood that crewing meant he would be busy helping us get ready to head back down the mountain. He came to life and grabbed our drop bags for us, helped me as I tried to stretch the cramp out of my quad, and refilled our water bottles. I was extremely pleased to see my dad stepping up to the plate to help us in this aid station. I felt blessed to have him as a father. Once we had changed into dry clothes, I put a fresh rain jacket on and we waited for Big Top to finish using the bathroom. After waiting a few minutes, during which Shifty and I shoved food in our mouths, we decided he must have left without us noticing. Shifty and I waved goodbye to my dad and we began the second half of the race.

I was amazed at how much better I felt in my dry clothes. I also swapped out my thin socks for thicker and warmer socks for the run down the mountain. I pulled the hood of my rain jacket over my head and felt the rain hit the hood in rhythmic droplets. I followed Shifty through the mud and noticed the trail had become even sloppier since we last passed it. The cramp in my right quad continued to squeeze that muscle in a painful grip. Shifty seemed to be out for a routine run through the woods. I was amazed the way he seemed to bound down the trail. We then approached the first rock ridge crossing and I craned my neck to see the view we enjoyed on our way up the mountain, but it was hidden by clouds.

The rocky ridge was a large slab of white rock that went about one hundred yards along the ridgeline of the mountain, bridging two states, before the trail returned to the cover of the trees and thick mud. The Virginia side of the ridge was a nearly sheer cliff drop for a hundred feet. The Kentucky side of the ridge was an extremely steep incline of about eighty-five degrees for a hundred feet down to the trees.

As I followed Shifty across the ridge, I noticed the rain had made the rocks more slick than the last time we crossed the ridge. I decided to try to step on the small mossy growths growing in the cracks of the rock to gain traction. As I placed my foot in one of the moss growths, my foot slipped and I began to slide down the rock face. I scraped my knee along the side of the rocks in an effort to keep from falling, reached up and found a rock, and clung to it for my life. I looked down to see if I could safely slide down the rock without injury and saw the trees a hundred feet below. I started screaming for help, realizing that sliding would mean mortal injury. I was terrified that I might die on this race. It was then that I noticed Shifty positioning his feet on some jagged rocks on either side of me below me on the cliff. He put his hands on my back and shoved me back on top of the ridge. Once on top of the ridge, I carefully gathered myself into a standing position and shuffled across the rest of the ridge. It was not until a mile further down the trail that I felt my adrenaline stop pumping and my heartbeat slow down. I realized Shifty had saved my life and thanked him. He just said, "You're welcome," in a very matter of fact manner.

A half mile later, Big Top caught back up with us. He had been in the bathroom changing into waterproof pants when we left the turnaround. I told him what had happened on the ridge as we continued down the trail. With the three of us back together, Shifty found a better response for his heroics than just "You're welcome": He told Big Top that if I fell to my death, he wouldn't be able to get my truck out of his driveway. We all three laughed pretty heartily at the comment as we continued through the muddy trail.

We finally came to an aid station that marked the end of the ridgeline. I thought this meant that from there to the finish would be completely downhill. At that aid station, I continued to avoid the junk food being offered by the workers. Instead, I continued to shoved a few pretzels in my mouth and ate a granola bar from my hydration pack. I had to keep my promise to my brother.

The next five miles, the trail was almost all downhill. By the end of that downhill, I felt the cramp in my quad leave my leg. I let out a sigh of relief as the pain left my body.

About a mile from the next aid station, I slipped into a deep depression where I felt insecure about struggling so much while my friends seemed to be just fine, which made me think I was not worthy to be in this race. I wished I were as strong as they were and admired their strength.

The rain caused the mud around the last aid station to be deep and difficult. As I took a step, the mud swallowed my leg up to my knee on each step. I had to move carefully to ensure I did not lose a shoe in the deep mud heading toward the aid station. Once under the tent of the aid station, I gorged myself on turkey sandwiches and more pretzels and drank a bunch of water. We left that aid station with renewed vigor. I was amazed how much the food improved our spirits. The three of us were back to our normal conversations.

We finally trudged back onto the gravel road for the last three miles of the race. I started to lead the three of us down the road when I saw headlights coming toward us and scrambled to avoid being hit by the truck. I thought maybe there had been an accident and that one of the runners might need to be rescued, then saw it was a lady in a red truck who was apparently taking a twilight drive up the mountain. She rolled down her window and asked why I was out here. I told her there was a race going on and then used a few choice words about her almost running me over. She threatened to run me over now. I quickly abandoned the false bravado and apologized, as I was in no shape to fend off what I later described to the guys as a meth addict looking for a place to get high. Luckily, she accepted my apology and sped down the mountain. I turned around to see Shifty and Big Top standing on the trail in the woods looking on through the glow of their headlamps. I told them the lady was gone and they caught up to me quickly. My boisterous berating of the driver provided great fodder for the next couple miles down the mountain.

We came off the dirt road and made our way through the town toward the finish line. Shifty led us through town and toward the baseball field that marked the finish line. As we entered the baseball field, I saw my dad cheering us on as we ran across the finish line. We had finished the race in fourteen hours and forty-five minutes. I was proud to have finished my first mountain ultramarathon with two of my best friends and my dad as my crew. The race director congratulated us on the race, put finisher medals around our necks, and handed us a plate with a barbeque sandwich, soda, and chips, because with the completion of the race I officially ended my diet. I stuffed my face as I sat in a chair surrounded by my dad and two great friends. As I sat there, I reflected on many things and realized the three of us had completed something that was completely epic.

The road trip home consisted mostly of griping about sore muscles and joints. Every time we stopped along the way, Shifty and I would painfully shuffle our way into the gas station, load up on food, and carefully climb back into the car like a pair of eighty-year-old men.

At the Trailhead happy hour the following Tuesday, I felt like a celebrity. A large group of trailheads greeted Shifty, Big Top, and I as we walked into the bar. They eagerly listened to our stories of the race and celebrated our race with us. It was an incredible feeling and I felt God smiling down on me in that very moment of celebration. I had gone from a boy learning to walk again to a man running up a mountain in the driving rain and I had found a great group of people to call my friends.

Afterword

Thank you for taking the time to read this book about my life, from my struggles learning to walk and play sports again, to being picked on in school, and finally finding and running on the path to happiness and self-love. One of the things I hope you discovered through reading is a sense of how you too can triumph over your struggles and find your own path to success and contentment.

I would not be in the position I am in without the love and support of my amazing friends and family.

If you found this book to be an easy read, you can thank Laura Miller, a friend from the Mizzou track team, as she proofread it before I sent it to a publisher. A few years ago, while I was still in the process of writing, another good friend from the Mizzou track team, Kate Greer, made a few edits to my then-unfinished book, so I feel the need to thank her as well. There are a lot more people who deserve to be thanked, as they helped me in some way to finish this book, but the list is nearly endless, and they know who they are and that I owe them a drink.

Made in the USA
Middletown, DE
15 January 2017